The Book of Magick Power

The Book of Magick Power

An Advanced Practical Manual for Adepts and Novices

by Jason Augustus Newcomb

The New Hermetics Press

Sarasota, FL

First published in 2007 by
The New Hermetics Press
P. O. Box 18111
Sarasota, FL 34276
www.newhermetics.com

ISBN: 978-0-6151-5263-9

Cover Design and typesetting by Fr∴ E. I. A. E.

14 13 12 11 10 09 08 07
8 7 6 5 4 3 2 1

Do what thou wilt shall be the whole of the Law.

A Warning: This book has been constructed on the basis of a number of models. These models are useful ways of looking at reality that may help you to more readily experience occult, psychic and paranormal phenomena. But these models should not be confused with reality in any sense of the word. They are simply convenient ways of looking at things that can be discarded when and if they are no longer useful to you.

OTHER BOOKS BY JASON AUGUSTUS NEWCOMB

Nonfiction:

21st Century Mage (Weiser Books, 2002)
The New Hermetics (Weiser Books, 2004)
Sexual Sorcery (Weiser Books, 2005)

Practical Enochian Magick: a Manual for the New Hermetics Adept (forthcoming)
The Advanced Adept Manual and Workbook (forthcoming)

Fiction:

The Brotherhood of Light and Darkness (forthcoming)

TABLE OF CONTENTS

LIST OF EXERCISES

Introduction

"Magick is the Science and Art of causing Change to occur in conformity with Will."

-Aleister Crowley[1]

This is a book of practical magick. By practical magick I mean the use of magical and psychic tools to cause and observe real changes in your environment. Quite a few books on magick spend little or no time on these subjects, and it is my intent to remedy this situation both for the magical community, and for anyone interested in exploring psychic and paranormal phenomena. This book represents the most complete exploration of practical magical and psychic tools that has ever been presented under one cover. What's more, I have dispensed with many of the complicated procedures that so often accompany these sorts of works, directly and honestly presenting you with the simplest techniques that you need in order to get results, and giving you just a minimum of my own personal philosophy.

When I first became interested in the dark and mysterious world of magick, psychic phenomena, and the paranormal, I was twelve years old. At that time, what interested me was developing and using magick power. I wanted to be able to create noticeable changes in the world around me with unseen forces. I wanted to create miracles. I wanted psychic powers. I eagerly consumed hundreds of books, but at best only received incomplete instructions on how to actually accomplish anything miraculous. In fact, I often read a lot more philosophy than instruction, even in books claiming to be practical in their approach. I attended dozens of workshops on psychic subjects, and found much the same problem. I became a member of several occult organizations, but there I still received little instruction on the practical development of useable power. In fact, much of the magical community seems to turn its nose up at psychic exploration and practical magick, either thinking it is beneath them or that it is all just a bunch of nonsense. Instead, many in the magical community seem much more interested in philosophy and religion. Many so-called magicians don't really seem to believe in magick at all. It's a very strange phenomenon in

[1] *Magick: Book 4 Liber ABA*, p. 126

the community. You may find yourself judged harshly by your peers if you admit that you are even interested psychic powers, as silly as this sounds.

But it is all fascinating, and I have found it to be neither nonsense nor beneath me. So, remember that I am on your side, no matter what anyone else says. We've all certainly heard stories like the following of strange, unexplainable experiences:

A young businessman feels an incomprehensible fear in his gut when he is about to board a plane. He decides to postpone the flight and *later learns that the plane crashed with no survivors.*

A woman in her sixties hears a disembodied voice telling her that her aging husband is hurt. She begins to pray. A few hours later she discovers that *her husband was having a heart attack at that precise moment, and only survived because a Good Samaritan rushed to his aid as if in answer to her prayers.*

A young woman has a vivid dream in which she visits her far away boyfriend in an unknown hotel. The next day her boyfriend calls, saying *he saw her as an apparition* the previous evening. At her request, he describes the hotel room *and it exactly matches her dream.*

These are all true stories, and I'm sure you've heard many more. It *is* possible to receive information through non-ordinary channels, and to influence events with your thoughts and energy. Psychic powers are *real.* Magick can really change your life. Whether you are interested in experiencing clairvoyance, telepathy, the out-of-body experience, magical influence, or transcendental communication with higher consciousness, this book provides clear and easy-to-follow instructions for successfully and quickly achieving results.

I have worked long and hard, sometimes secretly to avoid the derision of my fellow magicians, exploring myself, exploring consciousness, and applying the small palette of tools I managed to find in books and from teachers. Through all of this study and practice, over the span of almost twenty years, I have slowly pieced together a very wide array of psychic and magical tools. I've now taught hundreds of people at workshops, and their problems and questions have helped me further refine my approaches. This book is the practical fruit of all that work. Many people have used these techniques and their questions, troubles and triumphs have helped to perfect these step-by-step tools. This is the book that the twelve-year-old Jason was looking for so many years ago.

In my previous books, *The New Hermetics* and *Sexual Sorcery* I provided a number of tools that cover a few of the same subjects in this book. I have made every effort to not merely repeat myself at any point in this current work. Where something is similar or identical to something from *The New Hermetics,* I have tried to make reference to it, and hopefully offered another approach, or at least refined the technique. All these books ultimately have very different purposes. *The New Hermetics* is primarily focused on the experience of illumination and personal transformation, on guiding consciousness step-by-step along a clear path to connection with the cosmic mind and each individual's life purpose. This serpentine path takes you into the realms of practical magick, but only as stepping-stones to the development of your consciousness, on the evolutionary path to illumination and adepthood. *The Book of Magick Power* is simply intended to give you a set of tools for exploring the practical side of magick and psychic phenomena. In many ways, the techniques in this book can be seen as supplemental New Hermetics tools, and will hopefully be of great assistance to any adepts interested in exploring beyond the New Hermetics techniques. This book is intended to be useable for both beginners and advanced consciousness engineers. It contains a number of valuable new models. If you have not read and begun exploring the techniques of *The New Hermetics* and my other book *21st Century Mage,* I highly recommend that you do so. You will find them immensely useful in your exploration of your cosmic abilities. However, reading these other books is not absolutely necessary to benefit greatly from this present one.

Much of the material that you are about to read is about expanding psychic abilities. I tend to approach psychic phenomena and the paranormal primarily from a magical background, largely because I have been an initiate of the secret Western Mystery Tradition for many years. There will be some emphasis in this direction throughout this book, but you do not have to be from a magical background in order to get a lot of value from this book. I hope that it will be useful to all people who are interested in exploring the latent powers of the mind. I also do not make any distinction between any of the various philosophical branches of magick in this work. This is a book for everybody. Esoteric Theology will not play a significant role in these pages. Whether you are a Witch, Wiccan, Hermetic Magician, Thelemite, Pagan, Druid, Shaman, Toltec, Christian, Jew, Muslim, Chaote, Voodoo witchdoctor or just a regular old person I think you will find something useful in these pages.

In *The New Hermetics*, I basically dispensed with any outer ritual work, focusing purely on consciousness development through a series of mental exercises or meditations. However, in the present volume, you will find that there are ritual elements in some of the techniques. I have done this because it is often easier to get into the right mood for practical work when we have created an outer atmosphere that is conducive. But if doing ritual is not something that interests you, I have where possible provided alternative, meditative approaches. You can also adapt any ritual elements into meditations using your own creativity. Where I have given specific ritual elements and ritual words you can always feel free to change these to suit your personal needs, adding corresponding ideas from your own spiritual tradition to really make these practices your

15

own. There is no one correct way to do anything. Try them my way first, but please feel free to adjust these practices in whatever way suits your needs.

Since the time that I was twelve and desperately looking for instruction, many new how-to books on the subject of psychic and magical development have appeared on the scene. But most are incomplete, and often contain superfluous spiritual and philosophical material that obscures the instruction into a mystical mush. A definitive work that simply and clearly outlines the procedures necessary to open up the unseen world has yet to appear until right now.

What really separates this book from most others is its true emphasis on the practical rather than the theoretical. This book emphasizes the active use of mind power to create and manifest the life of your dreams. There is a certain amount of explanatory, and even some philosophical information in the work, but it is packed with over a hundred exercises that range from beginner level to advanced uses for the developing and expanding powers of the mind. Readers from beginners to professional psychics and energy workers will benefit greatly from the following pages.

The operational model that we will employ throughout this book is that human beings are seeing, hearing, and feeling creatures. Our experiences are completely defined by our senses, and even our 'sixth' sense experiences are processed through these main senses. By providing a plan of the exact things that one has to see, hear and feel when exploring psychic phenomena- where to look, how to listen, what our internal feelings might be, the results follow simply and easily. Although this book's subject is unusual, the approach is no-nonsense and grounded in reality. Practical techniques have been broken down by step, providing an exact model for success. Some of these practices are extremely simple and straightforward, but I have attempted to break them down into their basic experiential components wherever possible. Although these instructions are written out step-by-step, you should not feel confined to these steps. Success is the only desire I have for you, and these are merely tools that will help to guide you on your own personal, idiosyncratic path. Some of the techniques you will find in this book are not even particularly metaphysical, but they are all still useful techniques for accomplishing your desires.

Sadly, words always have a tendency to get in the way of meaning, and you are just going to have to forgive me if occasionally I use our limited vocabulary of ideas in slightly different ways. Words like 'energy,' 'consciousness,' 'aware-ness,' 'soul' and 'spirit' have so many different meanings in our culture, and they may be used in slightly different ways even throughout this volume. In my last book, *The New Hermetics,* I made frequent use of the term 'unconscious,' and in this book, I more frequently use the term 'subconscious.' While I basically mean the same thing when expressing these terms, I have a specific reason for the difference. In my previous book I wanted to emphasize getting in touch with those parts of ourselves that are deep within, layers with which we may be altogether unfamiliar, while in this book I am more concerned with those elements of consciousness that are just below the surface. When I mentioned 'parts' in *The New Hermetics*, I was generally referring to the subconscious. By 'unconscious,' I was generally referring to all parts of our consciousness that are beneath the threshold of our usual awareness. I only hope that the context of all of these ideas will help to clarify what I am trying to communicate.

This book contains the practices, beliefs, and thoughts of many different peoples, including a few of my own, going back thousands of years. Through experimentation and spiritual insight, millions of people have experienced telepathy, out-of-body travel, clairvoyance, precognition and magical phenomena. Contained in these pages are the fruits of their wisdom. However, their effectiveness will be a direct reflection of the energy and dedication you put into them. Some readers may apply some small portion of one of them, and halfheartedly try another, and then declare the whole lot of them useless. To them I say it is probably best that you do not attempt this sort of exploration in the first place- at least until such time that you are willing to dedicate yourself to it more fully. You must also keep your expectations realistic. If your intention is to be able to be 100% accurate in your clairvoyance, able to read minds like romance novels, levitate across the ocean and psychically hurl a rusty Buick at your neighbors you are probably going to be disappointed. These sciences are subtle and elusive, and although parapsychological research continually proves these phenomena to exist in a measurable way, they usually manifest at least somewhat inconsistently. Anyone who claims to be 100% successful with their practical work is either deluded or trying to con you. Aim for being above average, succeeding often enough that it is above statistical chance. As you begin to succeed more often than you fail, you will find yourself spontaneously growing in many ways, and experiencing intuition and insight that will be an invaluable guide in your life.

You must remember too, that the goal of these practices is not to gain power or advantage over others, but to understand others and the universe, so that we may better live in love and harmony. Psychic experiments should be conducted responsibly. These exercises are meant to contribute lovingly to the Universal Spirit, and should not be conducted in any way that impinges upon the privacy, happiness, or free will of any other being, human or not, in the Universe. In fact, behaving in this way seriously restricts our access to these magical regions of consciousness, as it is from our unity with all beings that the greater portion of our power proceeds.

I recommend that you conduct these exercises in such a way that they are contributing to your own spiritual unfolding, rather than ensnaring you more in the desires and power games of the mundane. There is an important axiom that you should keep in mind from the beginning: *If you desire power you become the slave*

17

of all the powers of the cosmos. By becoming desireless, you swiftly discover that you are the source of all the powers. In other words, the more you focus on the mundane desire to 'win the lottery' or 'levitate' in order to impress people, or have power over others, the more you are giving up your true center, the connection to divinity within you. The more you are operating from your spiritual center, the easier it will be to accomplish anything, without the hindrance of lack, need, or lower desire.

There is very little danger involved in these practices, but you may confront emotions, images and memories that you'd thought forgotten. If you feel that this might be at all detrimental to your psychological health, it is recommended that you consult your therapist before trying any of these exercises.

It might be very useful to find a partner who is also interested in these subjects, or a study group. Several of these exercises will work best if you have a partner. A few exercises even require one. And working with a partner or group will allow you to experience a much wider range of phenomena more quickly, there is a gestalt of power in a group, and your progress will be swifter.

Finally, you should try to do these exercises in order, because their effect is basically cumulative, especially within each chapter. If one of these exercises is really working well for you, by all means keep exploring it and leave the later exercises for later. If something does not seem to be working well for you, simply go on to the next exercise. Don't worry; soon you will be on your way. Take it slowly.

WHAT YOU WILL NEED
TO GET THE MOST OUT OF THESE PRACTICES

There are several physical items that are useful in preparing to explore the inner planes. None of them are absolutely necessary, because ultimately all of these practices are about consciousness. Really all that you need is yourself, your body and your mind. But many people find it far easier to create the proper setting for experiencing magick in their lives when they have a few ritual implements at their disposal. I do not think that you need to have a full magical temple constructed, or all of the weapons of a magician. Just a few simple items will suffice. The use of these implements reminds the brain that it is now entering the time for magick, a space between the world of the mundane and the infinite world of the spirit.

However, I must really emphasize that these things are optional. None of them are necessary for your success. Do not allow the lack of any of them to stop you or make you delay getting started. The more quickly you begin to do these exercises, the more quickly you will obtain results. Once you start working, you may find that tools just begin to miraculously manifest in your life. You may also discover that you are becoming so successful without them that you do not even need to bother thinking about them at all. However, if you have the means and/or already have these things, you may find the following useful.

Workroom or Temple

Ideally, you will set aside and completely dedicate a room or some particular space in your house to be your workroom or 'magical temple.' This need not be anything elaborate, but if you work in the same place consistently, you will quickly charge the area with an 'aura of power.' The more you work there, the more quickly you will enter the appropriate states of consciousness and achieve results. This is not really metaphysical at all. It is merely that by using a space exclusively for magick, your mind will quickly realize that when you go into this space you are going to be doing magick. You will then find yourself shifting quickly into a 'magical consciousness' every time you enter that space. However, if you do not have such a space that you can completely dedicate to your work, simply try to work in the same area as much as possible. This will have the same effect.

It may also be useful to have a small table or altar in the room that you will use; this can be as simple or elaborate as you choose.

But when it comes down to it, many of these techniques can be used simply and effectively anywhere in your everyday life. You can certainly look at auras or tune in to various psychic senses on a bus or at the mall, or even while having a boring meeting with your boss! The more often you use them, the more swiftly you will become accomplished and adept in their use.

Magical Circle

Some of the techniques in this book suggest the use of a magical circle. The circle represents the enclosing of your energy, protecting you from unwanted outside influence, and limiting your awareness to the confines of your working space. It contains and focuses your mental and magical energies, so that you can direct them most effectively. Entering and charging a magical circle is an excellent way of preparing for any exercise, as it tends to allow you to set aside your experiences in the outside world and concentrate exclusively on the present task at hand. It is, in essence, a simple mnemonic device that says to all the parts of your consciousness, "Now we are going to be doing magick."

I recommend that, if possible, you physically draw, paint, tape or engrave a magical circle in your temple or workroom. This physical circle will be a constant reminder of whatever psychic circle of your energy you create with your work. This simple diagram will be more useful to you in practical work than it might appear at first glance. While you can just trace an imaginary line around your working area, projecting a line of psychic energy around yourself, this circle will only be fully in effect while you are concentrating on it. When your thoughts turn to other work, you will have disintegrated your circle for all practical purposes. Most of the time this does not have much negative impact, as there is a 'residual' circle that you can call back to your mind as necessary, but the physical circle will prevent any and all possible problems.

Creating a psychic circle is a good practice for those times when a physical circle is impossible or undesirable. At those times you can simply imagine a glowing blue-white line of energy flowing out of your hand and being drawn on the floor around you as you walk around the edge of your working space. By having worked within a physical circle many times you will create a much more powerful psychic circle later on. You will also be able to just imagine a magical circle into existence while sitting meditatively, even while simply resting in the comfort of a recliner! This is also one of the simplest forms of psychic protection, which we will cover in a later chapter.

Magical Garments

Many people like to wear magical robes when conducting their work, and this can again have a positive mnemonic effect on your subconscious. "Oh, we're putting on our robes, let's open up those psychic channels and get ready for magick time." But you may make your own choice about this. Certainly you would probably not want to wear robes if you were seeing a psychic client, or out in the mundane world. People would surely know that you were cracked up then!

Magical Wand

The purpose of the magick wand is to direct magical forces. You can use a wand to draw symbols in the air, project energy out into the universe, or draw energy into you. It is not strictly necessary, but it can be useful in ritual contexts. There are many ways of constructing a wand, or one can be purchased from a new age or magick shop. There are those who say that there is one specific way in which a magick wand must be constructed, but I have noticed little difference in the effectiveness of one design over another. Three different possible designs are suggested in Appendix A of this work, or you can just use whatever you think will work best for you. You can also simply use a pointed finger or an outstretched hand in the place of the wand. It is just an object, and you are perfectly capable of operating without it.

There are traditionally four weapons of the magician, the wand, the cup, the dagger or sword, and the disk or pantacle. For this practical magick, the wand is usually all that's really necessary. "In fine, the formula of the wand is the only one with which we need more particularly concern ourselves."[1] Metaphorically and metaphysically the wand is really the will of the magician, the cup the understanding, the sword the intellect and the pantacle the body, so you really already have these things.

Incense

Your sense of smell is intimately connected to our memories, directly linking you up to your subconscious mind. Smell alone can change your consciousness drastically. I highly recommend finding an incense that you like and using it as much as possible in connection with your work.

You can also get or create special incenses for specific energies as you begin to work with planetary and other forces. I will cover this later on in the book. The more consistent you are with your use of incense, the more powerful it will become as a tool in your consciousness arsenal.

However, some people do not like incense, or find it physically irritating, and it is certainly possible to proceed well without it.

A Pendulum

You will need to have a pendulum for several of the exercises in this book. I used to think little of the pendulum, that it was just a new-agey contrivance of little import. But then one day several years ago, my mother asked if I could 'magically produce' some lottery numbers for her. I used the pendulum, and a technique that I will outline later in this book, and the numbers I produced won her six thousand dollars! I repeated a similar exercise with her a few months later, and she again won several hundred dollars. Since that time I have realized that the pendulum is an incredibly useful device for easily and directly connecting with your subconscious and other intelligences, and many practices in this book depend upon it. You can certainly just directly communicate with your subconscious, but a pendulum is a useful tool to filter out your conscious mind's tricky little desires and tendency to blur your communication.

A pendulum is really just anything that has a little weight attached to the end of a string. If you don't want to buy one, you can just tie a nail or a screw or a rock to a string. It can be that easy. But it is a tool with which you will commune with your subconscious, and your subconscious appreciates a little effort.

---

[1] Ibid., p. 149

21

I would recommend buying one. You can get a top of the line pendulum from any New Age shop for less than twenty dollars, and your subconscious will be ever so grateful for your gift.

Various other Psychic and Magical Tools

There are also several other little items that you may find useful throughout your work, such as crystal balls, either clear or opaque, magick mirrors, Tarot cards, psychic test cards, candles, parchment, etc. I will describe the use of some of these objects throughout this work, but they are only necessary if you want them, and can easily be replaced by other things. All of them are readily available at any Magical or New Age store.

Magical and Dream Journal

Start keeping a journal today. Record both your dreams and your practices in your journal, and keep track of all the new and exciting things that are manifesting in your life. You will want to refer back to what has happened to you over the course of your explorations, and you will treasure your journal once you start keeping it. There are long periods of my magical journey in which I failed to keep accurate records, and it is a shame. The records that I do have are truly fascinating. Don't rob yourself of this record. It is a true gift. The importance of our dreams is phenomenal in our explorations of psychic phenomena and magick. Immediately start recording any and all dreams that you recall. I have received so much magical teaching from 'dream masters' that I consider it a critical component of any magical and psychic training.

Write down all of your thoughts and observations as much as possible. Many of the ideas in this book came from chance observations that I made in my own journal, and the experiments that followed.

Your journal does not need to be anything fancy or expensive. Just a spiral-bound notebook will do just fine. If the book is too precious, you will think it only worthy of successes and important things. I'd like to see you recording everything. There is just as much to learn from unsuccessful experiments and random thoughts as there is from your great achievements. You could also keep your journal on your computer or with an audio recorder.

You may want to ritually consecrate your magical tools and space once you have obtained them. If you decide to consecrate one of your tools, I recommend that you consecrate them all. A very simple consecration ritual can be found in Appendix B of this book. However, using your objects lovingly for the one purpose of expanding your awareness is a consecration in and of itself. A ceremony is just an outer seal on this inner process.

With or without any of these things, you are now ready to proceed into the furthest reaches of infinity. But first, dear reader, I ask you to indulge me in a brief description of a useful metaphysics and a few new consciousness models. They will help you tremendously on your path, and provide the foundation for your work. There will be several practical exercises along the way, which I hope that you explore thoroughly before moving on to the deeper work.

CHAPTER ONE
A Brief Theory
of Mind and Magick

"The Mind, O Tat, is of God's very essence..."

-Hermes Trismegistos[1]

Latent within the constitutions of all human beings are wonders the likes of which we are totally unaware in everyday existence. Our minds are infinitely more than the tiny waking consciousness we traditionally consider the entirety of our being. Beneath this consciousness we are connected to a vast unconscious. What's more, this unconscious seems to extend beyond our personal mind, connecting us with all things. And when we learn to access this greater part of our minds, all manner of fascinating phenomena occur.

In the Ancient Mystery Schools, the aspirant was given the central and simple instruction "Know Thyself." As you begin your journey toward real inner knowledge your job is to truly start to learn yourself. You will discover hidden abilities, limitations, desires and dislikes. Take a few minutes now, and perform the following exercises. They are extremely simple, but gateways to true power.

Exercise 1 - Awareness of Yourself

Time Required: 5 to 20 minutes

This first exercise is really just a first stepping-stone toward your growing personal awareness. This is a process that takes a lifetime. You are, in the larger scheme, a microcosm of the greater universe as a macrocosm. So, learning to know yourself may eventually allow you to know the whole of the universe.

---

[1] *Thrice Greatest Hermes, Book II*, p. 127

By exploring this short, simple exercise, you will begin to notice how your consciousness exists in its natural state. Later, we will focus on modifying your consciousness, and getting deep within, but for now please take a moment and simply observe what's going on right now.

1. Find a comfortable place where you can relax for ten minutes or more without interruption.

2. You may sit in a chair, or lie down. It really doesn't matter. Simply choose a place that feels comfortable to you, in which you will not be likely to fall asleep. During the rest of the exercise, you must not move around much, so take a moment to find a position that is really comfortable.

3. Now, simply observe yourself. Are you tense? Relaxed? There is more going on than you think. What exactly do you feel? Do you have itches? Are there many thoughts running through your mind? What sorts of thoughts are running through your mind? Are you experiencing images? If you get distracted, observe what distracted you and go back into the exercise.

4. When you are finished, write down your observations in your journal.

Exercise 2 - Body Awareness

Time Required: 5 to 10 minutes

This exercise follows the last, and offers you another glimpse at exactly who and what you are at the present moment, focusing on what you think of yourself, and how you process your self-image. It will also help you to begin empowering your visualization skills, and your ability to think in a transformative way.

1. Stand completely naked in front of a full-length mirror.

2. Examine your body from top to bottom and back again. Notice the unique characteristics that make your body yours. Note any thoughts or associations or feelings you perceive right now. What do you think of yourself? Are there things you really like about yourself? Are there things you really dislike? This is the self that you and the universe have created as it exists right now.

3. Now close your eyes, as you draw in a breath, try to vividly remember your appearance in the mirror through closed eyes.

4. Hold onto this image of yourself as you hold your breath in for a moment. Are there parts of you that are harder to visualize? Let out your breath and open your eyes.

5. Repeat this several times, breathing in and closing your eyes remembering your appearance, then exhaling and looking at your reflection. Note the difference between your inward reflective, subjective reality, and your outward objective reality.

6. Now, close your eyes on an in breath, and focus on the parts of yourself that you like as you hold your breath a moment and visualize your body with closed eyes. Repeat a few times.

7. Now, close your eyes on an in breath, and focus on the parts of yourself that you do not like as you hold your breath a moment and visualize your body with closed eyes. Repeat a few times.

8. Finally, close your eyes again as you are breathing in, and imagine what you would be like if those parts you didn't like were different, or if you liked them better. Try to imagine yourself as lovingly as possible.

9. When you are finished, write down your observations in your journal.

There is one animating principle in the universe. Throughout the ages it has been called many things, most commonly, "God," or some specific name of God. There is nothing that exists outside of this singular animating principle. At the most fundamental and essential level, every man, woman, dog, rock and tree is God. But the term, "god" is problematic, especially in these times. As soon as one starts talking about God, everyone wants to make sure that this god is their god, or decides that it definitely isn't their god, and conflicts arise as theologies abound and it all ends in madness and death. Many recent tragedies have played this out on the world stage. Many educated people also insist that there certainly couldn't be anything as silly as "God" at all, feeling that this concept is just a superstitious throwback to a primitive age of darkness and foolishness. So, many modern sages do not use the term "God" to describe this one animating principle that lies at the core of everything, preferring to simply call it, "the All," "The One," "Unity," "The Good," "The Totality," or some such ambiguity.

27

But don't mistake this ambiguity for confusion. The principle is perfectly clear; the universe has as its source a conscious animating principle. Naming it is wholly unnecessary. Applying a name to anything results in a limitation. Once you have named something, it is defined, and the essential animating force in the universe cannot be defined, described, or limited in any way. It is everything. And, at the secret core of your being you are intimately connected with this singular source of everything, in fact you are this source, and your potential power is unlimited.

Infinite power is at your fingertips, right now. There is nothing that you are incapable of doing, because, in truth, veritably, and without doubt, you are the animating force of the entire universe. Every power of the firmament and of the ether, of the earth and under the earth, on dry land and in the water, of whirling air and of rushing fire, and every spell and scourge of God is obedient unto you. Of course you do not believe that, or there would be no need for me to tell you. Most likely, you feel that you have very little control over any aspect of your life. You have sacrificed your infinite power for opposition, misery, and decay, by shrinking yourself down into the space of a little body, and the span of a tiny life. And then you've set yourself at odds with anything outside your body, trying to control, manipulate or get the approval of a world that is ultimately not separate from yourself.

"I have done no such thing!" you may be saying to yourself, but in fact you have. How often have you crossed paths with a beautiful man or woman on the street and thought, "I wish I knew that person," and then passed by without a word, thinking that you were unworthy? How many times have you thought to yourself that your life would be perfect if you just had a better job, a nicer house, whiter teeth, and then done nothing about it? How often have you felt alone, misunderstood, angry or scared? Endless possibility presents itself, and endlessly you ignore possibilities to remain in a state of helplessness. You are the creator of your own reality, and you can be taught specifically the secrets of taking advantage of this fact.

However, in practical terms there are some limits on what we can accomplish, as long as we exist as separate bodies. Some people take to one thing more than others. Some of us are gifted at music, others at mathematics, and others still at sports or martial arts. The same holds true for magick. Some people's mere presence causes physical phenomena to occur, such as objects floating or falling, the appearance of apparitions or ghosts. For some, these things never occur, and their mere presence seems to stop them from occurring. But they may find that they can communicate telepathically almost as easily as talking on the phone. Some people find clairvoyance as simple as riding a bicycle, for others, they can only see the vaguest images, but their precognitive skills are nearly perfect. In this book you will find some things work easily for you, some take much practice, and some things seem impossible. I suggest that you work toward your strengths, and as you develop, you will find other abilities manifesting out of nowhere. I was not a born psychic. Far from it, I used to be quite lead-headed. So, I know that these things can be learned.

The methodology of this book is quite simple. By learning to observe and control the contents of your mind and the sensations of your body you will make contact with the subtler aspects of reality and learn to use these to your advantage. You will even eventually contact those pure and sublime portions of consciousness that have been called Gods, your Higher Self, The Augoeides, The Genius, Daimon, Holy Guardian Angel and many other names.

The practice of magick consists of the knowledge and application of psychic or invisible forces upon the world for the purposes of changing yourself and your environment. Practical magick consists of an array of techniques both mental and physical, to contact and direct invisible forces and beings. Most magicians use some magical techniques, but many fail to fully explore their own psychic potential.

Psychic phenomena have been separated off from magick as a whole for some time now, mostly co-opted by both the New Age movement and parapsychology. This is unfortunate because many magicians have nearly forgotten that these phenomena were once their central concern and exclusive purview. On the other hand, the studies of parapsychologists have given us many experiments that support the true validity of psychic phenomena, as well as many useful and simple approaches for developing abilities such as clairvoyance, out of body experiences and telepathy.

This book does not propose that any of these things take place outside of your own mind. On the contrary, as a wise magician once put it, "The universe is a projection of ourselves; an image as unreal as that of our faces in a mirror," and further, "We cannot affirm any quality in an object as being independent of our sensorium, or as being in itself that which it seems to us."[1] The whole of the universe, as we see it, is but a product of our own minds, colored by our own minds, and assuredly distorted by our own minds. This does not mean that what we see is real, or unreal. In truth, it is both and neither.

Many people ask me if there is *really* anything to all this psychic power and magick stuff, and sadly I am incapable of giving a *real* answer. When you have a dialogue with a God or some other disembodied spirit, is it simply a complex imaginary scenario, or something truly metaphysical? I cannot answer that question, or any other definitively. There is a subjective reality to these experiences, and they very often coincide with experiences in consensus reality. If you really explore the exercises in this book, you will continually be amazed, and sometimes disappointed. There is no way of knowing "for sure," what exactly is going on in any experience, whether magical or mundane. If you do a money

---

[1] *Book 4 Liber ABA* p. 217

spell, then receive an unexpected check, did you manifest that check, or would it have come either way? There is no way of knowing, nor is it something to really waste a lot of time on. Creatively participating in the unfolding universal process is your birthright, and a true gift. Checking to see if its teeth are rotten is an insult to the giver. Even if our experiences just seem imaginary, there is still power and meaning in them.

Most people secretly believe in magick, and use it all the time. How often have you thrown a crumpled piece of paper toward a garbage can, and then, seeing it going off to the side, willed that it manage to get in anyway? Hasn't this sometimes seemed to work? Whenever we play the lottery, throw a basketball, or wish for a new lover or a new job, we are hoping that somehow our minds and wills can influence these random circumstances outside our direct physical control toward our desired end. This is the essence of magick, and we are all magicians.

As a magician you must recognize that the world "out there" is ultimately an insoluble riddle. For every answer that you may gain from the great secret fountain of truth, a myriad of greater mysteries twirl forth in the boundless infinity. A magician, recognizing that the quest for infinite knowledge is futile, nonetheless knows that it is the destiny of our species to unravel what little we can in the span of a life. A magician is a wild, mysterious, wonderful creature in a wilder world of infinite wonder. Nothing in the world of magick is real, and yet nothing is unreal. Endless possibility awaits you.

The exact natures of psychic and magical forces are completely unknown, and will probably always remain so. In the past both were attributed to gods, spirits and angels and other worlds. Today parapsychologists attribute them to mysteries of the human mind. The Adepts of all times have always held both to be true.

We are all very lucky. We live in a mysterious and magical universe, whose mysteries still await our discovery. Even our most prestigious scientists and sages know almost nothing about anything! Most people ignore this fact, contenting themselves with a dull life of television and 9 to 5 jobs. It takes the mildly crazy people like myself to point this "magical-ness" out to everyone, and we are usually ignored, scorned and mocked, nailed to a cross or obliterated in some other gruesome way. I am going to risk any of these options to joyously share with you my wonder at this world of ours.

THE UNIVERSE IS AN ENERGY PHENOMENON

"It is prana that is manifesting as motion; it is prana that is manifesting as gravitation, as magnetism. It is prana that is manifesting as the actions of the body, as the nerve currents, as thought-force."[1] The wonder-filled world that surrounds us is truly a great mystery. It is not really a world of solid objects at all, but a world of energy. Any physicist or yogi will tell you that this is so.

All of our most basic human conceptions, religious, scientific, and mystic, about reality can be summed up in the phrase, "the universe is an energy phenomenon." The ancient magi and wise people of all early civilizations recognized that the universe was made up of energy thousands of years ago, and they began to map it out from it's subtlest to it's most gross aspects. Modern scientists are in fact the heirs of these ancient explorers, but the descendents have lopped off the heads of their own antecedents, and made every effort to remove any religious or magical implications from their work. Unfortunately, it took until late in the last millenium for science to even begin catching up with the ancients on the subject of energy.

This never ceasing flow of energy bombards us at every moment of our lives, and we perceive it as the world of objects that surrounds us. This energy is not only in everything; it is everything. We are patterns of energy that exist in a world of energy.

According to most theories of modern physics, what we perceive as matter is just a series of waves (or particles) that vibrate at specialized frequencies. In fact, the entire universe is basically just empty space. Huge gaps separate the meaningful particles (or waves) of the universe, yet somehow they are connected to one another, vibrating together, a giant sea of energy. But you do not perceive the world in this way. You see only solid, separate objects.

What physics fails to describe is the way in which we transform this flow of energy into the solidity of the world we perceive. This is a difficult task that begins at birth. Our parents and every person that we come in contact with instructs us until we perceive correctly what they perceive, the material world full of objects, basically in the same way that they perceive it. There are of course exceptions. Some people never fully learn to distinguish between certain colors. Some people can't ever learn to see the way others do. Some people experience breaks in the continuity of consensus reality throughout their lives. We pathologize some of them, and call others creative geniuses.

But it is always our thoughts that create the world that we see. When we touch a wall, we react to it in the way that we've been trained. We see a wall, and feel hardness. When we are small children, there are many breaks in the continuity, and strange and wonderful things occasionally occur. Perhaps you dimly remember a few of these, and that is why you've picked up this book. By the time we are adults, everything rigidly coheres to the intensive instruction we've received.

---

[1] *Raja Yoga*, p. 35

The important thing to remember is that it is all just a pattern of energy! We perceive only a small fraction of this energy. Layer upon layer of energy exists in the universe, just waiting to be witnessed.

But even if we accept all this, we continue to see only walls and objects. The reason is that we do not allow ourselves to really see reality. We see models. The only things we allow ourselves to witness are our ideas and descriptions about things. This is the way that you have been taught by all your experiences in life to perceive your surroundings. This mode of perception has served you well. It has protected you from walking into walls, and has given you a method of categorizing your different experiences in life.

In actuality, there are no walls, and nowhere to walk to. There is only a field of vibrating energy, of which you are a part. This is not to say that trees and cats and rocks and walls don't exist, for they certainly exist. They are all patterns of energy. You have merely learned to distinguish them in a rather unwieldy and meaningless way. You have separated them from yourself, and separated them from each other. So, we are left with these inadequate descriptions of everything, and a dim intellectual sense, thanks in large part to modern physics, that our perceptions about the solidity of matter may be incorrect.

There is a survival advantage to this separation of forms and apparent solidity of matter. It affords you the opportunity to avoid things that might be unpleasant or harmful. That is why you were taught these perceptions in the first place. This protection is necessary, however, only as long as you perceive this separation and potential harmfulness. You may eventually learn that all of your perceptions and ideas about what you see around you are totally meaningless, and then the truth will begin to unfold before you. For in reality, there is only energy. And there is nothing truly harmful in the entire Universe. This sea of energy is entirely you. When you discover your true oneness with it, you can feel only bliss, and something even beyond bliss. Becoming one with this energy is the goal of all eastern religion, and many contemporary western practitioners. The truth however, is that you are already at one with the Universe, because there is no other way to be. You have merely made the simple error of believing that you are separate.

THINKING AND ACCURATE PERCEPTION

The way to remedy this is to understand a fundamental difference between two modes of operating your consciousness: thinking vs. accurate perception. We humans always seem to place accurate perception in second place to thinking. In fact, most people would rather read about the exciting adventures of explorers and foreign places, rather than actually experience them. Watching television and movies has replaced most of life's adventures for many of us. The average person does not in any way regularly attempt to accurately perceive the world. The problem is that most of us accept the notion that the world is simply there. There is no need to "attempt to accurately perceive" anything, since perception is an automatic function of being. In reality, this could not be further from the truth. What we call perception is nothing more than a series of patterns of judgment and modeling based on our long term relationships with the outside world from the conditioned reality of our past experiences.

True perception is utterly impossible in this scenario. When we see a rock, we are not seeing a rock at all; we are seeing a set of models that we call "rockiness" which we established for ourselves long ago. In truth, a rock is a beautiful and mysterious energy phenomenon that we know almost nothing about.

The way to eliminate our limiting models, and perceive the world with accuracy is very simple. We must simply stop thinking, and start being. But this is easier said than done. Our conscious minds are thinking addicts. But our conscious minds are not the totality of our awareness.

CHAPTER TWO
A Brief Theory of
Consciousness and Perception

"Altered states of consciousness are the key to magical powers."

-Peter J. Carroll [1]

It is your own consciousness that is the key to unlocking your cosmic abilities, and by understanding your consciousness in new and novel ways, your magical capacities will quickly blossom. This is the beginning of our practical work.

The first thing that I really want to make clear is that all paranormal and/or magical experiences are subjective experiences in consciousness. Worrying about the objective validity of any experience is going to take you out of your experience, and this kind of validity is usually impossible to determine anyway. It is best to simply experiment, and judge any experience, if you must judge at all, only far in the future when you can look at it from a distance. Apparent failures can often produce very interesting results. I once conducted an astral projection experiment in which I asked a friend to place an object on the floor of a certain room of his house. I was then going to go there and try to identify the object. As I began the experiment, I quickly fell asleep. I woke up several hours later feeling a bit disgusted with myself, but I decided to try again. I couldn't quite get into the right state for a "full separation," so I used a technique that I'll describe later called the "body of light." I was basically just pretending to go, and when I entered the agreed upon room, I saw what seemed to be a "roundish" shape. But I couldn't really tell if I was making it up, so I returned to bodily consciousness, and wrote in my journal that it was a cylindrical object, perhaps either a hat or a drum. I went back to sleep feeling I'd failed. The next day when he called me, he told me that the object he'd placed in the room was a cooking pot. I immediately knew that was exactly what I'd seen. While "coincidence" could

---

[1] *Liber Null and Psychonaut*, p. 31

35

be argued, he could have placed a painting or a statue or a camera or any number of objects that aren't round or cylindrical. I've had too many similar experiences to disregard this kind of synchronicity. So, don't be too quick to judge yourself. On the other hand, I've had very successful seeming astral journeys in which I've seen things that definitely were not there in the physical world.

THE FOUR-PART MODEL OF CONSCIOUSNESS

The easiest way to break up the elements of consciousness within us is with a four-part model. These parts can be called the subconscious mind, the conscious mind, the super-conscious mind and finally the universal mind of "the All," which is beyond the other three, more a potentiality than a practical part of our awareness or work. This fourth part of your consciousness is the consciousness of the universe itself, and is not really something you really need to concern yourself with in this work. The Superconscious mind will interact with this ultimate part of your consciousness if need be, but you needn't worry about it. We will primarily focus on the first three components of consciousness in this book. Each of these parts of the mind represents deeper and deeper layers of energy, connecting us more and more fully with the totality of the energy world that surrounds us. This fits in very neatly with the four-part division of the world that I outlined in *21ˢᵗ Century Mage.*[1] You can see this model outlined in Diagram One.

Now if we further break each of these four parts into two pieces, we then have Timothy Leary's eight-circuit model of consciousness that I have described in both of my previous two books. This is depicted in Diagram Two.

This eightfold division fits very conveniently with our topic and is worthy of further study, but is beyond the scope of our present subject. You must also remember that these are all just models, and even if they are useful, do not necessarily represent reality. Still, you will hopefully find the following descriptions useful.

The Conscious Mind

This part of our awareness is often called the intellect, the waking mind, the ego, in Qabala it is called the Ruach, and in the popular Huna system it is called the Uhane. This is obviously the part of our consciousness with which we are most familiar, since it is traditionally the part we call, "I." However it is really only the tip of a very large iceberg of awareness that lies mostly under the threshold of our conscious mind's awareness. As I described above this is the part of

---

[1] *21ˢᵗ Century Mage* p. 10

FOUR PART MODEL	AREAS OF AWARENESS	21st Century Mage Model of the Planes
subconscious	Emotion, memory, Physiological Function	Astral Realm The world that we look at with our eyes closed.
conscious	Thinking, Reasoning, Decision-making	Physical Realm The world that we look at with our eyes open.
Super-conscious	Transcendence, True Creativity	Causal Realm The source that generates these Images.
Universal mind	Archetypal Source of all	Divine Realm The source of consciousness Itself.

Diagram 1 - Four Part Model of Consciousness

FOUR PART MODEL	AREAS OF AWARENESS	BIO-CIRCUIT	AREA OF CONSCIOUSNESS
subconscious	Emotion, memory, Physiological Function	I **Biosurvival**	sucking, nourishment, cuddling
		II **Emotional-Territorial**	power struggles
conscious	Thinking, Reasoning, Decision-making	III **Semantic**	learning, calculaion
		IV **Socio-Sexual**	morality, reproduction, pair-bonding
Super-conscious	Transcendence, True Creativity	V **Neurosomatic**	bliss, somatic rapture
		VI **Neuroelectric**	reprogramming self, relativization of reality
Universal mind	Archetypal Source of all	VII **Neurogenetic**	collective unconscious
		VIII **Neuroatomic**	non-local awareness, cosmic union

Diagram 2 - Eight Part Model of Consciousness

our consciousness that describes things, classifies them and helps us negotiate through the everyday world. It is this part of our consciousness that solves problems and makes decisions. But it is very dependent upon the subconscious to do so, because the conscious mind is really just the set of patterns and models we have been taught by the people around us, while the subconscious really runs most of the show.

The conscious mind is really just a point of awareness. Life's conditioning has artificially put all of the ideas that your conscious mind has about how great or how terrible you are, or how great or terrible the things in your life are. The subconscious mind holds onto all these ideas for you, but it is willing to discard any of them as soon as you are willing to. As soon as you start altering your state of consciousness, letting the subconscious take the reigns, most of your preconceived thoughts simply just don't get accessed anymore. The subconscious doesn't have the same ideas about the importance of your place in the world, how much money you make, or how attractive your sex partner is. It has its own ideas, which are quite possibly much closer to the real you, although the subconscious is also conditioned by outside forces.

The Subconscious Mind

The subconscious has been called many things, the soul, the anima, the Nephesh in the Qabala (although elements of the ruach constitute what we are considering the subconscious), the Unihipili in the Huna system, the lower self, the animal soul, the abdominal brain, the younger self, the unconscious, and of course the subconscious. These are all really names for one and the same thing. This is the aspect of your consciousness that is just below your awareness, running the physiological processes, storing and accessing your memories, and controlling your emotional energy. It is only through the subconscious that we can access connection to the next part of consciousness, the Super-conscious.

The subconscious is intimately connected to the superconscious in a way that the conscious mind is not. The reasons for this are not clear, but it is a simple fact that we can most effectively contact our superconscious through the subconscious. There are a number of theoretical models that offer explanations for this, Qabala, Vedanta, Theosophy and even Jung's theory of the collective unconscious. But we are going to concern ourselves primarily with the practical rather than the theoretical in this book. In order to experience higher consciousness, we must relax, slow down, and move within. When we do this, we are accessing the subconscious. Many of the techniques in this book will direct you to do just that. The subconscious tends to be very playful, almost childlike at times, but it is incredibly powerful and should be treated with the utmost respect. So take that attitude throughout your work, playful and respectful.

When doing any of the exercises in this book, it is really the subconscious that we are working with; the conscious mind is just going along for the ride. The subconscious mind is our energy mind, it is the feelings in our bodies, the emotions and the electrical impulses that travel through us. The subconscious mind has many abilities that the conscious mind does not, but it is neither all-powerful, nor all good. It can cause just as much trouble for you as your conscious mind. If you've ever had a bad habit such as drinking too much, smoking cigarettes, or eating too much, it is your subconscious that is actively keeping these bad habits up. The nice thing about the subconscious is that it generally listens, unless you've treated it very badly, so it is relatively easy to change habits if you firmly instruct your subconscious to do so, and you have a decent relationship with it.

The Superconscious Mind

However, it is really your superconscious mind that is in many ways the closest to what we might call "the real you." It's funny to say this, because most of us don't even notice that we have a superconscious mind, so how can it be the real us? Well, it is this part of your consciousness that is directly connected with the universe as a whole, and directs the course of your individual life. This aspect of your awareness has been called the Higher Self, the God-Mind, the Holy Guardian Angel, The Neschamah, and/or Chiah in the Qabala, the Aumakua in Huna, the Great One, the Genius, the Augoeides, the Daimon, the Wise Self, the Spirit, the Inner Sage and many other things. It is your cosmic mind, your personal connection with infinity. We depend upon this aspect of our consciousness for inspiration, true creativity, and transcendence. All real power to transform our lives comes from the superconscious. Your superconscious is connected with the subconscious below, and everything else above.

These three aspects of consciousness can almost be considered three or more separate beings that all share your life. They can conveniently be viewed as occupying three distinct areas of your body. These are just metaphors, and do not necessarily represent physiological facts, but I have continually found them to be extremely useful for practical purposes.

The conscious mind can be seen to occupy your head, the subconscious mind the torso, belly and sexual region, and the superconscious the crown of your head and just above. The reasons for this are simple. Our conscious mind seems to center its operations in the brain. Our thinking processes seem to issue from the brain, and our sense organs for dealing with the outside world are primarily located in the head. So, it is convenient to think of our conscious self as occupying the brain. This is not really true, because our conscious minds have full access to every part of our bodies, but it is a convenient central location to place this aspect of consciousness.

Our subconscious minds on the other hand seem to issue forth from the middle of our torso, somewhere around the navel or the solar plexus. This is in large part because there are several large bundles of nerves in this region, and it is from this area that our physiological functions run. We also tend to feel many of our emotions in the area of the torso, fear, longing, desire, joy and many others. These feelings move and play over our whole torso like a musical instrument, and feelings are run completely by our subconscious mind. Our conscious minds can think of something, and feelings will result, but it is because of the interaction of the conscious with the subconscious. It must be remembered that the subconscious also has access to all parts of our body. Just think how often once we really know how to do something, such as driving a car or washing dishes, it suddenly seems effortless. We barely feel like we are doing anything. This is because the subconscious mind has taken up the task, moving our bodies through the intricate set of procedures effortlessly. The subconscious is truly a great friend and assistant to the conscious mind.

The superconscious mind is traditionally placed just above the head. This is largely a psychological phenomenon based on the idea that inspiration rains down on us from the heavens above. In Yoga, superconscious-ness issues from the Sahasrara, the thousand-petaled lotus chakra at the crown of our head. In the Qabala, the superconscious is in Kether, which again means crown. In actuality the superconscious mind is just as intimately connected to each part of our body as the others. It is only a convenient place to locate it, for the reasons above, as well as a few other physiological reasons that we will get to later. At any rate, it is usually imagined to be occupying a field of light just above the head, with that light issuing down upon us and into us. This is a convenient way of imagining the superconscious, like a halo of divine light above us, and many exercises in this book will have you do just that.

Exercise 3 - Points of awareness

Time Required: 10 to 15 minutes

The following exercise will get you into touch with the areas of your body associated with the three personal parts of your consciousness

1. Stand with feet shoulder width apart.

2. Imagine that a string is pulling the top of your head toward the ceiling, making your spine stretch and align itself. Tuck your pelvis; let your shoulders fall down and back, relaxed.

3. Focus all your attention into your head, put all your consciousness into your head. Now walk around your house, keeping all your awareness in your head. See how this makes you feel. How does this affect your sense of self, sense of awareness and overall well-being?

4. Now focus all your attention into your stomach. Again, walk around your house, keeping all your awareness in your stomach. Lead with your belly. See how this makes you feel. How does this affect your sense of self, sense of awareness and overall well-being?

5. This time, imagine a globe of white light directly above your head, shining down on you. Focus all your attention up into this light. Walk around your house, keeping all your awareness on and in the light. See how this makes you feel. How does this affect your sense of self, sense of awareness and overall well-being?

6. When you are finished, write down your observations in your journal.

Exercise 4 - *Imagination, Breathing and Feeling*

Time Required: 5 to 10 minutes

There are three main ways in which the subconscious directly links to the conscious mind. These are through your imagination, through your breathing, and through your feelings. The conscious and the subconscious minds can both access these things fairly easily, and it is through them that the two minds communicate in both directions. Keep this in your awareness. It is of great practical importance.

1. Find a comfortable place where you can relax for ten minutes or more without interruption.

2. Close your eyes, and imagine a leaf with your conscious mind. Notice the detail or lack thereof. Now, ask your subconscious to produce an imaginary leaf. This may only appear briefly, but it will appear if you ask.

3. Notice the differences between the leaf that you created with your conscious mind and the one that your subconscious mind created. Which seemed more "real?" For most people, the subconscious produces a much more realistic image, although it might only appear for a moment.

4. Try this with a few more objects, such as a blue cube, a shimmering diamond, a pair of sneakers, and an elephant. Try to really notice the differences between your conscious and subconscious productions. For the most part, you will want to have your subconscious take an active role in visualization with the guidance and direction of your conscious mind throughout this book, because it is much more powerful at it than your conscious mind. Your subconscious will add energy to your visualizations.

5. Now, notice the feelings in your body. Take a few very deep breaths consciously. Then let your subconscious take over your breathing again. Notice the difference between the quality of your breath when it is controlled by your subconscious as opposed to your conscious mind. Also, notice the feelings in your body right now, after the deep breaths. You will find that physiological changes are taking place. One of the easiest ways of changing our emotions is by changing our breathing to deep breaths. Our subconscious minds react to the change. It is an easy and effective means of communication to the subconscious that you want to relax.

6. Take a few more deep breaths, then turn breathing back over, noticing how it changes the way that you feel. Repeat a few more times.

7. Think about something that makes you angry. Now ask your subconscious to come up with something that makes it angry. How are these different? Are they different things or do they just feel different? Try this with happiness, sadness, fear, and excitement.

8. When you are finished, write down your observations in your journal.

In this exercise, hopefully you have noticed that these tasks actually somewhat require the assistance of your subconscious mind even when your conscious mind is the active worker, and that you are really constantly communicating back and forth between these two aspects of your mind. But by directly communicating with the subconscious and through the subconscious the superconscious you can easily and quickly cause transformations in your life. If you wish to develop psychic and magick abilities, the very first thing you need to do immediately is to form a solid friendship with your subconscious mind. The subconscious mind runs your energy body, and through your energy body connects with the superconscious. Take a moment now, and perform this next exercise.

I also hope you will have noticed that your subconscious is much more powerful at producing these phenomena directly than your conscious mind. By describing what you would like to experience, and allowing your subconscious to produce the experience you will greatly enhance your imaginative capabilities. You may also wish to try combining multiple sensory modalities when using your imagination. If you are seeing, feeling, hearing, smelling and tasting your visualizations, they will become much more rich and dynamic.

Exercise 5 – The Subconscious and the Pendulum

Time Required: 10 to 15 minutes

You are already in constant communication with your subconscious every moment of each day, through the methods that you've just explored in the previous exercise. However, it is sometimes useful to isolate this communication, so that you are sure that you are giving your subconscious a voice, and not simply speaking for it. This simple method just allows you to remove most doubt from the process, by allowing your subconscious to communicate directly in an exterior form that you can view with your eyes. Of course, it's still possible for you to move the pendulum consciously, but if you allow your subconscious to control the pendulum, you will have an easy method of back and forth communication. This method mostly limits the communication to yes and no questions, but it is still of great value, and there are plenty of ways to expand its possibilities.

You will need your pendulum for this exercise, so if you have not yet obtained one, now is the time to get it. Your subconscious is very childlike, and enjoys playing games. The following should be done in the spirit of fun.

1. Sit holding pendulum, so that it dangles about three inches from your fingers, comfortably.

2. Talk directly to your subconscious, telling it that you are going to be playing this game with it. Tell your subconscious that a back and forth motion means yes, and a side to side motion means no. Then demonstrate the motions with the pendulum, again going over the meanings with your subconscious clearly.

44

3. Now, ask your subconscious if it understands these rules, telling it to show you a yes with the pendulum. Do not move the pendulum, but allow your subconscious to use the involuntary muscles of your hand to create the movement.

4. Now ask your subconscious to show you no.

5. Ask your subconscious a few simple yes or no questions that it will know the answers to (it does not necessarily have much more knowledge than you)

6. This simple exercise has now opened the door of communication directly with your subconscious mind.

7. When you are finished, write down your observations in your journal.

DELETION, GENERALIZATION AND DISTORTION

Neuro-Linguistic Programming (NLP) provides us with a couple of interesting models that you will find useful in your work. As I mentioned previously, over the course of our lives we have limited our awareness, and glued together the energy patterns of the universe into a rigid set of physical objects. The way in which we have done this is a threefold process of modeling: deletion, generalization and distortion. These are the three tools we humans use to model reality into chunks that are easily understandable for our conscious minds. These tools are not bad in any way, we need them to get through our everyday lives, but we must learn to at least partially circumvent them in order to experience alternative information and psychic realities.

Deletion

It is simply not possible for our conscious minds to process all the bits of information that surround us. We are constantly experiencing millions of pieces of information every second. In order to have meaningful relationships and negotiate our way through consensus reality, we must delete huge portions of potentially available information. Out of the millions of potential pieces of information, our conscious minds can handle just a few at a time. Our subconscious can handle vastly more, and tends to help us sort through what we may find useful at the time, giving us all that we can handle. Occasionally, the subconscious feels that we are ignoring something important, and gives us a little pang or internal pressure to become aware of something. It is fairly easy to instruct the subconscious to make new and different information available that we have previously ignored, and the trainings in this book will help us to do just that.

Generalization

We use generalization positively to access pieces of past information when we are presented with similar problems in the present. For instance, when we were first learning to write the letters of the English alphabet, we were equally struggling with the shapes, and the physical process of holding the pen or pencil. But, a few years later, when we learned to write in cursive, we were able to apply our previous experience with the writing instrument, and just have to learn to create the new shapes. If you have ever ridden a skateboard, it makes riding a snowboard much easier in the future and vice versa. On the negative side, we often simply don't really notice the things around us, because they are similar to things we have already seen. When we see a chair, we don't really notice that specific chair, but just generalize it as a thing we may or may not sit on. We often do this with people and experiences. "Yes, I'm making love to Betty again, I have done it a million times, and this is how it always feels." Thus we do not allow spontaneous new experiences to enter our lives, and we must always consider everything new if we are going to develop real power.

Distortion

Distortion is our mind's ability to take something that is one way, and transform it into something else altogether. This can happen with both objects and situations in our lives. It can be a very positive tool, as in the "suspension of disbelief" that we engage in while watching a movie, play or looking at a painting. It is also the way in which we create new things and new ideas. All dreams and fantasies are distortions. All inventions are based on distorting possibilities. One hundred years ago, the idea of information traveling through the air was impossible, but a few dreamers were capable of thinking outside this paradigm and we now have a global information network that is truly astounding. On the other hand, distortion can be extremely negative because we humans can transform the meaning of anything into a totally disempowering mess.

Exercise 6 - Observing Reality

Time Required: 2 to10 Minutes

To get a little bit of a practical idea about these processes, take a moment right now and do this brief exercise.

1. Gather a few small objects from directly around you. It doesn't matter what they are. They do not need to be anything meaningful to you. Pens, jewelry, remote controls, any objects that you have near at hand, that you recognize and know well, but that you haven't ever given much thought to.

2. Take one of the objects in your hand, and really look at it. I mean really look at it, as if you've never seen anything like it before. Notice the shapes, textures, colors and ways that it reflects or absorbs light. Try to discern every detail of the object. What is the object made of? How was it gathered from the earth, and shaped into the object you now hold? What was it like in its natural state? Is it completely man-made? Where did the chemicals come from? Truly, it is a fascinating object. Do you understand it? Do you really know what the meaning of this object is? Does it have a meaning? Is it a meaningless object? Now look at it intensely, allowing your eyes to de-focus a little, and staring intently, until the object begins to have a bit of a halo around it. Is it now a magick object?

3. Repeat this same process with the rest of the objects you have chosen.

4. When you are finished, write down your observations in your journal.

You may not understand exactly why you are doing this exercise, but that is unimportant right now. As you become less and less connected to the surface deletions, generalizations and distortions you use to define the things you see, you will become more and more connected with reality. As reality begins to dawn in your life, you will notice that you begin to have power over yourself, and the situations of your life.

It is our subconscious minds that really run these modeling patterns, so we must persuade our subconscious that it is okay to view the world in novel new ways. The easiest way to do this is through altering our state of consciousness, which we will cover in a few moments.

VISUAL, AUDITORY, KINESTHETIC

NLP practitioners consider our senses to be of utmost importance in communication and change. Each of us has favorite sensory modalities for processing information, and by understanding which of these modalities we prefer, it makes the process of communication much easier. Some of us are very visual. We like to see diagrams and pictures and read instructions, we like to look at how things work, we are attracted to bright colors, attractive images, and we process information largely through visual pictures in our minds. Some of us are more auditory, we like things explained to us verbally, we are attracted to soothing tones; we process information with words in our heads. Some of us are more kinesthetic, we like a hands on approach, we like to touch things, are attracted to textures, sensations, and enjoy processing information with our feelings. These senses, Visual, Auditory and Kinesthetic, form the building blocks of our waking consciousness.

The senses of taste and smell are of equal importance, but most of us do not use these senses to actively process information. Instead, our subconscious uses them primarily to decide whether we like or dislike something or someone. We all of course use all of these senses to a greater or lesser degree, but each of us has sense modalities that we use more often than others. What's more, the sense modality that you favor most likely indicates the psychic modality that you will find easiest to develop. For instance, if you tend to be visual, you will probably favor clairvoyance (psychic seeing) above clairaudience (psychic hearing) or psychic empathy (psychic feeling) and so on.

Exercise 7 - Are you VAK?

Time Required: 5 to 10 minutes

Take a look at these lists, and you will notice that you favor one of them at least a little above the others, especially in times of stress. Keep in mind that we all favor different modalities in different situations, so you are not strictly one or the other. This is just to give you a simple idea of which one you tend to favor most. These are again just tendencies, and certainly not hard and fast rules. You will of course find that you have tendencies associated with more than one modality, but try to get an idea of which one dominates your cognitive processes.

Take a moment and notice which of these items seem to apply to you.

Visual:

You like to write things down
You like movies and TV
You read billboards
You like written instructions or diagrams
You like to daydream fantasize
You follow written recipes for cooking
You like to draw and doodle
You are good at planning, visualizing problems and solutions

48

You memorize things with pictures or writing things down
You like to read
You like maps for finding your way in new places

Auditory:

You prefer verbal instruction
You work out math problems aloud or with words in your head.
You repeat things over and over to remember them
You use rhymes to remember things
You like to talk over plans and decisions
You like to ask for driving directions
You like talk or news radio
You are a good listener
You are a good talker
You love to ask questions
You want to be understood

Kinesthetic:

You like to make things
You like to get hands on things
You sway to music
You like to move
You like to touch textures
You like to be touched
You love hugs
You like to learn by experiencing
You like to take things slow
You are sensitive to others feelings
You like comfort
You like to make people happy
You seem to just know when others are sad, happy or angry

Write down your observations in your journal. Are you more visual, auditory or kinesthetic?

Exercise 8 - The Importance of the Imagination

Time Required: 10 to 15 minutes

The power of subjective experience is amazing. Whatever you pretend to be true is considered your truth to all parts of your consciousness except in many cases for your conscious mind. So, if you are thinking positive and empowering thoughts, your subconscious and superconscious minds will believe these things to be true, and these things will start to manifest in your life. If, on the other hand you are constantly thinking limiting negative thoughts, your subconscious and superconscious will believe that is what you want to experience, and bad things will continually happen in your life. As we explored a short while ago, our imagination directly connects our conscious and our subconscious. By using our imaginations alone, we can profoundly affect our emotions, physiology and ultimately our experience of life. "When a man imagines he actually creates a form on the Astral or even some higher plane; and this form is as real and objective to intelligent beings on that plane, as our earthly surroundings are to us."[1] Explore the following brief subjective experience exercises and you will see what I mean.

1. Find a comfortable place where you can relax for ten minutes or more without interruption.

2. Now, close your eyes, and begin to imagine that you are in a super-market, in the produce section. Try to imagine this as vividly as possible. In front of you is a shelf of bright yellow, juicy lemons. One of them has been conveniently cut in half for you. Pick up this lemon half in your imaginary hand, and look at its sections, examining the juicy corpuscles, and feeling the cool, bumpy texture. Squeeze it a little, imagining the juices flowing into your hand. Now stick the juicy part right in your mouth, and squeeze. Taste the incredible sourness of the lemon juice flowing into your mouth, and running down your chin. How does it taste?

3. Now imagine that you are being whisked away into the recent past in India, and you are on a dusty street in a very poor village. You can smell animals, and in the distance you can see a small crowd of very hungry looking children. In the center of this throng, you can see Mother Theresa handing out bread to the children from the bag. Walk up to Mother Theresa, and see her smiling at you kindly. Then punch her in the stomach and steal the bag of bread. How does this make you feel?

---

[1] *Ritual Magic of the Golden Dawn*, p. 47

4. Now imagine that you are in a dark and gloomy old house. We all have secret fears, things that scare us unreasonably. As you turn a corner in the house, find yourself face to face with something that you truly fear. Choose something that you really find horrible and scary, your most secret and awful fear. Allow yourself to get close, to look this fearful thing right in the face. How does this affect you?

5. When you are finished, write down your observations in your journal.

If you've really done the preceding exercise you will notice that these brief reveries set off all sorts of physiological, electrochemical responses in your body. Your salivary glands produced saliva, you felt guilt or perhaps mischievous pleasure, and you produced adrenaline. But none of these experiences were technically "real." Your subconscious behaved as if these experiences were real even though you were just pretending, and produced the appropriate emotional and physiological responses. How many unreal things have you made real with this same power? How many times have you avoided doing things you wanted to do because you allowed this power of imagination to negatively limit yourself? You can now use this incredible power for good, imagining great things for yourself, and making them happen easily and naturally.

Imagination is what magick is all about. It is the astral light, the "Azoth of the Philosophers," as Eliphas Levi called it. It is through the imagination that we connect with our psychic abilities, communicate with angels and spirits, and express our magical wills. It is not "just imaginary," but rather it is through our imaginations that we connect to the subtle underpinnings of the world of energy that surrounds us. Our consciousness is connected with all things, and our imagination is that connecting link between everything. But this power is most easily accessible to us when we have shifted our awareness more fully into our inner worlds.

ALTERED STATES OF CONSCIOUSNESS

Consciousness is a continuum. It is through shifting our consciousness into unfamiliar areas of this continuum that our minds and imaginations give us access to paranormal experiences. But our minds are not mechanical instruments that clink from one gear into another, one moment in consensus reality, the next in some magical realm, although this does happen occasionally. For the most part, these experiences happen in a more fluid way. Strange things actually happen around us all the time, but we frequently do not recall them, because when we shift through states of consciousness, we often seem to forget what occurred in the previous state. How often have you woken up from a dream,

51

feeling that something important or interesting had just been happening, but you are completely incapable of recalling what it was?

We are in fact conscious at all times. It is just that we are operating out of different states of consciousness, and there is some trouble translating between the layers. A sort of amnesia seems to block our recall between the states of consciousness, unless we are very careful to make sure that we remember what has taken place. I use terms like subconscious, unconscious, superconscious, but they are all your consciousness, and you are always aware on one or all of these levels. Even in the deepest sleep states, it is still possible to obtain meaningful communication with the sleeper. I have experienced this sort of communication both as the sleeper and as an alert communicator, conversing with a sleeping subject. In my hypnosis office I have had communications with a client, either through words or body signals, and the client has had absolutely no recollection of the communication. But meaningful information was passed in both directions, so the person was conscious on some level, and the therapeutic result was obtained. Some part of our essential consciousness is always aware. I have occasionally had full conversations with my sleeping girlfriend that she does not remember. If I ever realized she was asleep, I'm sure I would ask much more interesting questions!

One explanation that psychologists offer for altered states is that there seem to be different patterns of brainwaves associated with the basic distinct phases of consciousness when a subject is connected to an electro-encephalograph (EEG) machine. Again, consciousness is a very fluid and elusive thing, so this model is a bit simplistic. All of these states blend into one another, and it is not possible to strictly say that one thing is always this and another that. Still, it is useful as a way of classifying general experiences. There are five basic distinct types of brainwaves: Beta, Alpha, Theta, Delta and Gamma.

Beta — brainwave frequency: 14 to 30 cycles per second

These are the kind of brainwaves that are observed by an EEG machine when we are in an active and alert state of mind. Many of us actually spend far less time in this state than one might suppose. This is a state of outer awareness in which we are focused on what is going on around us. This is the state we are in when we are jolted into full awareness such as when we must solve a problem, or when someone swerves in front of us while driving. It is the state we are in when we are seeking solutions, facing opposition, doing deductive thinking or any conscious, reactive state of mind.

Magick that may be conducted in the Beta State: for the most part, you should at least be in a light alpha state for any serious work, but occasionally you may have success with telepathic sending, intuition, insight, prophecy through flashes of insight, magnetic charisma or fascination in the Beta State. These lists are only meant to be suggestive. Please judge by your own experiments.

Alpha — brainwave frequency: 8 to 13 cycles per second

These are the brainwave patterns observed when a person is deeply relaxed and focused inwardly. It's often called the light trance. This is the state we are often in when watching TV or a movie, meditating, doing yoga, or driving long distances on the highway. Many of us spend a lot of time in this state.

When performing magical rituals, it is ideal to be in the alpha state of consciousness, but when we first start to do rituals, we are usually in the beta state, trying to remember all the steps, words and gestures correctly. Over my life, I have noticed that more complex rituals tend to actually not be as effective as simple ones, because it is the state of consciousness, not the ritual that is doing the magick. This is one of the many reasons why I have tried to keep all of the ritual elements in this book as simple as possible. However, that is my predisposition, and for you it may be that complicated ritual tasks help you get into the best state for you. There are plenty of sources for very complicated rituals in many good magick books. I am not going to reprint them here. But, no matter what rituals you use, allow yourself to do things wrong, attempting to remain in the relaxed and focused state rather than concerning yourself overmuch with ritual details. State is the key to success. This is true of all ritual, not just those to be found in this book.

Magick that may be conducted in the Alpha State: The majority of your work will be conducted in the alpha State, such as clairvoyance, clairaudience, clairfeeling and empathy, mental influence and fascination, intuition, traveling in the spirit vision (body of light), telepathy, spell-casting, manifestations, automatic writing, evocation, communication with other planes and so on.

Theta — brainwave frequency: 4 to 7 cycles per second

This is the state associated with extreme relaxation and the deeper trance states of advanced meditation or deep hypnosis. It is sometimes called the "hypnagogic state." This is that usually brief time between waking and sleeping when images, sounds and mini-dreams seem to come into your mind of their own volition. When you focus your consciousness in this state you often have "peak experiences" associated with illumination and transcendence. You may also be actually asleep in this state. You usually do not have much awareness of your body in the Theta State, although you may feel vibrations, ripples or slowly spinning sensations. Many writers on the paranormal and the occult ascribe these sensations to the loosening of your astral or ethereal body. I will leave that to your own exploration to find out what you think. You will generally not move your physical body at all in this state, unless your subconscious causes some sort of twitch.

Magick that may be conducted in the Theta State: out of body experiences/astral projection, illumination, inspiration, intuition, channeling, communication with other planes, and past life experiences.

Delta — brainwave frequency: .5 to 3 cycles per second

This is the state of deeper sleep, sometimes both dreaming REM sleep and the deeper so-called dreamless sleep. However, dreamless sleep is a misnomer. Our untrained minds are always generating images, sounds and feelings even in the deepest sleep states. After nearly twenty years of exploring my mind I can say with confidence that we are always dreaming, always aware. We usually do not consciously remember Delta experiences without training and effort.

Magick that may be conducted in the Delta State: Out of Body Experiences/Astral Projection, Channeling/Mediumship.

Gamma — brainwave frequency: over 30 cycles per second

This is the state of hyper-alert mental activity. The Gamma brainwave has been observed in certain monks and yogis in states of higher consciousness, and may play a useful part in some remote viewing experiences. But we will not have occasion to focus on this state particularly in the techniques of this manual.

So, let's take a look at these states in actual experience. The following exercises will give you a practical impression of these states associated with the different brainwaves and their functions.

There are numerous light and sound mind machines, and other gadgets, gizmos and computer programs designed to entrain the brain to these different states, and I think these can definitely be useful. Many of the techniques in this book can easily be adapted for use with these brainwave entrainment devices. This can be a very useful method of working. However, I recommend that you also learn to get to these states without outside assistance, because these electronic tools can become crutches, just as drugs (and thinking) can become addictive. It is very simple to get into the alpha, theta and delta states, and we are free to use them anytime, once we are used to them.

Exercise 9 - Beta State – Waking Consciousness

Time Required: 2 to 5 minutes

Beta consciousness is the state of full conscious awareness, when your conscious mind is running things. No complex exercise is necessary to experience it. You are in this state right now. Any time that you are trying to understand something new, or deal with a difficult situation your brain will be functioning primarily with Beta waves. This state of consciousness is perfect for critical thinking and operating effectively in the outside world. We actually spend less time in this state than you might think. So much of our time is spent watching TV or doing mundane tasks that we are often in the alpha state in our daily lives. Here are a few examples of times when you will be operating in the beta state:

Working on a crossword puzzle
Rock climbing
Making a speech
Trying to seduce someone
Telling a funny story
Doing math
Really listening to someone talk about something important
Driving in difficult traffic
Building a piece of furniture
Solving a problem with your computer

Even in these tasks, we can often slip into trance or the alpha state.

1. Take a few moments and observe your state of consciousness at this moment. If you spend too long on this, you may actually slip into the alpha state. Keep your mind active. Go ahead and think about your day. What are you going to be doing with the rest of your day? How long do you have to spend on *The Book of Magick Power* today? This is your waking state, and on an EEG machine you would primarily be registering beta waves right now.

2. Record your experience in your journal.

Exercise 10 - Alpha State - The Light Trance

Time Required: 15 minutes to an hour

As I've mentioned above, we often find ourselves at least on the borderline of this state, so it won't be an unfamiliar place. This state has been called many names, the light trance, the magical trance, magical consciousness, daydreaming, meditation, introspection and countless other words too. It is simply the state of consciousness in which we limit our attention, relax and focus inward. Even if we are still looking outward, we are generally referencing inner states when we are in this state of consciousness. The brain slows down, and alpha waves begin to predominate. In this state our subconscious mind becomes more active, while our conscious mind becomes more docile. This is why this state is so perfect for exploring magick and the paranormal. As our brain slows down and moves inward we begin to notice things through our subconscious that we usually simply tune out. These are the beginnings of psychic and magical awareness. We are often naturally in the alpha state when we are:

Watching TV or a movie
Cleaning
Making love
Driving on the highway
Daydreaming
Meditating

This is the simplest method I have come up with so far for entering the Alpha State in a magical context. It may look a little long at first, but it is in many ways simpler and more direct than the technique I used in The New Hermetics. This exercise, or the next slightly faster modification of it, will be the first thing you do anytime you wish to conduct magick or psychic exploration. This exercise will actually provide two separate things for you. It will put you in the Alpha State, but it will also begin to connect you up with your superconscious mind, by visualizing a globe of light right above you, and this light shining down into your body. As the light travels into your body, you will be connecting up your subconscious and your superconscious, and this is a gateway to real power. You will count down very slowly from ten to one, as you send the light down through your body. As you are doing this, allow each part of your body to entirely relax. This exercise can be very healing and balancing as well as providing you with a useful skill. The key to success with this technique is to really allow yourself to relax as you are doing it.

1. You should find a place where you will not be disturbed for at least a half an hour. This may mean unplugging the phone. Don't worry! Those calls from the coast can wait!

2. Sit in a very comfortable chair, or lie down in bed. This latter may not be the best idea because it is very easy to fall asleep, and we do not really want that to happen.

3. Once you are seated, (or lying down) close your eyes and notice the feel of your body. Are there any pains or itches that jump to your awareness? Do you have to go to the bathroom? Take as much care of these things as you can before you begin. Once you start you do not want to be disturbed or move much if possible. Itches may plague you in the early stages of this exercise, but you will eventually overcome them.

4. Now that you are ready, you must simply begin to relax and focus inward. Take three or four deep breaths, allowing your body to relax deeply with each exhale, and then turn your breathing back to your subconscious.

5. Begin to focus on a spot right above your head, imagining a grapefruit sized globe of bright white light a short distance above you. This light is an access point to your superconscious mind. It is a connection to spirit and the divine, so attempt to feel a loving feeling emanating from this light, and allow yourself to feel love toward this globe of light. Your visualization does not have to be clear or perfect, just pretend that you are doing it right. It will work as long as you pretend and feel loving toward the light, allowing yourself to have fun and be relaxed no matter how dim or wobbly the image is. Your subconscious mind can also assist you in visualizing this light above you. Ask, and see what happens.

6. Imagine this light as shining down on you, and as the light touches your head, imagine that your head is beginning to fill with light. As your head fills with light, allow this light to relax the top of your head, your forehead, eyes, cheeks jaw and the back of your head, mentally saying to yourself, "ten."

7. Allow the relaxing light to move down to your neck and throat, relaxing your neck and throat, saying "nine."

8. Allow the relaxing light to move down to your chest and shoulders, relaxing your chest and shoulders, saying "eight."

9. Allow the relaxing light to move down to your arms, hands and fingers, relaxing your arms, hands and fingers, saying "seven."

10. Allow the relaxing light to move down to your belly and back, relaxing your belly and back, saying "six."

11. Allow the relaxing light to move down to your groin and buttocks, relaxing your groin and buttocks, saying "five."

12. Allow the relaxing light to move down to your thighs, relaxing your thighs, saying "four."

13. Allow the relaxing light to move down to your knees, relaxing your knees, saying "three."

14. Allow the relaxing light to move down to your shins, relaxing your shins, saying "two."

15. Allow the relaxing light to move down to your feet and toes, relaxing your feet and toes, saying "one."

16. When you have finished, you will be in the Alpha State. It may not be extremely deep into alpha, but you will be there. If you would like to go deeper, simply go through steps 5-16 again. You may find yourself experiencing odd sensations, and completely relaxed. If you fall asleep during any part of this, do not worry. You will be able to continue as soon as you wake up, and at that point you will definitely be at least in the alpha state.

17. At this stage, you should just become acquainted with this state. Truthfully, you may not even be aware that you are in an altered state. You may just feel relaxed and hopefully filled with loving energy and light. All that has happened is that you've very slightly changed your perceptual conditions, and reduced the usual overwhelming number of signals from your physical body. Your focus has been turned inward, toward higher states of consciousness and your psychic abilities.

18. Simply observe this condition for a few minutes. You may hear voices, and you may see images. These will be of the same nature as the hypnagogic imagery that you may experience when drifting off to sleep. Although this will most likely not be anything of significance, you should attempt to remember what you have seen, and write it down in your journal. This habit cannot be emphasized too much, since it is the only way that you can objectively gauge your progress.

19. After a few minutes, or however long you feel comfortable with, you should begin to return to normal waking consciousness. This will certainly happen on its own after about twenty minutes or so, especially when you are first starting to work with this exercise. Still, you should endeavor to be in control of the situation. To come out of the trance is simply to reverse the process. Become aware of your feet, and slowly jiggle them. Become aware of your legs, and gently tense and un-tense them. Move all the way through the body, reawakening it. Finally, open your eyes and stand up. You will probably feel very relaxed.

20. Record your experiences in your journal.

You may find it difficult to relax satisfactorily at first. Don't worry. The pressures of modern life tend to overwhelm us all. If you have finished with the last step and still are holding on to a lot of tension, simply repeat the directions until you begin to notice a shift in your awareness. When you shift into the altered state you may notice a number of sensations:

- tingling
- warmth
- coolness
- sense of lightness
- sense of heaviness
- a lack of desire to move
- minor twitches in your fingers or toes
- feeling of slipping
- sense of floating

You may experience one or more of these sensations or something that is uniquely your own experience.

It is also possible to leave the trance state by slipping off into sleep. This is not at all dangerous, but it is not recommended for two reasons. First, you are attempting to learn control of your consciousness, and yielding to sleep is counter to that end, and second, it does not allow you to make an entry in your journal. The conscientious maintenance of your journal is paramount to your success in this endeavor. This state can be very refreshing. Even a few minutes in this state can be as rejuvenating as a long nap.

Exercise 11 - Creating an Anchor for the Alpha State

Time Required: 20 minutes to one hour

Once you have gone into the alpha state several times with the above method, you will want a quicker way to enter this state in any circumstance. This will allow you to use your developing powers whenever you need them.

I covered the subject of anchors and how they work in *The New Hermetics*, so I will not spend a great deal of time here in explaining them, but I will basically give you the same instruction for creating the anchor in this book. If you are in any strong state of emotion or experience, any unique stimulus at that time will create an anchor. Anytime you experience that stimulus again, you will be drawn back to that same state.

You can really use any triggering method you like to signal to your brain that you want to instantly go back to a particular state, but you must use the exact same trigger each time. So, for the sake of simplicity and continuity, I will teach you basically the same trigger mechanism as I used in *The New Hermetics*. I will use the words "Alpha State" rather than "Altered State," but you can also use whatever words are most comfortable for you. You must be in an intense and pure state for anchoring to work properly, so be sure that you get into a nice deep Alpha State before activating your anchor, and be sure to activate it at the peak of the experience, in other words when you are most deep.

The anchor we will use consists of three parts, visualization, words and a kinesthetic touch. The kinesthetic touch portion consists of pressing your index fingers, your middle fingers and your thumbs together firmly, but not too firmly, like a yoga mudra, or an "okay" sign, as you press say, "Alpha State," (or "Meditation") mentally to yourself. At the same time, you will be visualizing the light of super-consciousness descending through your body.

1. Enter the Alpha State as above.

2. You should now be in a relaxed but alert state. Deepen your relaxation to the deepest that you can relax while continuing to focus. You may do this by repeating the light descending relaxation visualization, or by just letting yourself drift deeper.

3. When you reach this very deep state of relaxation and focus, Again visualize the light above, sending it briefly through your whole body again, letting it relax you, then as it reaches your feet, filling you completely, press your index and middle fingers against your thumbs together firmly and say to yourself, "alpha state," (or any other word, as long as you are consistent).

4. Repeat the above process several times, coming up out of the alpha state, and going back down, then anchoring at the peak.

5. You will then want to test your anchor. Get into normal waking consciousness, then visualize the light above, sending it briefly through your whole body, letting it relax you, then as it reaches your feet, press your index fingers, your middle fingers and your thumbs together firmly and say to yourself, "alpha state."

6. You should be back in Alpha State again. If not, start at the beginning again, and work through this until you can quickly move into the alpha state at will.

Taking the time to master this will be well worth your while. From now on, you can simply use this exact anchor, visualizing the globe of light above, sending it briefly but relaxingly through your whole body, then as it reaches your feet, press your index fingers, your middle fingers and your thumbs together firmly and say to yourself, "alpha state."

Exercise 12 – Theta State – Deep Trance

Time Required: 40 to 50 minutes

Getting even deeper, right to the hinterlands of consciousness, is very easy once you've mastered the above. You will simply use the exact same technique you used for the alpha state with a slight modification. You will use colored light instead of white light, and these colors will progressively relax you even deeper. You will start with energetic red light, moving right through the rainbow to calm, spiritual violet light. This will eventually bring you very deep. You may in fact begin to go too deep, somewhere in the middle of this exercise. If you do, simply observe your state and continue to focus. In this state you will see mini-dreams, and it may become difficult to focus. Simply do your best to stay on track.

1. Again, sit or lie down somewhere where you won't be disturbed.

2. Enter the Alpha State as above.

3. Focus again on the globe of bright white light a short distance above you. Now imagine that the light is turning bright red.

4. Imagine this red light as shining down upon your head, and as the light touches your head, it begins to fill your head with light. As your head fills with red light, allow this light to relax the top of your head, your forehead, eyes, cheeks jaw and the back of your head, mentally saying to yourself, "ten."

5. Allow the relaxing red light to continue filling you, moving down to your neck and throat, relaxing your neck and throat, saying "nine."

6. Allow the relaxing red light to continue filling you, moving down to your chest and shoulders, relaxing your chest and shoulders, saying "eight."

7. Allow the relaxing red light to continue filling you, moving down to your arms, hands and fingers, relaxing your arms, hands and fingers, saying "seven."

8. Allow the relaxing red light to continue filling you, moving down to your belly and back, relaxing your belly and back, saying "six."

9. Allow the relaxing red light to continue filling you, moving down to your groin and buttocks, relaxing your groin and buttocks, saying "five."

10. Allow the relaxing red light to continue filling you, moving down to your thighs, relaxing your thighs, saying "four."

11. Allow the relaxing red light to continue filling you, moving down to your knees, relaxing your knees, saying "three."

12. Allow the relaxing red light to continue filling you, moving down to your shins, relaxing your shins, saying "two."

13. Allow the relaxing red light to continue filling you, moving down to your feet and toes, relaxing your feet and toes, saying "one."

14. Repeat the same process through your whole body with orange, then yellow, then green, then blue, then indigo, then violet light. Again, your visualizations of these colors do not need to be at all perfect. The idea is what is important, and the relaxation.

15. When you have finished, you will be at the Theta level of brainwaves. You may find dreams, voices or images swirling into your awareness somewhere in the middle of this exercise; this is a sure sign that you are getting to the right state. Keep relaxing, and make sure that you don't drift off into actual sleep.

16. After a few minutes of enjoying this state, or however long you feel comfortable with, you should begin to return to normal waking consciousness. Be in control of the situation. To come out of the trance simply become aware of your feet, and slowly jiggle them. Become aware of your legs, and gently tense and untense them. Move all the way through the body, reawakening it. Finally, open your eyes and stand up. You will probably feel very relaxed.

17. Record your experiences in your journal.

Exercise 13 – Delta State – Sleep Consciousness

Time Required: must be performed when retiring for the night

The Delta state is less useful for practical work than the Alpha and Theta states, unless you have a partner to communicate with you, because you will generally find it difficult to recall or be active in this state.

Still, the following exercise may be helpful, especially if you have trouble sleeping at night. However, be cautious, because you don't want to start falling asleep all the time when entering the Theta state.

1. When you are going to bed for the night, enter the Alpha then Theta states.

2. From here, simply allow yourself to drift even deeper. You will eventually black out entirely, or get lost in a dream.

3. If someone is with you, they can now ask you questions, and they may be able to speak directly with the unconscious aspects of your mind, unhindered by the conscious mind. Sometimes, the unconscious is grumpy and refuses to play along, but this technique may become useful later on, in communicating with non-human intelligences and obtaining past life memories.

4. If someone is with you, they can record any conversation in your journal for you. If you are alone, record anything interesting that you recall in the morning as soon as you awaken.

THREE TRANCE TIPS:

- Take advantage of opportunity. Do trance work in the morning or evening when you're relaxed and perhaps very mildly sleepy. But you don't want to be too sleepy.

- Trance is Relaxation and Focus. If you are "working" on getting into trance you are going wrong. Simply observe and go with the flow, remaining alert, and allowing yourself to naturally relax.

- When you want to visualize something, say what you'd like to yourself mentally. In other words, say "I would like to see an apple," if you'd like to visualize an apple. Then, just let an apple appear. Let your subconscious do the work. That's its job. Just ask. Don't worry if your visualizations are not crystal clear like a television screen, with time your abilities will improve.

Almost all psychic phenomena take place in trance states. All clairvoyance from remote viewing to precognition to Astral Travel to Lucid Dreaming are all variations on the same phenomenon, that of interfacing your conscious with your unconscious self, and gaining at least partial access to your totality, which is infinite.

YOUR ENERGY BODY

As we have discussed before, the universe is made up of energy, and our consciousness and everything around us is made up of this energy. Our bodies are also made up of energy, and energies flow through us as emotions, electrical impulses and the vital fluids of our physiology. The Chinese call these energies "chi," the Hindus, "prana," and there are dozens of other names and types of energy description that have been proposed and worked with by philosophers, scientists, and magicians for thousands of years. We need only concern ourselves with the basic idea that these energies can be useful to us in understanding ourselves and the world around us from a psychic perspective. We can also collect and direct these energies to make magical transformations in our lives. The next few exercises will practically introduce you to the "psychic vehicle" of humanity, your energy body and aura.

The easiest way to gain access to the vast stores of energy within us is through our sexuality. With the possible exceptions of eating and breathing, sexuality is the fundamental urge of all complex life forms. This drive is so powerful that huge portions of our time are spent suppressing or indulging in it. I have discussed some of the following information and exercises in my book, *Sexual Sorcery,* but since these are so integral to psychic and magical development, I will go over them here as well. Since sexuality is the most direct and powerful energy function that we possess, if we can harness it we will be able to do nearly anything. We can arouse the "Kundalini Effect" fairly easily through these means.

According to many adepts, sexual fluids are in fact the subtle evolutionary energy that builds the universe in its most physical aspect. Blood is also a gross physical vehicle for this energy. This is the reason why blood and sexual fluids are so often used in ancient magical practices. They are raw magick power in its most uncontrolled form. The sex act is like a generator, a dynamo that builds this sex energy up in the extremities, and then blasts it into the world in an unstable and tenuous explosion. Unfocussed, this energy dissipates.

When you learn to use this energy it will become a potent tool for magick and psychic development. The subjective feeling that you get from this energy is somewhere between a physical and a mental sensation. It can be experienced as a pleasant sensation in every part of your body, but the easiest access points to begin this flow of energy seem to be the top of the head and the base of the spine/sex organs. We will discuss energy centers further in a few moments.

These next few exercises are in a more or less cumulative order, so it will probably be a good idea to do them sequentially. You won't have much luck with the later few until you've had some luck with the former.

Exercise 14 - Conscious Breathing

Time Required: 5 to 10 minutes

We will begin by simply discovering the energy that surrounds us in the air that we breathe, and learning to focus our minds on our breathing. You are now going to spend a few minutes focused entirely on your breath. Breath is the key to vitality, but we so often ignore it.

1. Sit or lie down in a comfortable place.

2. You may enter the Alpha State using your anchor if you desire, but this is not absolutely necessary.

3. Begin to visualize vitality surrounding you in the air all around. Imagine it as sparkling phosphorescence or a soothing glow.

4. Now, as you breathe in, feel this vitality entering your body. Feel this vitality flowing into your whole body. Feel the vitality entering through every pore of your body. Take complete breath, filling down to your belly and up to your shoulders.

5. As you exhale, imagine everything toxic within you exiting through every point of your body. Exhale completely, emptying your lungs and ejecting all of the negative energy within you.

6. Repeat this for several minutes. If you get distracted by other thoughts, simply come back to the exercise as soon as you realize that you've become distracted.

7. When you have practiced this for a few minutes, notice how fantastic you feel!

8. Record your experiences in your journal.

Exercise 15 - The Sex Energy Channel

Time Required: 2 to 5 minutes

This exercise will be the key to unlocking your internal energy pathways. It is a very simple matter. Located between your sexual organs and your anus is a small area known as the perineum. The pubococcygeus muscle surrounds the perineum. This is one of the muscles that we use to urinate. Bearing down on it opens the urethra, and contracting it closes the urethra.

This muscle is intimately associated with sex, because when it is strong it increases our sexual sensitivity. It allows a woman the ability to contract her vagina, increasing pleasure for both partners, and a man to have a stronger erection, and the ability to hold out for longer before ejaculating. Who knew that such a wonderful little muscle existed?

Within this context, the perineum will become important because by focusing on its contraction we will draw energy up through our root or Muladhara chakra. That is another exercise however, first we must simply learn to locate and use the muscle.

1. Sit or lie down somewhere where you won't be disturbed.

2. First simply attempt to contract and let go of the muscle a few times. Simply imagine that you holding in urine, but instead of squeezing the whole groin muscle, just isolate the muscle beneath your sex organs. Squeeze your perineum several times. At first it may be hard to isolate, and you might squeeze other muscles too- anus, groin, abdominals, or even your shoulders. Just do your best.

3. When you able to mostly isolate your perineum, use the complete breaths of the previous exercise and coordinate these with contracting and releasing your perineum. As you inhale, contract the muscle. As you exhale, push down and release muscle.

4. After doing this a few times, you may begin to hold the breath in and hold the perineum contracted. Then exhale completely, and hold the breath out while pushing down on the muscle for a few seconds. When you are doing this correctly you will find yourself becoming experiencing a mild sexual arousal.

5. Record your experience in your journal.

Exercise 16 - Sex Energy Breathing

This next exercise builds directly on the last one.

1. Find a comfortable place to sit or lie down where you won't be disturbed.

2. Take three or four deep complete breaths, as in the previous exercises.

3. Begin to add the perineum contractions to your breathing, imagining that your breath is actually coming into your body through your perineum or Muladhara chakra. As you breathe out, imagine that the breath is flowing out your perineum. You will feel a definite sensation of energy in your pelvis and groin when you are doing this correctly, a tingling sexual feeling flowing up into your torso.

4. Continue to breathe in and out through your perineum region for several minutes, exploring the sensations that come up as you awaken this flow.

5. Record your experience in your journal.

THE SEVEN CHAKRAS

Now that you have begun to awaken your direct awareness of some of the energy that is flowing through you we can discuss the seven main chakras, or energy centers of the body. You are more than likely aware of these energy centers, but I will briefly describe and discuss them for the benefit of anyone who is unfamiliar with them. I will also share with you a few brief but important insights on them that will hopefully allow you to quickly and powerfully access their power.

The seven chakras are an integral part of Yoga philosophy and they have been drawn up into New Age literature and magick in the last several decades. They are often described as globes or whirling energy vortexes, and you may find these ideas useful in visualizing them, but that is not the only way that the seers in India originally envisioned them. They also saw them as lotus flowers. This lotus flower metaphor is useful, because it gives you the idea of something that opens, spreads and becomes beautiful in the light of the sun. The chakra lotuses also have different numbers of petals corresponding with letters and seed mantras in Sanskrit and pathways of energy through the body and into the universe. We don't need to concern ourselves much with these latter concepts in terms of practical work, but I just think it should be mentioned that our western ideas about the chakras are much more simplistic than the complex and beautiful descriptions of the tantric yogis. Sometimes the locations of these chakras are moved around slightly by various authors, and this is also the case amongst different schools of ancient yoga philosophy. But I will attempt to give you their locations according to the most common tradition.

But what are these chakras anyway? For our practical concerns they are energetic fields within our bodies that can block or enhance the flow of vitality through us. They are the containers and purveyors of our emotional energy, the paths through which our power and life forces flow. They are metaphors, but they are also very real. They issue forth from our spines, and you can actually somewhat see where they are located if you look at an anatomical drawing of our nervous system. Some like to compare them with glandular systems in our bodies, but I think it's much more appropriate to compare them with nerve plexuses.[1] They are centered in the spine, but it is usually easiest to find them as they radiate to the front of your body.

We feel all of our emotions in these chakras, our joys, our sorrows, our angers and our fears. In a moment, we will conduct a brief exercise that will show you what I mean, but first let me briefly describe these energetic areas.

---

[1] Shortly after writing this passage I opened a yoga book, *The Sivananda Companion to Yoga*, and found that the author made a similar comparison. See p. 71.

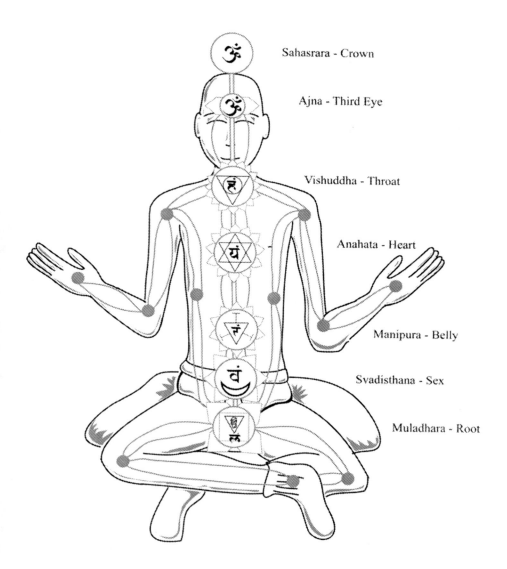

Sahasrara - Crown

Ajna - Third Eye

Vishuddha - Throat

Anahata - Heart

Manipura - Belly

Svadisthana - Sex

Muladhara - Root

Diagram 3 - The Ancient Hindu Chakras

Muladhara

The first chakra we have already worked with, and somewhat opened. It is called the root chakra, or Mulhadhara chakra which means "root support." This Chakra is located in the area of the perineum, between the genitals and the anus at the base of the spinal column. It is also called the Adhar-Padma, or fundamental lotus, and has four petals according to the ancient Indian seers.

It is said that there is a beautiful triangular yoni at the center of this chakra, where the goddess Kundalini dwells. Her tail is wrapped three and a half coils around, blocking the entrance of the Sushumna nadi or central channel of energy, which is basically our spinal cord. This can be considered for our purposes a metaphor for the evolutionary quasi-sexual power that can be released into the rest of your body from this chakra. This chakra is also linked with the element of earth. It is our connection with the physical world when we are seated in meditation, and it provides the firm base on which we rest. This chakra can be grounding and empowering to our lives in the physical world. According to yogic tradition, constant contemplation of the Muladhara chakra can also cause levitation, freedom from disease, cleverness and omniscience, and freedom from all sins. Feel right now in this area for a moment, until you discover some internal experience in your perineum. Contract it a little if you wish, until you feel that now familiar sensation.

Svadisthana

This Chakra is located at the base of your sexual organ, and is often referred to as the Sex Chakra. The name Svadisthana means, "her special abode." According to yoga philosophy, this lotus has six petals, and that daily contemplation of this chakra will make you beloved by all the beautiful goddesses, and makes it possible to travel on the astral plane, and have the highest psychic powers. It is associated with the element of water. This chakra can help us to turn our sex energy into a powerful spiritual force, as we raise that energy up into our higher chakras. Feel this area right now, experiencing the sensations at the base of your sex organ. This is just a few inches above your perineum, on the other side of your genitals. Contract your pelvic muscles to discover this point. By contracting these muscles you may feel a watery, liquid sexual sensation in your groin and pelvis.

Manipura

Located below the navel, though some authorities place it as high as the top of your solar plexus, Manipura means "City of the shining jewel." According to

70

tradition, this chakra has ten petals, and meditating on this chakra destroys sorrows and disease, makes the lord of desires, cheats death, gives you the ability to enter another's body, to make gold, to see the hidden adepts and see hidden treasures. It is associated with the element of fire, particularly the fire of the digestive processes. This chakra is the location of our "abdominal brain," the complex network of nerve channels that run our physiological functions. It is the natural home of our subconscious minds, and as we raise energy into it, we empower ourselves tremendously. It is our will, our center of balance, and our alchemical cauldron of transformation. Feel right now in this area for a moment, until you discover some internal experience in your belly. You can contract your stomach muscles for a few seconds to awaken some sensation in your abdomen.

Anahata

Anahata means, "Not struck," which implies the musical sounds and vibrations of the universal mind, which are "not struck" on an instrument, but rather issue forth mystically from the eternal silence. These are the sounds you can hear if you close your ears with your fingers. The Anahata is your heart chakra, located in the center of your chest. This chakra legendarily has twelve petals, gives you the powers of knowing past, present and future, clairvoyance and clairaudience, as well as the ability to walk on the air, and makes you desired by the daughters of the gods. This chakra is associated with the element of air. This is where we feel love and compassion, and when we raise our energy to this chakra from the lower centers, we naturally feel more loving and kind. Feel right now in this area for a moment, until you discover some internal experience in your heart. If you think about someone that you love very deeply it may help you to become easily aware of this chakra. You may also spread your arms wide to direct your awareness into your open chest.

Vishuddha

Vishuddha means, "Purified." This center is often simply called the Throat chakra. It is found directly below the larynx, by the thyroid gland. It has sixteen petals, and is associated with the element of spirit, or ether, or Akasha. It can be a gateway to the astral plane, as well as into dreaming and fantasizing. According to tradition, this lotus gives you wisdom, knowledge of sacred texts and their mysteries, strength, and the ability to live for a thousand years or more. This is the center where we create words and communication, literally where we vibrate words into existence. Feel right now in this area for a moment, until you discover some internal experience in your throat. If you intone the sound, "Eeeeeeee," you can cause a vibration in this chakra.

Ajna

Ajna means, "Command." This center is located between your two eyebrows, and is often called the Third Eye chakra. It is said that if you always secretly contemplate this chakra you will destroy the karma of your past life, and obtain the highest success. It is the location of your mind, and particularly the connection of your mind with your subconscious and superconscious. This is where you focus your attention during clairvoyance, or any time you are trying to see something psychically such as auras or spirits. Feel right now in this area for a moment, until you discover some internal experience in your third eye. If you intone the sound, "Mmmmmm," or "AUMmmmm," you can cause a vibration in this chakra.

Sahasrara

The word Sahasrara means, "Thousand-petaled," but this does not mean that there are exactly one thousand petals on the lotus. Rather, there are infinite petals. One thousand is just a convenient, descriptive and evocative word implying a multitude of petals. This is the seat of superconsciousness, the connection point for cosmic power and awareness. Feel right now in this area for a moment, until you discover some internal experience at the crown of your head. If you intone the sound, "AUM," deep in your throat you can cause a vibration in this chakra.

When these areas are blocked up by negative thoughts, painful emotions or suppressed feelings it prevents the flow of energy through us fully, and limits our awareness and joy in life. Interstingly, the avante-garde psychiatrist Wilhelm Reich rediscovered these exact same regions, and called them the segmental arrangement of character armor. There are even seven segments in his model.[1] By working to remove these blockages, and learning to access and flow energy through these regions we will awaken our powers, and improve our lives tremendously.

---

[1] *Character Analysis* pp. 406-430

Exercise 17 - Personifying Emotion

Time Required: 15 to 20 minutes

Let us take a look at where we experience specific emotions, and how they effect our energy bodies. The purpose of this exercise is to discover for yourself which parts of the body are crucial in expressing, feeling and holding specific emotions.

1. Stand up, and act out the following emotions. Don't verbalize; just physically and emotionally get into these states. Feel free to move and contort as dramatically as you need to in getting into these emotions.

2. Try this with: Jealousy, Anger, Love, Passion, Ecstasy, Irritation, Fear, Judgment, Pity, Hate, Inspiration, Joy

3. Observe the postures that your body assumes to get into these states. Where do you feel them? Where do you tense up? What does the energy feel like? How do you release the emotion when you are finished? Are there places where it gets stuck?

4. Record your experiences in your journal.

In terms of working through blocks and getting energy to move through our bodies I must recommend taking up a regular practice of yoga or the martial arts. These wonderful practices will awaken and charge you with energy in a totally positive and empowering way while they get you into great physical shape at the same time. I would love to see you find a class today! But, from our limited relationship in this book, you can use the following exercise to engage each of your chakras in turn, and start the process of clearing and engaging them more fully.

Exercise 18 – Breathing Up Through the Chakras

Time Required: 5 to 10 minutes

This exercise will be your first attempt at directing your energy consciously within your body. Hopefully, the previous exercises have given you a taste of what it feels like.

1. Sit or lie down in a comfortable place.

2. Breathe in and out a few times to relax, not concentrating on anything, just relaxing.

3. Then breathe in slowly, drawing in energy using your perineum. As you are inhaling, move this vibration of energy from you perineum up into your spine, radiating into your sex organs, your Svadisthana chakra then up through each of your other chakras, the Manipura or belly chakra, the Anahata or heart chakra, the Vishuddha or throat chakra, the Ajna between your eyes, and the Sahasrara at the crown of your head. Feel the energy palpably flowing up through each of these chakras, through the whole diameter of your body, as if you are entirely filling up with energy.

4. Breathe in slowly and deeply so that you can observe the energy as it flows through each chakra. You may discover blocks or unexpected images or feelings may arise in your mind. You will want to take note of what you are experiencing in each chakra over several long slow deep breaths, sending the energy up through your body with each breath. You may find it hard to pass the energy through certain chakras. At this point simply relax and observe the experience.

5. Each time you reach the crown of your head, or run out of breath, reverse the process. Send the energy down through all of your chakras, and out of your perineum.

6. Continue this for several minutes, observing the changes in your consciousness over time.

7. Record your experiences in your journal.

Exercise 19 - Chakra Breathing

Time Required: 30 to 40 minutes

This exercise is for exploring each of the chakras in detail, so that you can begin to more fully awaken your connection with these regions. You will also be able to clear away blocks as you discover them. If you experience difficult feelings, emotions or tightness as you perform this exercise, you can briefly stop, getting up and shaking your body, bending, twisting, stretching to release stress, moving and opening the particular area of your body where you are feeling blocked up. If you feel numbness or find it hard to find certain chakras, you may also wish to do this in order to open yourself up to greater connection with the chakra.

You may find it useful to imagine each of the chakras as a small sphere (or lotus flower) in an appropriate color. The most popular colors for visualizing the chakras are red for Muladhara, orange for Svadhisthana, yellow for Manipura, Green for Anahata, Blue for Vishudda, Indigo for Ajna, and Violet or White for Sahasrara. You do not need to feel confined to these colors. These are not really even the traditional colors of the chakras. These were added to the system at a late day, most likely through the Theosophical Society. In traditional yoga philosophy, there are several different versions of the colors for the chakras, but none are a rainbow. The Muladhara is often viewed as yellow, the Svadhisthana white, Manipura red, Anahata smoke colored, Vishudda blue, Ajna white, and the Sahasrara is usually seen as being beyond color.[1] If some other color, shape or feeling appears more appropriate to you, explore it.

1. Find a comfortable place where you won't be disturbed for at least thirty minutes.

2. Breathe in and out a few times to relax. You may use your Alpha state anchor if you wish.

3. Use your sex-energy breathing to concentrate energy into your Muladhara chakra, containing the energy right there in the area of your perineum. Imagine a set of imaginary hands, using them to pull open this area. Allow yourself to feel a sensation like you are opening a flower that is intimately a part of yourself. Experience any feelings, images or thoughts that come up as you open this chakra, letting them flow through you. Continue this for several breaths, experiencing the sensations of this region.

4. Now, move your awareness to the base of your genitals, the Svadhisthana chakra. Imagine that you are now breathing in and out through your Svadhisthana region, just as you were imagining with the Muladhara before. You can contract your genitals a bit as you breathe to help you focus. Use your imaginary hands to pull open this area, feeling the sensation that you are opening a flower. Breathe with your Svadhisthana for several breaths, experiencing the sensations and images that come up.

---

[1] *The Sivananda Companion to Yoga*, p. 71

5. Follow this procedure with each of your chakras in this way, opening and experiencing all seven chakras, allowing the sensation of each chakra to flow the whole region of the body where they reside.

6. Record your experiences in your journal.

Exercise 20 - Arousing Kundalini

Time Required: 15 to 45 minutes

Once you have thoroughly explored the previous exercise, and cleared through a lot of your inner blockages, you will finally be ready to really start drawing a powerful charge of energy in through the following technique. This technique may result in an immediate charge of "kundalini force" surging through your system, or not, but you will certainly begin to awaken this force eventually once you start working with this technique. If you still have a lot of blocks, you may find yourself having some pretty strange energy experiences at night or while you are resting or meditating. A number of people have had very disconcerting out of body experiences and energy overloads as a result of using this technique before they were ready. This is just one method for awakening the kundalini directly. There are many others.

To prepare yourself for this technique, you may want to spend a few minutes doing alternate nostril breathing to balance out your right and left hemispheres. I gave extensive instructions in this practice in *The New Hermetics*, but here is a very brief description.

Close your right nostril with your thumb, and exhale your breath completely through the left nostril. Then inhale through the same left nostril. Seal the left nostril with your middle finger, and exhale through the right nostril. Then, keeping your left nostril sealed, inhale through the right nostril. Then seal the right, and exhale your breath completely through the left nostril once again. This is one cycle, and can be repeated for as long as you like. Ten minutes of alternate nostril breathing regularly should balance you very well.

1. Find a comfortable place where you won't be disturbed for at least thirty minutes.

2. Breathe in and out a few times to relax.

3. If you wish, spend a few minutes doing alternate nostril breathing, as described above.

4. Spend a few minutes breathing energy up through all of the chakras, as in Exercise 18. Really feel the energy flowing through you.

5. Then, on an inhale, breathe in deeply contracting your perineum. Draw the energy up through your chakras. Hold your breath as long as you can, continuing to draw energy up through your body.

6. Exhale, holding the perineum contracted, holding on to the energy. Don't let it sink out as you exhale.

7. When all your air is out, hold your breath out, the perineum still contracted. As you are holding your breath out, draw in your abdomen, as if you were trying to get your navel to touch your spine. As you are doing this, draw energy up into your spine as if your spine were a straw.

8. Keep drawing up energy as you contract your perineum and abdomen. You may begin to shake. A tingling sensation will begin to move up through your spine. Hold for as long as possible, then exhale. Continue to draw energy up your spine throughout.

9. As you breathe in again, draw more energy up into your chakras through the perineum, and then follow the above directions again.

10. You will want to repeat this until your whole body is filled with an incredibly powerful force of energy. But this may be too much if you are not fully prepared. Try beginning with five breaths, but you can expand it to more if you are not feeling uncomfortable.

11. Record your experiences in your journal.

You will want to regularly perform these energy exercises until you feel quite adept at moving these inner forces. You may find yourself having spontaneous psychic and magical experiences as a result of just using these exercises including but not exclusively, out of body experiences, premonitions, visions and even 'poltergeist' type phenomena such as objects falling off the walls or moving around seemingly of their own accord. I have personally experienced most of these things in this way, and know of several other people with similar experiences. These are not necessarily to be sought out at this point, because they will be out of your control and perhaps not even healthy. It is better to experience them within the controlled confines of the exercises later in this book. They are a sign that you are moving energy, but that it is being channeled out of you through leaks and blockages.

THE AURA

One way in which the energy of the universe manifests in our bodies is through what is often called the aura, the subtle field of energy created by and around the human body. This aura is generally about a foot taller and wider than the physical body, and its shape is approximately that of an egg. The aura is the essence and discharge of the states of consciousness beyond the physical. It is the magical mirror of the universe. It is the body of light. It is your astral body. It is the psychically visible product of your emotions, your consciousness, your thoughts and to a certain degree your superconscious mind.

The aura may in fact be something that is largely imaginary. However, it is something that is possible to experience, and you can discover useful information about people through examining their auras. The aura may just be an imaginary way in which the subconscious can communicate and understand information about people and things. The important issue is that you learn to recognize it. Once you do so, you will be able to learn a great deal about a person, simply by perceiving their aura. You will find energy centers, stresses, desires and fears all have their place in the aura, and learning to perceive them is of utmost importance.

The aura can be perceived in many ways. We will explore three techniques. The first is with a pendulum, the second with the psychic eyes, and the third with the sense of psychic touch, wherein we use the subtler aspects of the physical consciousness to perceive the aura.

Exercise 21 - Feeling the Aura with a Pendulum

Time Required: 5 to 10 minutes

In this exercise you will use a pendulum in your hand to discover the edges of someone's aura. So, first you must find a person who is willing to allow you to experiment on them. This may be the difficult part of the exercise. You could try to do this on yourself, but this won't be the most effective way of doing this.

The convenient thing about this exercise is that your subconscious does all the work for you, and you will have a clear and visual indicator of what is going on in the form of the swinging pendulum.

1.   Have the person you will explore sit down and relax.

2. You must now also relax a little too. You can use your anchor to enter the Alpha State if you wish, but this is not totally necessary for this exercise.

3. Let your subconscious know what you are about to do, and make sure that it is willing to play along by asking. Once your subconscious has agreed, you are ready to proceed.

4. Hold your pendulum about a foot and a half above the head of the person you are going to explore, and gently lower it toward their head. Stop when the pendulum starts to swing. This may take more than one try, while you are just getting used to the process. You have found the edge of their aura when the pendulum swings to life.

5. Move the pendulum over the edge of this aura and explore. Find areas that seem tense, and areas that seem active, energy centers. These will cause the pendulum to swing differently, but you must learn for yourself exactly what these changes are. Your subconscious will react to different kinds of energy indifferent ways. After trying this technique a few times you may become very adept at learning a great deal about a person from their aura.

6. Record your experiences in your journal.

Eventually, you may find the pendulum very useful, but at first this might still be a difficult task. You must relax and try to have fun with the process. Good results will come eventually, but fun should always be had in the process.

Exercise 22 - Seeing the Aura

Time Required: 5 to 10 minutes

The second technique for perceiving the aura is the process of learning to "see" the aura visibly. You will not be seeing it with physical eyes, but rather sensing it with the inner eye, the third eye that we all have locked inside. Proficiency with this technique will most likely occur later, but it is possible to get a sense of the rudiments of it now. You must again find a person to observe, but in this case, you could simply go out into the world and look at the auras of the people you see. It is probably easier to start this process in a controlled way with someone who will sit still and play along.

Many instructions on seeing the aura suggest that you have the person you are viewing sit in front of some sort of blank or neutral colored wall. This is in fact totally unnecessary. It can actually help you to make the mistake of believing you are seeing an aura when you are in fact just seeing the after-image that burns into your retinas when you stare at something for a long time. You don't want to mistake this for an aura. It is just an optical illusion. The aura is not something you see with your physical eyes. You see it psychically, with your third eye, with the images projecting somewhat over your eyes.

1. Have the person you will explore sit down and relax.

2. Go into the Alpha State using your anchor.

3. Take a moment to do a little sexual energy breathing, to open up your energy body. You may also use the arousing Kundalini breathing technique if you wish.

4. Let your subconscious know what you are about to do, and make sure that it is willing to play along by asking. Once your subconscious has agreed, you are ready to proceed.

5. Don't look directly at the subject. Instead defocus your eyes and look just past them, over their shoulders or above their heads.

6. Move your attention to your third eye, and relax your attention there. Don't use your physical eyes to hunt for impressions, just attempt to receive images through the third eye. Don't focus hard on anything, just relax and keep your attention on your third eye, having fun.

7. You will soon get aura impressions. At first this may just be a sense of a sort of halo around the head and shoulders, but this will soon result in more impressions.

8. Record your experiences in your journal.

Exercise 23 - Feeling the Aura

Time Required: 5 to 10 minutes

We have not discussed this so far, but there are powerful energy channels in the palm of your hands and your fingertips. In this exercise you will use these channels to psychically sense the aura. To awaken the psychic senses in your palms, you may wish to gently rub your palms with your fingers in a circular manner until you feel a gentle tingle in both your palms and fingers. You will once again need to find a willing subject.

1. Have the person you will explore sit down and relax.

2. Go into the Alpha State using your anchor.

3. Take a moment to do a little sexual energy breathing, to open up your energy body. You may also use the arousing Kundalini breathing technique if you wish.

4. Let your subconscious know what you are about to do, and make sure that it is willing to play along by asking. Once your subconscious has agreed, you are ready to proceed.

5. Hold your hand about a foot and a half above the head of the person you are going to explore, and gently lower your hand toward their head. Stop when you feel any sort of change in your hand. This will be very subtle, and may take more than one try to find. It may be a warmth, or a vibrating sensation, or just a mental sense that this is the place to stop. You have just found the edge of their aura. What does it feel like?

6. Now, run your fingers over the edge of this aura and explore. Try to find areas that seem tense, and areas that seem active, energy centers. After trying this technique a few times you may become very adept at learning a great deal about a person from their aura.

7. Record your experiences in your journal.

Once you have learned this exercise well, you can ask the person you are exploring to concentrate on sending energy out of a particular area of their body. You will find that with practice you will always be able to tell from where they are sending it.

You may find this technique somewhat difficult at first, since it requires a certain level of sensitivity. This sensitivity will come, but you must be patient. There is no time clock for the rate at which your abilities will develop. Each of us have built blockages throughout our lives, and only by constant practice and work can we break through to our inner selves.

THE THREE KEYS TO SUCCESS IN MAGICK

There are three keys or pillars to success in magick and psychic development. These are image, energy, and inspiration. If you look back at the rest of the chapter, you will see that you have been introduced to these concepts already, but I want to draw your attention to these things specifically before we move on. If you make sure that all three of these keys play a part in all of your work, you will be rewarded with success. If you have two of them in your work, some things will work, but others won't. If you are ever having trouble, consider which of these factors is missing. One of them certainly will be. The three combined will guarantee your success. Let's take a brief look at each of these ideas.

Image

By image I mean a useful piece of information that communicates between the various layers of our minds. If we desire something to manifest in our lives, we must communicate that desire meaningfully to our subconscious. This can be through a visual picture, symbol, color, a feeling or a set of words. All of these fit into the category of image as I am using it in this context. In the case of psychic awareness, your conscious mind must receive a useful piece of information from your subconscious. Again, this can be through a visual image, a sound or voice, or a feeling. It is essential to either process. The image is the part of the experience that is either generated or received by the conscious mind.

Energy

Energy is your emotions, and the other subtle forces and energies within that we have just been working with. In order to accomplish anything, it requires energy. Energy is your will, your desire and your enthusiasm. You cannot get something for nothing. In order to do magick, you must arouse and direct your inner energy where you want it to go. In order to receive anything psychically, you must open up your energy channels, releasing blocks and allowing yourself to receive information from the energy all around you. Energy is the particular domain of the subconscious mind.

Inspiration

By inspiration I mean approval and assistance from higher consciousness. This is the exclusive job of the superconscious mind. Just about all psychic information comes from higher consciousness. All magick depends on the influence of higher consciousness in order to work. You must cultivate this connection with your superconscious mind in order to succeed with anything. Continued use of the earlier Alpha and Theta meditations will help with this connection immensely, as will all of the other exercises in this book.

As you can see each of these three keys corresponds with one of the three parts of your consciousness, and each of them are required for true magick. Image without energy and inspiration is a dead thing, inert and useless. Energy without image is uncontained and dissipates, as enthusiasms that fade quickly, lacking supporting ideas. Inspiration without image is incomprehensible, a pointless reverie. It is when these three combine that amazing things can happen.

CHAPTER THREE
Dreaming True

> "The Dream Delightful is then a Pageant of the Fulfilment of the True Will, and the Nightmare a symbolic Battle between it and its Assailants in thyself."
>
> -Aleister Crowley[1]

Dreams are such an important part of your consciousness work and psychic development that I want to include a brief chapter on this subject right at the beginning of our practices. So many schools of yoga, magick and shamanism teach the importance and power of dreams. I do not have space to devote more than a few pages to this subject. There are several recommended books in the bibliography that can give you a more thorough grounding in this exploration. Dreams unlock gateways in consciousness, pathways to hidden worlds and hidden powers. Dreams can combine the three principles of image, energy and inspiration in such an immediate and powerful way that their force can be unbelievable.

I'm sure that many of us have woken from a dream and felt that what had just happened in the dream was so powerful that even though we recognize it as fantasy, it still haunts our emotions for hours. When we can learn to direct this dream force, we can explore so many things. We can visit people, places and events through astral travel; we can heal lifelong issues within ourselves and play out our secret fantasies and desires. We can learn about our future and our past, and get creative inspiration. We spend almost half our lives dreaming, and learning to understand and work with our dreams can literally open us up to another life. And in our dream lives we are all powerful!

Dreaming has been a very important part of my own spiritual journey, but I have mostly left it out of my previous writings for many reasons, mostly because it was somewhat off track from the subjects I previously covered. I am

---

[1] *Liber Aleph,* p. 14

still often amazed to have a profound insight or magical lesson come to me spontaneously in the night. I have had many dream teachers, who have helped me to learn astral projection, cosmic consciousness and other wonderful experiences. For the past few weeks, I have been devoting more attention to my efforts at dream work, and I can tell you from experience that it is like riding a bicycle. Once you've got it you can use it whenever you'd like with just a small bit of effort.

From the time I was a small child, I've always had occasional spontaneous lucid dreams and frequent flying dreams, but I never could predict or control their occurrence. When I was a teenager I spent a huge amount of time and energy learning to achieve these experiences at will. In the next few pages, I will give you what I hope to be the practical advice that is the fruit of all that effort. There are many books that explain a number of these techniques, and you can read them if you like, but the core principles can be explained very simply and quickly.

DREAM RECALL

But many people do not even remember the vast majority of their dreams. Some people don't even think they dream much at all. The truth is that researchers have proven that we all dream many dreams each night. We just don't generally access this information and memory when we are awake. As you awaken from a dream you are quickly traveling up through three distinct states of consciousness from the Delta to the Beta state. It is often hard to remember what's happened when moving between two states of consciousness, such as when we've drifted into a reverie on a long car trip, and forget much of the journey. With such a wide gap in the consciousness continuum between the sleep and waking states, it is no wonder that we often forget our dreams. But once we learn to remember our dreams and become familiar with the dream state, it is easy to turn your dreams into powerful transformative tools.

The first thing that you need to do to start exploring dream work is to start recalling as many of your dreams as possible. You will sometimes remember five or six in a single night once you get the hang of it. If you are one of the many people who do not remember the majority of your dreams it is a very simple matter to start remembering your dreams, even tonight. The key to recalling your dreams is really just to start keeping a dream journal. Once you are starting to remember at least a dream or two each night you will be ready to start setting up lucid dreaming and dream programming.

Exercise 24 - Dream Journaling for Recall

Time Required: must be performed when retiring for the night

You will need a journal for this exercise. If you have taken my advice and started keeping a journal of your practices, you can use this same journal for your dreams. You can also keep a separate journal for dreams if you wish, but you may find it useful to keep all your work together. This will alert your subconscious to the fact that you are considering dream journaling to be a part of your magical work.

Not all of our dreams are particularly interesting or magically enlightening. Many times dreams are quite dull and ordinary; they are just a sort of shuffling of events and thoughts that we've experienced recently. However, we must endeavor even to record and remember these dreams too, so that our subconscious minds will really get the idea that we are wanting to have access to this part of our lives.

1. As you are getting ready to go to bed, open up your journal to the next blank page, and write at the top a sentence describing your intent, such as, "Tonight I will remember my dreams."

2. Look at those words on the page and repeat them to yourself a few times.

3. Pick up your pendulum, and consult with it about whether it understands your intention, and is willing to play along. Your subconscious houses your memory access, so you will need the support of your subconscious in order to succeed. Consulting with the pendulum will make your subconscious really understand that you are considering this important.

4. Close your journal, and keep it close by your bed as you lay down to sleep. You may even keep it under your pillow. Be sure you have a pen with it!

5. Close your eyes, and start drifting, as you are relaxing, repeat to yourself that you are going to recall your dreams with the same words you wrote in your journal. Do this in a relaxed and pleasant way, and do not obsess over it.

6. Go to sleep.

7. Immediately upon awakening, write down all you can remember of any dreams you've been having underneath the statement of intent you wrote in your journal. Do this even if you awaken briefly in the middle of the night. You will often wake from a dream about 5 or 6 hours into your sleeping and this is an excellent time to recall dreams. You may also simply awaken in the morning, in which case you should again endeavor to remember anything you can. Do not get up or move around much at all until you've written something down from your dreams. Just getting up and stretching can cause you to forget things you remembered vividly moments before. You do not have to write huge essays, even just brief notes and images so that you can remember later what the main points of the dream were.

8. If you are not recalling anything, or very little, close your eyes again in the position you were in when you were sleeping. Try to recall what you were just doing. Try to remember a scene, an image, or anything that might jog your recall Don't struggle, just simply relax and think back quietly on where you just were...

This is a very simple and extremely effective way of starting to remember your dreams. But you may not remember anything at first, in which case you should calmly and patiently repeat this exercise until you do start remembering your dreams. It will come eventually, and you will be grateful, once you start remembering powerful and evocative dreams.

Exercise 25 – Throw Out Your Alarm Clock

Time Required: must be performed when retiring for the night

One of the biggest hurdles to remembering your dreams is the disruptive wake up created by your alarm clock. This fast awakening and irritating noise will cause you to forget your dreams more than anything else. In order to set up dreaming most effectively, you must really try to stop using your alarm as much as possible. But, at the same time, you don't want to start being late to work because of me. You'll end up getting fired and then you'll throw this poor book out in disgust!

So to prevent this calamity, please use the following tool to teach yourself to wake up automatically. Your subconscious mind has an excellent built in time clock, and can wake you much more effectively and peacefully from your dreams than an alarm. It is just a simple matter of setting it up.

1. Choose a night when you do not have any pressing business the next day, such as sometime over the weekend, so that there is not too much pressure. Pressure is sometimes useful to jog the assistance of your subconscious, but you don't want to mess up your life.

2. Take your pendulum, and ask your subconscious mind if it will wake you up at a specified predetermined time.

3. Get a "yes" response from the pendulum. If it says "no," you will have to inquire why. Usually you will receive an impression, feeling or thought that will indicate the reason if you direct your attention to your belly and ask.

4. Once you have figured out the reason, come up with solutions and find out if your subconscious finds the solutions acceptable.

5. Once you have received a definite 'yes' answer from your subconscious that it will wake you, set a particular time, and get approval. Choose an appropriate time. If you don't allow yourself enough rest, your subconscious may rebel and not wake you, even if it says it will with the pendulum. Your subconscious is responsible for your physiological well-being, and this may supersede your conscious desires. Also, make sure that you give yourself sufficient time to record your dreams before you need to be somewhere.

6. Once you have agreed upon a time, you may go to sleep. In all probability you will wake up within five minutes of the time you have set with your subconscious.

7. If you have not woken up at the correct time, do not get angry at your subconscious. This will inhibit, rather than help your progress. Simply consult with your subconscious why, using the pendulum, and receive answers from your belly. Try the practice again and again until you get it to work.

Once you have set this up you will be able to recall your dreams much more easily.

Exercise 26 - Dream Programming

Time Required: N/A

This is a simple process for encouraging yourself to dream about a particular topic. It can be used any number of ways, and various modifications will be found throughout this book.

The following exercise is very flexible and useful, but you must keep in mind that it will not always work, because dreaming is an important function of consciousness, and sometimes you will need to be dreaming other things aside from your conscious desires.

1. First, you will need to pick a topic that you would like to dream about. This can really be anything from a particular place, to a person to some sort of scenario. Gather together some objects or pictures that remind you of this subject that you'd like to dream about, and look at them repeatedly throughout the day, thinking almost obsessively about the subject you'd like to dream about.

2. In fact, think about this subject constantly throughout your day.

3. When you are getting ready for bed, write at the top of a blank page of your journal, "tonight I will dream about…(your subject)."

4. Consult with your subconscious using the pendulum about whether it understands your intention, and is willing to play along. Consulting with the pendulum will help your subconscious understand that you are considering this important.

5. As you are drifting off to sleep, continue thinking about this subject, letting images relating to this subject play through your mind until you fall asleep.

6. When you awaken, write down any dreams whether they relate your subject or not.

You may have to do this exercise for several consecutive days in order to really program your dreams successfully.

LUCID DREAMING

The next step in our process is to become aware that you are dreaming while in the midst of a dream. This has been popularly named, "Lucid Dreaming." It is far easier to accomplish and commonly occurring than its detractors might have you believe. You may have had lucid dreams that you don't even remember, strangely enough. I have had numerous experiences upon awakening where I thought I had not dreamed lucidly, only to discover as I was writing out my dreams that I'd been lucid earlier. The amnesia effect seems to affect even the lucid state.

There are many varieties of lucidity as well. It is possible to have the conscious and clearly lucid thought, "I am dreaming now," and yet still react to elements of the dream world as if they were real. I consider this a sort of pre-lucidity, and once you are recalling your dreams and familiar with your dream world you will have experiences like this constantly. In some ways, I think this state is the one preferred by your subconscious because it still allows the information processing of your unconscious to go on while you are a more active witness than usual.

All your lucid and pre-lucid dreams will have a much more vivid and powerful quality than your usual dreams. By this I mean that your "physical" and emotional reactions to things will be much stronger. Many lucid dream books describe these sorts of dreams as being particularly colorful and detailed, but I have found in my experience that while they will sometimes be more visually vivid and colorful, it is the dramatic, emotional impact that is the strongest. This may of course just be me.

There are three main methods of accomplishing lucid dreaming. These are becoming lucid in the midst of a dream, waking up from a dream, and going back into the dream state immediately to experience lucidity, and going from the waking state directly into a lucid dream. There are numerous tricks and techniques that people have come up with over the years, but I will just cover the three that I think are best and easiest.

Exercise 27 - Reality Check

Time Required: N/A

I'm not sure where I first heard of this exercise, but I think it may have been created by Dr. Stephen LaBerge. My version is slightly different from those I've seen elsewhere. A similar idea can be found in Tibetan dream yoga practices, though with somewhat different intentions. Generally this process is the best way to begin the process of becoming consciously aware in the dream state.

The way in which this works is that you will regularly check in with yourself throughout your entire day, asking yourself if you are dreaming. By doing this constantly and repeatedly over the course of a week or so, it will become a habit, and you will eventually find yourself asking this question in your dreams.

This may in fact not happen exactly in this way for you. Personally, I never say to myself, "Am I dreaming?" Instead, I just seem to have an, "aha," where suddenly I recognize that I'm in a dream. At the same time, this happens far more frequently when I'm regularly doing the reality checks throughout the day, so I know it is related to this technique.

1. Carry some object with you that will constantly remind you to check in regularly. I personally write the letter "c" on the back of my hand, to remind me that I am conscious. Some people simply check in with themselves at certain times each hour. Some people use a ring or some other piece of jewelry. The nice thing about writing on my hand is that people regularly ask me what it is. This gives me another stimulus to do a reality check.

2. Every time you notice this object, or notice the time, or whatever device you choose, mentally ask yourself, "Am I dreaming, or am I awake?" Really ask yourself, and examine your environment. This is your reality check. Who knows, you may actually be asleep. Do this religiously, as often as possible. Ask yourself at least once per hour.

3. Eventually, you will find yourself checking your reality in the midst of a dream.

This method will lead you naturally into lucid dreaming. It may take a little while, but your focused effort will eventually pay off. You may also wish to combine this effort with the next technique, to jumpstart the process. However, do not omit the reality checking. It will help your consciousness to be more alert in general, and a number of later techniques will require this alertness.

Exercise 28 - Wake Up Return

Time Required: must be performed in the middle of the night

This is an exercise you can use to enter into lucid dreaming in the middle of the night when you've woken out of a dream. It is very simple and effective, but it is easy to fall back asleep without succeeding, so don't beat yourself up if this happens. Just keep trying.

1. As you are going to bed, write on a new page of your journal something like, "Tonight I will recognize I am dreaming while dreaming," or, "Tonight I will dream lucidly."

2. Consult with your subconscious using the pendulum about whether it understands your intention, and is willing to play along.

3. As you are going off to sleep, repeat the words you wrote, affirming your strong intention to dream lucidly.

4. In the middle of the night or early morning, as you rouse from sleep, remember what you were dreaming. Without getting up, close your eyes and think about the dream, repeating your words from your journal, and firmly intending to be lucid. You may begin dreaming the same dream again, or enter a new dream. In either case, stay alert and you will become lucid.

This technique may best be tried in the early morning at first. I find this the easiest time to dream lucidly.

Exercise 29 - Directly Into Lucidity from Waking

Time Required: 40 minutes to 2 hours

1. This technique begins just like the Delta state pattern except that you will attempt to remain fully aware throughout. It's probably a good idea to do this at a time other than bedtime.

2. Enter the Alpha then Theta states.

3. From here, simply allow yourself to drift even deeper. Try to remain focused. Focus on the sensations in your body, and try to follow your inner stream of thoughts and images. You may eventually black out entirely, or get lost in a dream briefly, but as soon as you become aware again, you will be dreaming lucidly. Try to relax and stay with the dream, and try to stay alert.

With either of the preceding techniques, you will probably find your lucidity interrupted by waking up at first. You will be excited that you have succeeded, and this will bring you up to waking consciousness. You must endeavor to remain relaxed and simply enjoy the experience. Time will make you expert in this.

DREAM SCHOOL

Before leaving the subject of dreams I want to mention a few final things. There is a popular notion in certain circles that we are actually involved in some sort of consciousness school when we are dreaming at night. While it is not possible to say whether this is technically true or not, I have had too many experiences of working with dream teachers and even being involved in specific and useful dream lessons to totally disregard this notion. I have had many experiences in which dream adepts have taught me something about consciousness, or worked with me on astral projection, or initiated me into a new level of consciousness. Perhaps you too will find your own dream lessons. You will certainly notice recurring themes and recurring settings, and with any luck you will learn a tremendous amount of important material in your nightly sojourn into the unseen world of the mind.

It is also supposedly possible to experience shared dreaming, in which you are having the same dream as another person. I have never had such an experience, so I cannot write about it from first hand experience. When I am lucid, I tend to get so fascinated by the experience itself and the enhanced abilities of my consciousness that the idea of trying to contact my friends or lovers has just never come. If you wish to experiment with this, simply try to find one of your friends when you become lucid. They may or may not remember the experience, so you might want to call them as soon as you awaken.

As a final thought on dreams and sleep I highly recommend the following simple practice. Each night, as you close your eyes, send out love and forgiveness to everyone in the world when going to sleep. You will enrich your life tremendously.

CHAPTER FOUR
Psychic Receiving

"Generally speaking, clairvoyance means the second sight as it is popularly named, or the power of seeing, without the use of the eye, events taking place at a distance, actually or in the future or having taken place in the past, or seeing deceased people."

-Franz Bardon[1]

You are already receiving information psychically. We all occasionally do things "on hunches," "gut feelings," or have a little voice in our heads that tells to do or not do certain things. Some of us receive little images in our thoughts and dreams that guide us. Becoming psychic is simply a matter of becoming more aware of these phenomena, and learning to activate these experiences at will.

I must warn you that developing the gift of psychic awareness is sometimes as much of a curse as it is a blessing. We all have darkness within ourselves as well as light, and you will sometimes experience dark things when you explore psychic reception. I once gave a reading to a young woman who was concerned about the psychosomatic illness of her mother, and I found myself quickly plunged into a scenario of childhood sexual abuse. The young woman confirmed that her mother had been abused, but it was a very difficult experience for both of us, and I only hope that I gave her some comfort. This is not a plaything. As you become more and more "psychic," you will begin to know things about the people in your life that are unsettling and often disturbing to your relationships. You may suddenly "know" which friends are cheating on their partners, and who is becoming a drug addict or alcoholic. You may foresee unsettling political information in the world. However, you must observe caution in believing anything that you receive psychically, because it is very easy

---

[1] *Initiation into Hermetics*, p. 142

to confuse psychic awareness with fantasy. And fantasies can lead you to all sorts of unhealthy paranoia. I know of several people who have really fouled up their lives, convinced that they "knew things" about their friends that turned out to just be their own fears and projections.

It is also in almost all cases completely inappropriate to share information you receive about another person unless they specifically ask for it. People should not be given metaphysical information that they don't want. It could even be harmful. And, even if they do ask and you share, you will constantly be put into precarious situations. Many people are in denial and won't believe things you see, and they will resent you for saying them, and sometimes you will be wrong, exposing yourself to even more problems. Most people that hang up a shingle as a psychic are frauds, so they don't have to worry about ethical and moral issues. But you will. Genuine psychics are usually very cautious about sharing their gifts, and they are almost never in it for the money.

That being said, opening up to psychic receiving is also a delight. It can bring you closer to your loved ones through deep empathy and it can prevent you from taking wrong steps in your life. You must simply take a balanced and cautious approach, being sure to test the validity of anything you receive as much as possible.

In this chapter we are largely going to focus on the three main types of psychic receiving, clairvoyance, clairaudience and clairsentience, or psychic seeing, hearing and feeling. We will also cover some alternate ways in which you can use these psychic senses along the way. As I mentioned in a previous chapter, you will probably gravitate more toward one or another of these psychic tools, based on your own dominant sensory modalities, but you should really endeavor to develop all your senses as much as possible, because once they are all working together each one will be empowered by the others. In the exercises that follow, we will focus on one of the psychic senses at a time, but once you have some experience with each of them individually you can start using them in various combinations as you see fit.

As you are learning to awaken these latent powers, you must keep a few things in mind. Your impressions may at first be only vague and fleeting, but you must make every effort to pay attention to any chance image, feeling or inner sound that comes up. Your true psychic message will probably be the first thing that comes to you, before you have a chance to set your expectations. This first fleeting impression will be a genuine message from your subconscious, while later ones may be impressions that your subconscious is creating in order to please you. Your subconscious will try to make you happy, even if that means lying to you. You may not like what you see initially, or it may seem irrelevant, or it might be so vague that you don't understand its meaning. It is a mistake to ignore these first impressions.

Instead, if you do not understand something, ask for clarification or explanation rather than ignoring an impression. If you are not in the habit of inner exploration, (which I hope you are by now!) you may not really even feel connected with the inner pictures sounds and feelings that will come up. It is just a matter of practice to start getting a sense of these things.

The absolute worst mistake you can make is to feel that what you are getting is not good enough. This will make your subconscious feel that it has to impress you in some way, and the information you receive may become more glamorous, but it will most likely be less accurate. You want to receive useful information, not just experience interesting pyrotechnics in your mind. Just relax and enjoy the process. Over time, your inner senses will evolve as you grow closer and closer to your own unconscious, and the impressions that you get will become stronger, clearer, and easier to understand.

You must be careful about preconceived expectations in your work, because it is very easy to influence your subconscious in this way. If you think Peggy is cheating on her husband, and seek information on this clairvoyantly, your subconscious may show you scenes of infidelity just to make you happy. This is why in "scientific remote viewing" the viewer is usually not given any information whatsoever about the target. The target is sealed in an envelope, with a series of random numbers as a target coordinate. That way, no preconceived notions can influence the impressions received. So, when you are conducting your psychic experiments, try to be as open as possible, with no specific expectations. When you have emotionally charged questions that you really want an answer about, you could even try sealing a few of them in envelopes so that you don't know what question you are getting psychic impressions about. Your superconscious and subconscious minds will know perfectly well which question is within the envelope. You could also conduct your experiments with a friend, and do your psychic questioning for each other, each of you giving a series of sealed questions to the other. But, for the most part, just keeping a clear and open mind, and making sure that your subconscious knows that you want accurate information should keep you out of too much trouble.

There is no easy way to tell whether something is genuine psychic information or just imagination, projection or fantasy. The one thing I can say on this subject is that it will generally just seem right. You will know it when you experience it. But even this isn't entirely accurate because there have been plenty of times in my life when I have felt something to be accurate when it was not, and vice versa. Generally, the more you trust your psychic powers, the more often they will start to be correct. Your subconscious seems to benefit from this sense of trust. Like a child or family pet seeking praise, your subconscious desires to please you. If it feels like you are dubious no matter what it does, your subconscious will stop bothering to worry about giving you accurate information. Likewise if your subconscious is sure that you want some specific preconceived answer, it may give you the answer you want even if it is wrong. So, I would say that the best course of action is to assume that all impressions you receive are in some way related to the information you need, and simply try to understand what that message is communicating.

Exercise 30 – Developing Clairvoyance

Time Required: 10 to 15 minutes

Clairvoyance is the art of "seeing" distant places, people, and things. It is also the art of receiving symbols and visions of a practical or spiritual nature. Eventually, clairvoyance can lead to traveling on the inner planes, the out of body experience or astral projection. This will be covered later. As with looking at auras, you will not be using your physical eyes for this practice, but rather you will be using your inner eye, or third eye, located between your eyebrows. The basic technique is very simple.

Diagram 4 - The Third Eye - Psychic Seeing Region

Always do this and all other psychic exercises in a relaxed and playful way.

1. If possible, use your pendulum to make sure your subconscious is willing to work psychically right now. There will of course be times when this is not convenient or necessary.

2. Use your anchor to go into the Alpha state.

3. If possible, do a few Kundalini arousing breaths.

4. Tell your subconscious and superconscious that you want to obtain clairvoyant images, and that you would like them to be accurate, rather than just trying to please you.

5. Specify what you would like to know about, if you have something specific in mind.

6. You may have your eyes closed or open, but shift your gaze to your third eye and relax your attention there, allowing whatever comes into your mind to appear. Images may be brief, momentary.

7. You may again ask for the specific information if you are not receiving anything, or clarification of anything you receive. But you should not refuse or ignore any images that you see no matter how vague or momentary. If you do not understand something, or feel that you have missed something, simply ask for more.

8. Do not analyze, simply observe what comes, keeping it in your mind, not forgetting anything.

9. Return to normal consciousness slowly and deliberately, intentionally remembering all that you have experienced.

10. Immediately write down whatever you have observed. It is important to write it all immediately, because you will tend to forget it quickly, much like dreaming.

With this exercise, you may simply see shapes or colors or other symbolic images. At first you may not know what these mean. Your whole unconscious may have a way of communicating to itself and to you that is unfamiliar. Over time, you will get a sense of what these communications mean. You may also see memories from your own life that relate to the question at hand, and require further interpretation. At first, there may be no clear connection between the memories and the question, but if you stay with it, there is some message there. You may also see real time images or complete images of future events. Sometimes it may be a little hard to distinguish what is what. You can always ask for greater clarification, but sometimes this clarification may itself be just as confusing. Simply observe for a while in these practices, recording everything, and your powers will slowly expand.

The images may be so very brief and fleeting, particularly at first, that you don't even notice them. We are all in the habit of ignoring large parts of our inner senses. We are in fact constantly generating images, and once you get in touch with this flow of imagery, your powers will grow immensely. Try your best to note every passing image, turning it over in your mind, examining it in detail.

You can also try adding your other senses, touching, smelling tasting and hearing these images, to give them greater life and depth. You will want to use this technique frequently, to really get the hang of it, so go ahead and try using it with any or all of these experiments:

- Choose a few friends, and receive some clairvoyant images relating to them. These may be symbolic images, or what they are currently doing, or where they are currently heading in life. Follow up with your friends if you wish, but do so with subtlety. Don't tell them that you are psychically spying on them. No one wants that!

- Choose a few people you don't know, and receive images relating to them.

- Choose a few celebrities, and receive images relating to them.

- Get a symbolic image for your day. This is a fun technique, in which you just ask for an image that will define your day. You will find that these images will be very meaningful and often helpful in situations that come up through your day. You can also receive an image relating to your upcoming week, or your whole year. You could use this on New Year's Day, to get a sense of how your year is going to go, and how best to deal with what you will face.

- If you have a goal or project you are working on, get some insight through clairvoyant images.

- If you have a friend in need, get some images of how best to help. Be cautious however, and keep the information to yourself.

- Try to determine what a friend or a few friends are doing right now. Follow up to see if you were right, keeping the nature of the experiment to yourself.

- Try to get future visions for your friends and yourself. Simply record these, and follow up later when you can clearly see what has happened. If you see something nasty in the future of a friend, keep in mind that it may be more symbolic than literal. You can try to support this friend, but don't be a busybody.

- Try to get symbolic images relating to some of your friends. Again, use subtlety and common sense, avoiding psychic invasion of their privacy.

Exercise 31- Remote Viewing

Time Required: 30 minutes to one hour.

This is just a simple variation on the last exercise. Remote viewing is a buzz word that is fairly popular to describe any kind of clairvoyance that is in a controlled "scientific" setting. The term was coined by a government funded research project at the Stanford Research Institute back in the 1970's. It has come to be adopted by many parapsychological research groups and a number of new age teachers. Many different writers have produced different instructions on the "correct" way to do remote viewing, but they are all quite different and all work to varying degrees. Technically, all of the exercises in this chapter fall under the general heading of remote viewing. However, for our context, I am using the term to describe the exercise of trying to get information from a distant place without any prior knowledge of what or where this may be. This will be an extremely simple exercise, not following any particular protocols, but generally just using a blind target format. You could use this same technique for any of the exercises in this chapter.

For this exercise, you will need to have someone seal a piece of paper identifying a location, person, thing or event into an envelope without telling you what it is. You could also do this yourself by choosing a number of different things and sealing them all into identical envelopes. If you do this you will want to make a large number of envelopes and wait a while until you've mostly forgotten what you created so that you do not feel tempted to make a guess as to which one it is.

1. Place the envelope with the target in front of you.

2. Before you even begin, your mind may produce a little guess as to what might be in the envelope. Ignore this for the most part, because it is most likely not accurate. Write it down before you start, but don't let this guess color the rest of your experiment. It is most likely just a trick of the mind rather than a genuine psychic hunch. We all want to guess as quickly as possible, so the subconscious will throw something up. It might be useful, so write it down, but after that forget about it.

3. Use your pendulum to make sure your subconscious is willing to work psychically right now.

4. Use your anchor to go into the Alpha state.

5. Do a few Kundalini arousing breaths.

6. Tell your subconscious and superconscious that you want to obtain information about the sealed target, and that you would like the information to be accurate, rather than just trying to please you.

7. Shift your gaze to your third eye and relax your attention there, allowing whatever comes into your mind to appear. Images may be brief, momentary.

8. Don't try to receive anything, just relax. Allow low-level impressions to come to you at first such as shapes, colors, textures and sensations. Allow other senses to participate, smell, touch, hearing. Simply be open to any information.

9. If you are working with a partner, share with them aloud whatever you are receiving, and let them write it down. Do not let your partner lead you if they know what the target is.

10. Do not analyze, simply receive what comes, keeping it in your mind, not forgetting anything. Don't try to figure out exactly what you are receiving about. Just receive impressions. Your first few times with this technique you may only receive vague senses of things. Do not worry. Simply keep these impressions in mind.

11. Return to normal consciousness slowly and deliberately, intentionally remembering all that you have experienced.

12. Immediately write down whatever you have observed if you do not have a partner who has been recording for you.

13. Analyze it later. Don't rush. Collect a few experiments before you bother about whether any of it is accurate or not.

The great advantage of this technique is that it forces you to really open up to pure impressions. When you know what you are psychically seeking there is a much greater chance of just making things up or making conscious guesses in order to feel that you've received something. With this technique, you will only receive images produced by the subconscious mind.

This doesn't necessarily ensure accuracy. Sometimes, what you received will have nothing to do with the target. Do not become concerned about this. Simply keep trying. Eventually you will be amazed, and this will happen more and more frequently the more often you experiment.

Exercise 32 - Crystal Gazing

Time Required: 10 to 15 minutes

This is simply another variation on clairvoyance. Some people find that having an external point of focus helps to jog the visual sense. You can use this technique with a crystal ball of any size or color. You could also look into a bowl filled with black ink, a dark mirror or magick mirror, or even just stare at the wall or any blank surface. Hermetic Adept Franz Bardon actually suggests the use of magically coated paper to create a magick mirror.[1] In many ways this technique is similar to aura gazing, because while your eyes will be open you will primarily still be using your third eye to receive information.

This technique can be a bit tiring, so try not to do it for too long at first. Be sure to have patience and fun, and your experience should be enjoyable and educational. If at any time you feel the urge to close your eyes, go ahead, continuing to receive information directly.

1. Use your pendulum to make sure your subconscious is willing to work psychically right now.

2. Use your anchor to go into the Alpha state.

---

[1] *Initiation into Hermetics*, p. 201

3. If possible, do a few Kundalini arousing breaths.

4. Tell your subconscious and superconscious that you want to obtain clairvoyant images in the crystal, and that you would like them to be accurate, rather than just trying to please you.

5. Specify what you would like to know about, if you have something specific in mind.

6. Open your eyes, remaining in the relaxed and tranquil Alpha state.

7. Look into the crystal or whatever object you are using as your focal point.

8. Shift your gaze to your third eye and relax your attention there, allowing whatever comes into your mind to appear in the crystal.

9. You may again ask for the specific information if you are not receiving anything, or clarification of anything you receive. But you should not refuse or ignore any images that you see no matter how vague or momentary. If you do not understand something, or feel that you have missed something, simply ask for more.

10. At a certain point, one of two things will happen. Either is perfectly okay. First, you may find your eyes closing, in which case you will simply receive information through normal clairvoyance. Or you may find yourself becoming so totally absorbed in the object of your attention that it seems to grow and envelope you into a stream of psychic images.

11. Do not analyze, simply observe what comes, keeping it in your mind, not forgetting anything.

12. Return to normal consciousness slowly and deliberately, intentionally remembering all that you have experienced.

13. Immediately write down whatever you have observed. It is important to write it all immediately, because you will tend to forget it quickly, much like dreaming.

Exercise 33 - Developing your Clairaudience

Time Required: 10 to 15 minutes

Clairaudience is "hearing" paranormal information through your inner senses. The key to this is really just to turn your attention away from your physical ears, instead becoming aware of your inner voice, allowing your subconscious mind to communicate to you through this voice. Inner self-talk and psychic hearing will be in the same area, although sometimes the psychic hearing will seem further in back of the inner voice. So think to yourself aloud in your head for a moment. Say, "This is where my psychic hearing happens." Wherever you are experiencing this inner talk is the location where your psychic hearing will come from, or just in front. This may be just above your ears, just inside of them, or at center of your brain. The only challenge in this is separating this communication from your own conscious stream of self-talk. These things tend to blend in with one another. You actually hear this voice quite frequently, but may not have clearly distinguished it.

Diagram 5 - Psychic Hearing Region

105

The voice you will hear in clairaudience is generally that of your own subconscious mind. Your superconscious will generally speak through your subconscious. But the voices you hear will sometimes definitely be from an outside intelligence. You will only want this to happen when you are specifically choosing to intentionally communicate with outside intelligences such as angels or spirits. You do not want to allow other intelligences to speak to you without your asking. This can be somewhat dangerous if allowed to go on without your permission and request. If a voice that you are hearing seems extremely alien, be cautious. We will cover this topic further in the chapter on communication.

The clairaudient ability can be somewhat difficult to develop because it is so similar to self-talk, and because in this culture sound is given lower priority than image and feeling. Many of us are very familiar with inner pictures or feelings, but inner sounds are less familiar. I myself am least proficient with this psychic modality, but when it comes, it seems very powerful, and usually contains very unusual and surprising information.

I was once sitting in silent meditation, when a very clear and unusual voice said to me distinctly, "You are Athanasius." It almost sounded like the voice was coming from the air behind me. At the time, I was seeking a new magical motto, or magical name, so I decided to adopt it. Why not? However, two days later I received a knock on the door, and I found a police detective, and another uniformed police officer, were standing on my porch. The detective said he wanted to ask me a few questions, so I cordially invited them inside. After peering warily around my apartment, they proceeded to accuse me of defacing a local church with a number of spray-painted pentagrams. It was somewhat well known in the community that I was practicing the occult, and I think they were just trying to find a scapegoat. Of course this was ridiculous, and I quickly persuaded them that I had nothing to do with this vandalism. However, I was nearly dumbstruck when they told me the name of the church, "St. Athanasius."

The following procedures, quite similar to those for clairvoyance, should be very helpful in starting to develop this ability.

1. If it is possible, use your pendulum to make sure your subconscious is willing to work psychically right now. There will of course be times when this is not convenient or necessary.

2. Use your anchor to go into the Alpha state.

3. If possible, do a few Kundalini arousing breaths.

4. Tell your subconscious and superconscious that you want to obtain psychic information clairaudiently, and that you would like them to be accurate, rather than just trying to please you.

5. Specify what you would like to know about, if you have something specific in mind.

6. Shift your attention to your ears or the best area you've determined and listen to your stream of thoughts. Listen for whatever comes into your mind to appear. It may be quiet or fragmentary, or difficult to distinguish from your thoughts, but you will receive some kind of information instantly from your subconscious.

7. Try not to analyze what you are hearing, wondering whether or not it is imaginary. Just accept what comes, keeping it in your mind, not forgetting anything.

8. Return to normal consciousness slowly and deliberately, intentionally remembering all that you have experienced.

9. Immediately write down whatever you have received. It is important to write it all immediately, because you will tend to forget it quickly, much like dreaming.

Just like clairvoyance, you will want to use this technique frequently, to really get the hang of it, so go ahead and try using it with any or all of these experiments:

- Choose a few friends, and ask how they are currently, or what they are doing now, or where they are heading in life. Follow up with your friends if you wish, but do so with subtlety. Don't tell them that you are psychically spying on them.

- Ask your inner voice for how to deal with near future circumstances.

- Your inner mind, your subconscious, and/or your superconscious, may have a name that it would like to be called when you are communicating. Ask for the name of your superconscious and your subconscious minds. You may also ask the name of your Guardian Angel if you prefer this model of thinking.

- If you are interested in such a thing, ask your inner voice for a magical name or magical motto.

- Ask your inner voice if any of your friends need a call.

- If you have a friend in need, ask for a message about how best to help.

- Ask for a message about how to approach your day.

- Ask how to solve a problem or how to approach a new project or idea.

- Ask for a new idea.

Exercise 34 - Developing Clairsentience, Empathy or Psychic Feeling

Time Required: 10 to 15 minutes

Clairsentience or psychic feeling is most easily understood as those times when you receive paranormal information through your kinesthetic senses, either your feelings or your physical sense of touch. You have already had a little practice at this with feeling for an aura with your hands. When you receive psychic feelings they will mostly be in the belly, although sometimes they will manifest in the face or forehead as well.

This is one of the easiest psychic senses to develop for most people, since we all have feelings, and the subconscious is very at home providing you with information through sensations. However, some people are not as in touch with their feelings, and there is nothing wrong with this, so don't feel badly if you find this challenging.

This sense can and will become very powerful, and you will start to receive all sorts of feelings about people and situations that will be very useful once you understand them. This psychic ability is easy to use in any situation, whether out in the world or in your personal temple or workroom, but it is sometimes difficult to shut off your psychic empathy once you develop it fully. In a moment I will give you a simple grounding and closing exercise that may help you to at least quiet this sense down.

Learning to trust these subtle bodily sensations will be very helpful in your life. There have been many times in my life when I have ignored initial bad impressions of someone and the person turned out to have a really negative influence in my life over the long run. Once you start receiving these messages, really try to understand and heed them.

When you are familiar with this exercise, you will most likely not have to enter the Alpha state to receive clairsentient feelings. Most likely they will just come quickly and easily of their own accord. Still, these methods will help you avoid falling into pitfalls.

Diagram 6 - Psychic Feeling Region

1. If you can, use your pendulum to make sure your subconscious is willing to work psychically right now.

2. Use your anchor to go into the Alpha state.

3. If possible, do the chakra opening breathing, and a few Kundalini arousing breaths.

4. Tell your subconscious and superconscious that you want to obtain clairsentient feelings, and that you would like them to be accurate, rather than just trying to please you.

5. Specify what you would like to know about, if you have something specific in mind.

6. Shift your to your belly and relax your attention there, allowing whatever feelings come.

7. Do not analyze, simply notice what comes, keeping it in your mind, not forgetting anything.

8. Return to normal consciousness slowly and deliberately, intentionally remembering all that you have experienced.

9. Immediately write down whatever you have felt. It is important to write it all immediately, because you will tend to forget it quickly, much like dreaming.

As with the other psychic senses, you will want to use this technique frequently, to really get the hang of it, so go ahead and try using it with any or all of these experiments:

- When you are going out to do something, try to sense what is going to happen before you go.

- Sense for hidden dangers when you are out in public.

- When meeting people for the first time get a psychic "vibe" from them.

- Get a feeling for people that you know- What feeling comes? Follow up with your friends if you wish, but do so with subtlety. Once again, please don't tell them that you are psychically spying on them.

- Try to feel what one of your friends is feeling right now.

- First thing in the morning, try to get an overall feeling for your day.

- Sense for the overall emotional atmospheres in rooms and houses you are visiting. You will get a sense of what sorts of feelings predominate in these places.

Exercise 35 - Grounding and Closing

Time Required: 5 to 10 minutes

If you are ever feeling overwhelmed by one of your psychic senses, most likely clairsentience, or you just simply want to take a break from them, you may use the following exercise to calm things down.

1. Sit down and close your eyes.

2. Use your anchor to go into the Alpha state.

3. Visualize a channel of energy or a sort of root extending down from your Muladhara chakra or perineum down into the earth. (You can also draw in healing light from above at this time too).

4. Send all of the extra unwanted energies and feelings into the earth through this shaft, as if you were draining the air out of a balloon.

5. Once you feel you have drained out the excess, use the same imaginary hands that you used earlier in opening your chakras to close them one at a time in the same way that you opened them. Imagine that you are sealing up a hole, or closing the lotus flowers.

6. Return to normal consciousness and relax.

Exercise 36 - Psychometry

Time Required: 10 to 15 minutes

Psychometry is the practice of reading information by touching physical objects. As mentioned in the section on aura feeling, there are powerful channels in your fingertips and palms that you can use to receive psychic information. The following is a simple technique for discovering information about an object or its owner by holding it in your hands.

1. Place the object in front of you or in your lap.

2. Go into Alpha using your anchor.

3. Arouse Kundalini if you wish, or at least open your chakras. Rub your hands together briefly to awaken the energy centers in your hands.

4. Pick up the object and hold it in your hands. Feel its texture. Turn it over in your fingers.

5. Start with your gut, what general feelings does this object give you? Is it happy, sad, angry, frightened, scary, cold, warm, or any other feeling? Once you have gotten a general feeling for the object you can move into images or sounds, using whichever psychic modalities you prefer.

6. Do not analyze, simply notice what comes, keeping it in your mind, not forgetting anything.

7. Return to normal consciousness slowly and deliberately, intentionally remembering all that you have experienced.

8. Immediately write down whatever you have observed. It is important to write it all immediately, because you will tend to forget it quickly, much like dreaming.

Exercise 37 - Psychic Tests

Time required: varying

Once you are familiar with the preceding exercises you may want to try using your different psychic modalities for the following simple tests. You may see the exact image you are trying to get when using clairvoyance, or just something symbolic. You can use clairaudience to try to verbally get answers from your unconscious, or perhaps hear different unique sounds associated with the objects. The different test choices may have different feelings, or you may just feel the correct response. Experiment with all of these possibilities:

•   Do some coin tosses, using your psychic awareness to determine which side will come up. Try perhaps fifty tosses. Try to discover which psychic sense is best at this. Also try to note whether you have a higher percentage of correct guesses at the beginning middle or end of your series.

- Try the same with throwing dice.

- Put some differently shaped and textured small objects into identical boxes. Try to determine what is in each box with your different modalities.

- Take a deck of cards, playing, Tarot or psychic test cards, and try to guess which cards are next. If you are using Tarot cards or playing cards, start by just guessing the suit, rather than the exact card. With practice you can try working up to guessing the exact card.

You can also do these same experiments directly using the pendulum with your subconscious mind. If you do this, choose, toss, roll, or pick beforehand, because your subconscious may get confused if it hasn't already occurred. Your superconscious may know the future, but your subconscious may not.

The point of these tests is not to be one hundred percent accurate. This won't happen. However, you will be able to make correct guesses that are statistically higher than random chance. Even if you are only 60-70% accurate with the coin toss prediction that is still significantly higher than straight guessing! Some people, especially when new to psychic exploration, will actually get only 30% correct, which is still statistically significant, because it proves that you are receiving non-chance related information. You are just interpreting it backwards.

NOTICING NONVERBAL COMMUNICATION

Being psychic also involves looking with your eyes and other physical sense organs, not just receiving information from inside your own head. Having extra sensory perception also implies seeing, hearing and feeling normal perceptions in a more highly sophisticated way. The importance of paying attention to all sensory input, psychic as well as ordinary cannot be stressed too much. The following techniques can only be used when you actually have a person present, sitting or standing in front of you, and you are having an active dialogue with them. You will want to use these techniques once you have advanced to the point that you are ready to give someone a "reading," or if you are covertly trying to ascertain information about someone you are with.

Many fraudulent, fake psychics use the techniques I am about to give you in order to fool their clients into believing they are receiving paranormal information when they are simply using their normal senses and trickery. These techniques are sometimes referred to as "cold reading," by mentalists and other fakers. However, you, as a real psychic, should still avail yourself of these techniques, as they will greatly assist you in avoiding mistakes and being able to tell when you are "missing." So many psychics, even professional ones, go off on wild tangents that are really just their own fantasies. By using the following techniques you will be able to observe what is real and what is not. At first, these may seem to impair your psychic channels, but they will soon place you in much deeper rapport with the person you are reading and you will find yourself producing amazing information.

Be observant, notice who you are talking to. If you are talking to a multi-millionaire, most likely they are not worried about money. If they have on a wedding ring, they are probably not looking for a new love in their life. By observing exactly who you are talking to you can keep yourself from going too far astray with your psychic impressions.

Look at the little details of the person you are sitting with. Does the person look sad, tense, dubious, curious or scared? Are their fingernails manicured, bitten, or dirty? What about their hands? Are they clean, rough, or dirty? Is their jewelry expensive, cheap, or tacky? What is their hairstyle like? How are their clothes and shoes? Uptight? Frumpy? Tailored? How are their vocabulary skills and the tone of their voice? All of these factors can help you in assessing who and what the person you are about to read is all about, and can be invaluable to keep you from simple blunders.

Also, listen carefully to what they say. They may give you vital information as they are talking to you casually that will help you to guide your own psychic senses toward the correct sorts of information for them. Put two and two together. Don't be afraid to use normal reasoning in your psychic reading. This can be extra sensory perception too.

Exercise 38 – Calibrating Positive and Negative Body Language

Time Required: 2 to 5 minutes

When you are reading another person who is in front of you, there are only two possibilities with any information that you receive. It is either correct or incorrect. So, if you say something that is wrong, by saying something different you will often be right. You could use this to easily give fake psychic readings, and many very famous people do just this. They use binary information, like hot or cold, man or woman, short or tall, and if they miss they just switch choices and it seems like magic. They might say something like, "I'm seeing a man, and he's walking toward you on a sunny day, and he's someone that you know, and he's a nice man," and so on. With all of the statements in that sentence, if any one of them are wrong, you could easily make it right by simply saying the opposite. "Oh wait, actually I think he's not a nice man, yes he's definitely not so nice..." By observing subtle and sometimes not so subtle body language cues about whether you are on track or not, it is very easy to fake a reading in just this way. But you will use this same skill for a positive purpose instead.

Frequently the subconscious mind of the person you are reading will give you signals about whether you are right or wrong about any information you receive in the form of unconscious movements or other changes in their body. Often a client's subconscious thinks differently than their conscious, and if you learn to read the signals, the client may verbally say that what you are saying is inaccurate, while their subconscious cues you that you are really on the right track. This non-congruent behavior is very common, and learning to detect it will help you in a multitude of ways. The method of learning this unconscious communication is simple to describe, but requires some practice to put into effect.

1. Ask some non-offensive, simple yes and no questions, such as verifying where they are from, their name. "So you're from Wisconsin? Oh, Minnesota? Was that a nice place to grow up? And your middle name is MacKenzie? Is that Irish? Oh, Scottish? Do you have relatives in Scotland?" etc. etc. etc.

2. Observe differences in their body language, looking for consistent 'yes' and 'no' cues.

3. Watch for the person's head movements, body movements, skin tone changes, changes in breathing patterns, characteristic gestures. Very often, people will simply unconsciously nod or shake their heads in response to things that you say. It is often very easy to pick up the cues. However, some people require much more careful observation.

4. Once you have done this, you will know their subconscious cues for whether you are on target or not, and can proceed with your reading.

5. When you are giving them your psychic information, try to watch for this subtle feedback and it will help you to give the most accurate reading that you can.

READING AURAS

One very simple way to get psychic information from a person that is in front of you is by reading their aura. You have had some experience with this in an earlier chapter, but now that you are really developing your psychic senses you will be able to get much more detailed impressions of the auras of people around you. As I mentioned before, auras, in the way that we experience them, may in fact be largely imaginary. But your subconscious can communicate a lot of valuable information to you about people quickly and easily through the practice of aura reading. To do this, you need simply use the aura reading exercise from earlier, but now you will try to get a bit more in depth.

The first thing you may notice is the general shape of the aura. If it is large and bright, this generally will mean that the person is healthy and probably relaxed. If the aura seems small and dim, something is wrong. The person may be upset, ill or tense. If the Aura seems overlarge and seems invasive, this may be the sign of a very needy or egotistical person. If the shape of the aura is very clear and sharp, the person is most likely very goal-oriented, focused and completely conscious in the present moment, and perhaps somewhat aggressive and domineering. If the aura is fuzzy or looks like an irregular blob, the person is most likely out of focus, unclear or not paying attention to what's going on around them. They may be flaky and irresponsible, or perhaps just momentarily drifting. An extremely irregularly shaped aura or one that is full of holes may be the sign of serious illness, either mental or physical. A very bright aura might be the sign of an advanced consciousness, or may be the sign of a manic personality, especially if it is very bright but also misshapen. If the aura seems dingy or grayish, the person is most likely feeling sad. Even these simple generalizations may not be true for you. Trust your own instincts. You may also notice any number of other things as you begin to examine the world around you in this way.

Once you've noticed the shape, you may begin to notice colors in the aura. These colors may be generally pervading throughout the aura, or else in various patterns or patches within the aura. As far as what different colors might mean, I would suggest going by your feelings more than any list. What does the color seem like? Is it bright? Dark? Dull? Shiny? These will be the most indicative things. But here is a general sort of list:

Black and *White* are very culturally biased and charged colors. In our culture white means purity but in other, particularly Eastern, cultures white sometimes means death. Black is not necessarily bad, it may just suggest earthiness or some other thing entirely. So, don't be too sure that these particular colors mean what they might seem at first glance. Check in with your gut.

Red- vitality, force, vigor, energy, warmth, sometimes anger

Orange- courage, will, success, communication

Yellow- openness, happiness, creativity, self-confidence

Green- life and growth, balance

Blue- sensitivity, caring, peace, maturity, calmness

Violet- spirituality, deep thought

But again, these are only meant to be suggestive. Use your own growing instincts, and you won't go astray.

CHAPTER FIVE
Psychic and Magick Influence

"When the Imagination creates an image- and the Will directs and uses that image, marvelous magical effects can be obtained."

-V. H. Frater Resurgam[1]

In this chapter, you will be taught a number of methods for using the power of the mind to influence the world around you. I must highly caution you to be sober and deliberate in the use of these techniques, and not to use them to harm other people. There is a very gray area when it comes to magical influence, and you will have to use your own conscience and connection with the deeper aspects of yourself to decide what is an appropriate use for these powers.

Exercise 39 - Consulting Your Subconscious

Time Required: 2 to 5 minutes

Before engaging in any active magical process, whether it is one from this chapter or any other, you must consult your subconscious every time to determine if it approves of what you intend to do. If your subconscious does not approve of what you are undertaking, it will not succeed, because your subconscious provides the energy for everything. Your subconscious will also decline the operation if it goes against the will of your superconscious, because the will of your superconscious is your true will. What goes against your true will is impossible. You must allow your subconscious to communicate honestly. Do not attempt to manipulate the pendulum toward your desired answer, because this will just make everything useless, and could damage your further relations with your subconscious.

---

[1] *Ritual Magic of the Golden Dawn*, p. 47

1. Before you begin anything from psychic influence to magical spell work, take your pendulum in your hand and ask your subconscious, "Are you comfortable with us doing this operation?" If yes, proceed to step 6. If no, go to step 2.

2. If no, you may ask why, and wait for some sort of answer. This may be a thought that pops in, an image, or a feeling somewhere in the body. If it seems unclear, keep asking until you understand why your subconscious is uncomfortable.

3. Once you understand the problem, ask your subconscious, through the pendulum, "Can we find a way of making you comfortable about this, so that we can proceed?" If no, abandon the operation. It is useless to proceed. You can resort to more yes and no questions to get greater clarity if you need to.

4. If your subconscious is willing to go ahead if you make some adjustments, then try to come up with some ways that your subconscious could be more comfortable. Your subconscious is just trying to protect you from causing harm to yourself. You might try perhaps adjusting a few details, changing the scope or scale of the operation, or else coming up with a different way in which your subconscious can continue protecting you while still allowing you to go forward with the work.

5. Ask your subconscious, through the pendulum, "Do these changes make you comfortable about doing this?" If the answer is no, you must either come up with other alternatives or abandon the operation.

6. If yes, ask your subconscious if your superconscious is really comfortable with the operation. If no, abandon the project. If yes, you are now ready to proceed.

I suggest that you consult your subconscious at the opening of nearly every exercise in the rest of this book, just to remind you that it is a good idea. However, there will be times when you may find it unnecessary. At some point in your work you will also become so connected with your subconscious and superconscious mind that it won't really be necessary to use the pendulum except on the rarest occasions. Your communication will be easy and automatic between the layers of your consciousness. You will simply know when your subconscious is opposed to what you are proposing to do, and you will be able to easily address the problems directly.

MAGICAL PREPARATIONS

These next exercises will not be strictly necessary for some of the more simple types of magical influence, but I want to introduce them to you early so you will be familiar with them once you start trying to achieve more dramatic effects.

Exercise 40 - Purification

Time Required: 1 to 15 minutes

For any serious work you will want, at very least, to ritually purify yourself, to help bring your consciousness into focus on the operation you are about to conduct. Water has the magnetic property of absorbing negativity. For most operations, a few simple sprinkles of water should be enough to get the sense of purification, even if it is just somewhat ceremonial. But for larger operations, you may want to take a purifying bath or shower, fully immersing yourself in cool, cleansing water.

If you are just sprinkling yourself with water, you can do this in your temple or work area, before or just after you've started your work. If you are fully bathing, you can do this simple ritual in the bathroom. You can also repeat it ritually in your workspace after your bath to really emphasize the purification.

1. Use your anchor to go into the Alpha state.

2. Take a small basin of water in your hand, or immerse yourself in a bath.

3. Sprinkle a little water on yourself, being sure to let go of all images, thoughts and worries that don't relate to the work, saying to yourself something along the lines of "I cleanse myself, so that I may purify myself, so that I may accomplish my work," or something similar. You could also specifically mention the work you are about to do.

4. Visualize and feel the water drawing away all negative energy and anything that does not relate to your work.

You can use this simple technique in any circumstance, and the more often you use it, the more psychologically powerful it will become. I will not emphasize it very much in the upcoming chapters, but don't forget or ignore it. It is a great simple aid to focusing your mind.

Exercise 41 – Consecration

Time Required: 1 to 5 minutes

After you purify yourself, it is traditional and useful to consecrate yourself to the work you are about to do. Purification is ridding yourself of unrelated thoughts, while consecration is actively dedicating yourself to the work at hand. As purification is usually done with water, consecration is performed with fire. We will use incense for consecration in this book, but you could also use holy oil to represent fire, if you have such a thing.[1]

You can use a special incense, related to the nature of your working, or just a general incense that you find pleasant such as Frankincense or Nag Champa incense.

1. In the Alpha state, after purifying yourself, take up some burning incense in your hand (In a censer or incense holder. Don't burn yourself!)

2. Let the incense smoke flow over your body and your face, smelling it and feeling the energy of your work filling you, saying something such as, "I consecrate myself to this work, and this work alone that it may be accomplished with the power of the great animating consciousness of the universe."

3. Feel and visualize the light from your superconscious filling you as you say this.[2]

In the next few exercises, these two techniques of purification and consecration will not necessarily be required, but for advanced workings you will certainly want to use them. They will help supercharge your consciousness and your powers whenever you do so. You could even use them for particularly important psychic receiving work.

---

[1] This is usually what is called the Oil of Abramelin. It is obtainable at many occult and New Age shops, or a recipe can be found in my book *21ˢᵗ Century Mage*, p. 27

[2] You can find more information on purification and consecration in my book *21ˢᵗ Century Mage*. Also, according to Aleister Crowley, appropriate words in the new aeon for purification are, "pure will, unassuaged of purpose, delivered from the lust of result, is every way perfect," and for consecration, "I am uplifted in they heart, and the kisses of the stars rain hard upon thy body." See, *Magick: Book 4 Liber ABA*, p. 215

Exercise 42 - Circle Casting

Time Required: 3 to 5 minutes.

For many of the upcoming exercises in this book, you will want to create a limited area of working, to focus and contain your power and energies, and to create a safe space where you will not be bothered by outside forces. The traditional manner in which this has been done for millennia has been by creating a magical circle within which to work. With this exercise you will use your imagination to create a safe, sacred circular space for your work. If you have a circle laid out in your workspace, you will simply trace the perimeter of this circle. If you have trouble visualizing any of these things, you can also simply use the sense of feeling to establish this space, or hear the rushing or buzzing of energy as you go through these steps. Of course, ideally, you will do all three, but simply do your best, and your circle will be impregnable to anything but that which you specifically invite. You may do this before, after, or sometimes instead of purification and consecration.

1. Go into your Alpha state, using your anchor.

2. Imagine light entering you again from above, and moving down your arm.

3. If you have a Magick Wand, you should be holding it in your hand at this point, and directing the light into the wand.

4. Imagine the light flowing down your head into your shoulders, down your arm into your wand or outstretched fingers, until there is a very strong sense of this light powerfully flowing into your wand from above.

5. Go to the East of your work area. The East is the traditional place to begin your circle, because light rises from the east, and it is considered the place of beginnings. Point your wand (or hand) down at the ground, imagining the light coursing from above, through your arm, projecting down to the ground.

6. Slowly circle the room in a clockwise manner, tracing a glowing line of energy on the floor in your path.

123

7. When you get back to the East, finish the circle completely, then move to its center, the center of the room. If you have an altar set up, it should be right in the center, so move behind the altar facing east.

8. Continue to allow the light to flow into you, imagine that it is beginning to accumulate in your heart. Visualize it as a bright ball. Let it continue growing and expanding until it is expanding past your body.

9. Send this light turning in a counter-clockwise direction, as it continues to grow, imagining that the turning light is sweeping away all outside energies.

10. Continue this growing and sweeping light until the globe of light fills the whole circumference of your circle, going above your head, and below the earth to completely surround you with a globe of light.

11. All energies other than your private connection with your subconscious and superconscious have now been swept out of your working area.

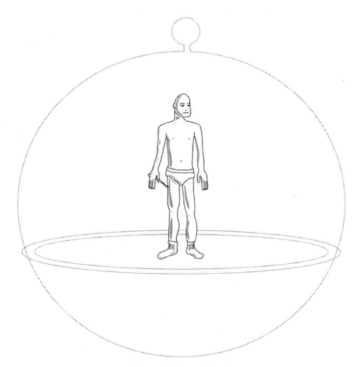

Diagram 7 - Sphere of Protection

You could also simply go through this procedure sitting in meditation, imagining the whole circle and sphere into existence from a seated position.

For most work, this simple exercise is sufficient preparation, but for some operations I recommend that you perform some sort of full temple opening. The following is a modification of the Lesser Ritual of the Pentagram based on the New Hermetics Grounding and Centering tool. You could also do the traditional Lesser Ritual of the Pentagram, or else some other temple opening of your choosing.

Exercise 43 - Pentagram Ritual

Time Required: 5 to 15 minutes

As in aura gazing and crystal gazing, you will want to use your third eye in this exercise to visualize the various elements while keeping your eyes open, although you can close them at appropriate moments. You may begin by imagining an inner temple forming in the space of your workroom, which is four-square, each of the walls facing one of the four direct-ions. As you trace the pentagrams and say the words of power, you will visualize the walls disintegrating, revealing the elemental worlds behind them. At first, this exercise may seem dauntingly complex, but once you get the hang of it, you will find it to be a powerful and moving experience.

I have abandoned the Hebrew words that usually go along with this ceremony in preference of English words that clearly evoke the powerful principles of practical magick that you will be working with. However, if you are familiar with and would prefer to use the traditional Lesser Banishing Ritual of the Pentagram or one of its derivatives, you can still use the visualizations that follow to assist you in making your intent more powerful.

1. Stand facing east. Take a few breaths to relax yourself.

2. Use your anchor to put yourself into the Alpha state if you have not already done so.

3. Begin breathing into your crown chakra, opening the Sahasrara, visualizing the ball of white Light, burning like a star, directly above your head. This is your connection to your superconsciousness. Raise your right hand above your head, and draw a shaft of light down into your head from the globe of white light above you, just like in the Alpha state exercise, only this time imagine it with as much intensity as possible, as if you are drawing the power of the whole universe into

yourself. You can also visualize that a shaft of white light is rising vertically from the globe of light above your head to the infinite consciousness of the universe itself, and that you are drawing on this infinite source of power. Touch your forehead, saying the words, "As above."

4. Inhale deeply, feeling the light above your head burning with intensity as it sends its rays down into your head, then as you exhale slowly, continue drawing the shaft of light down with your hand to your the groin area, saying the words, "So below." Visualize the vertical shaft of white light descending all the way to another globe of light beneath your feet, and onward, through the center of the Earth, to infinity once again.

5. Touch your right shoulder, saying "To accomplish." Breathe into your shoulder, like you were breathing into one of your chakras, opening a channel of energy there, and visualizing another globe shining where you are touching your shoulder. See a shaft of white light, extending horizontally to your right, and on to infinity.

6. Touch your left shoulder, saying, "The miracle." Now breathe into your left shoulder, as if breathing into one of your chakras, opening a channel of energy there, and visualizing another globe shining where you are touching your shoulder. See a shaft of white light, extending horizontally to your left, and on to infinity.

7. Bring both your hands to your heart, Begin breathing energy from all four points (Above head, feet, left and right shoulder) into your heart, forming a sphere of brilliant light and energy. This should feel quite ecstatic. Say, "Of the one thing."

8. Interlace your fingers, standing at the center of a blazing Cross of white Light, which extends to the ends of the Universe, as you vibrate the sacred word "AUM," flowing light to the whole universe from your heart.

9. Go to the Eastern edge of your circle. Send energy from the glowing orb at your heart up through your arm as you exhale, and trace a large Banishing Earth Pentagram.

Diagram 8 - Banishing Earth Pentagram

Make sure that you are tracing it clearly and consciously, not just flailing your arms around. As you trace, visualize a blue-white flaming glow forming the pentagram in the air before you. As you trace the pentagram, be aware that you are setting in motion forces that will prevent any hostile influences from entering your circle. Inhale deeply, drawing energy down from the star above your head into your heart. You may visualize the letters "KNOWLEDGE" glowing brightly in white light coming down into your body with the energy. As you exhale, send the energy up and through you as you throw your arms outward toward the pentagram, saying "Knowledge!" while you visualize the energy bursting through and past the pentagram blasting away all negative energy as it fills a quarter of the entire universe. See a vast golden yellow plain of gently waving grass materializing beyond the pentagram. The sun is rising. Visualize billowing clouds of yellowish air playing over this scene before you, an airy atmosphere, and as you see this become aware of the power of your mind, the process of thinking. Draw your right hand to your lips, inhaling, and continuing to visualize the scene in the east behind the pentagram.

10. Pierce the center of the Pentagram. Send some of your energy out of your body as you exhale, tracing a line of blue-white light around the circle as you move to the South, (to the point where the center of the next Pentagram will be).

11. Inhale deeply, drawing energy from the globe of light above your head into your heart. Send energy from your heart up through your arm as you exhale, and trace a Banishing Earth Pentagram. As you trace, visualize a blue-white flame forming the pentagram in the air before you. As you trace the pentagram, be aware that you are setting in motion forces that will prevent any hostile influences to enter your circle. Inhale deeply, drawing energy down from the globe of light above your head into your heart. You may visualize the letters "WILL" coming down into your body with the energy. As you exhale, send the energy

up and through you as you throw your arms outward toward the pentagram, saying "Will!" Visualize the energy bursting through and past the pentagram blasting away all negative energy as it fills a quarter of the entire universe. See a vast, blazing hot, red desert materializing beyond the pentagram. It is noon. Visualize burning red flames before you, playing over this scene before you, a fiery atmosphere, and as you see this become aware of your will, your passions and desires. Draw your right hand to your lips, inhaling, and continuing to visualize the scene in the south behind the pentagram.

12. Pierce the center of the Pentagram. Send some of your energy out of your body as you exhale, tracing a line of blue-white light around the circle as you move to the West, (to the point where the center of the next Pentagram will be).

13. Inhale deeply, drawing energy from the globe of light above your head into your heart. Send energy from your heart up through your arm as you exhale, and trace a Banishing Earth Pentagram. As you trace, visualize a blue-white flame forming the pentagram in the air before you. As you trace the pentagram, be aware that you are setting in motion forces that will prevent any hostile influences to enter your circle. Inhale deeply, drawing energy down from the globe of light above your head into your heart. You may visualize the letters "DARING" coming down into your body with the energy. As you exhale, send the energy up and through you as you throw your arms outward toward the pentagram, saying "Daring!" Visualize the energy bursting through and past the pentagram blasting away all negative energy as it fills a quarter of the entire universe. See a vast ocean beach with glorious blue waters beyond the pentagram. The sun is setting on the water. Visualize undulating waves of watery energy before you, playing over this scene before you, a watery atmosphere, and as you see this become aware of your emotions and feelings. Draw your right hand to your lips, inhaling, and continuing to visualize the scene in the west behind the pentagram.

14. Pierce the center of the Pentagram. Send some of your energy out of your body as you exhale, tracing a line of blue-white light around the circle as you move to the North, (to the point where the center of the next Pentagram will be).

15. Inhale deeply, drawing energy from the globe of light above your head into your heart. Send energy from your heart up through your arm as you exhale, and trace a Banishing Earth Pentagram. As you trace,

visualize a blue-white flame forming the pentagram in the air before you. As you trace the pentagram, be aware that you are setting in motion forces that will prevent any hostile influences to enter your circle. Inhale deeply, drawing energy down from the globe of light above your head into your heart. You may visualize the letters "SILENCE" coming down into your body with the energy. As you exhale, send the energy up and through you as you throw your arms outward toward the pentagram, saying mentally, but not uttering a sound, "Silence!" Visualize the energy bursting through and past the pentagram blasting away all negative energy as it fills a quarter of the entire universe. See a vast land of green mountains and rich dark earth beyond the pentagram. It is midnight. Visualize rocky structural energies forming before you, playing over this scene before you, an earthy atmosphere, and as you see this become aware of your plans, goals and your physical life. Draw your right hand to your lips, inhaling, and continuing to visualize the scene in the north behind the pentagram.

16. Pierce the center of the Pentagram. Send some of your energy out of your body as you exhale, tracing a line of blue-white light as you move to the East. Complete the Circle by finishing the line in the center of the first Pentagram (where you began).

17. Now spread your arms at your sides at shoulder level, facing toward the east again, and say, "Before me, Intelligence." Visualize a giant golden yellow angelic being forming in the billows of cloud in the east. This is your guardian of the element of Air.

18. Say, "Behind me, Understanding." Visualize a giant pulsing blue angelic being forming in the flowing watery energy behind you in the west. This is your guardian of the element of Water.

19. Say, "To my right hand Creation." Visualize a giant fiery red angelic being forming in the flames of the south. This is your guardian of the element of fire.

20. Say, "and to my left hand Manifestation." Visualize a giant earthy black angelic being forming amongst the structures in the north. This is your guardian of the element of Earth.

21. Observe the energy in and about you, saying, "about me flame the Pentagrams, and in the column shines the Six-Rayed Star."

129

22. Repeat steps 3-8.

23. You may now begin your work, or return to normal awareness whenever you are ready.

Again, all of this can simply be imagined into existence from a seated position.[1]

MAGNETISM

The first and most important form of magical influence that you should learn is the capacity to have great personal magnetism. Having charm and charisma will get you far in life, opening doors, creating opportunities, friendships and far-reaching influence. It is really a simple matter. Mostly it comes down to simply being yourself. However, this must be your best self. Really love yourself, and others will love you. Attempt at all times to empower yourself, emphasizing your best qualities in your own mind whenever possible. Take a few moments, and think of those things that you like most about yourself. Liking yourself and feeling confident are really the keys to per-sonal magnetism, but the following may also be helpful.

Dress the part. Try to look your best at all times, defining a personal style that will enhance your comfort and confidence. Further, you must really desire magnetism. Think constantly to yourself, "I will be popular, famous, sought after."

You may think that you want to be popular and well loved, but your subconscious may not agree with your conscious desires. Check in with your subconscious using the pendulum. If your subconscious does not find the idea of popularity and personal magnetism agreeable, figure out why, and come up with ways of making your subconscious comfortable with this prospect.

You must have good and positive reasons for wanting to create personal magnetism. If you are merely seeking to manipulate others for petty reasons, your subconscious and superconscious minds will rebel. Be generous, altruistic in your thinking, interested in being helpful and useful to the world. Selfish motivation will eventually hinder your magnetism, even if you seem quite charming at first.

Be enthusiastic. Enthusiasm is contagious. If you are high on life, others will want to be around you. Intense emotion in general will help draw people to you, as long as this emotion is positive. Regular work with your chakras will greatly help to open up your intense, positive emotions.

---

[1] Such a meditation can be found in my *The New Hermetics*, called "The New Hermetics Grounding and Centering." p. 99

Exercise 44 - Personal Magnetism, Charisma, and Irresistible Charm

Time Required: 5 to 10 minutes

When you are about to be in a situation in which you wish to be highly charismatic, you will find the following simple procedure helpful.

1. Go into the Alpha state using your anchor.

2. Fix in your mind that you are going to be fascinating, visualizing and feeling this desire building within you as a palpable energy coming up from your gut.

3. Feel even more enchanting energy flowing down into you from the light above your head.

4. Feel the power from above and below mingling in your heart, combining this with images of yourself being very charming and well loved. Build up this energy in yourself as a palpable glow of captivation that swirls around you.

5. Send it emanating out of you into your aura, imagining yourself glowing with a charismatic glamour.

6. Record your experience in your journal when you get home.

Exercise 45 - Fascination or Enchantment

Time Required: 2 to 10 minutes

This is a variation on the preceding in which you are interested in influencing a particular person. Some may say that this technique borders on negative magick, but as long as you don't abuse this it can be useful in certain situations. You will have to use your own moral compass to decide what the right sort of situation might be. Remember that it will not work well if it goes against your own best interests.

1. If possible, consult with your pendulum before you begin.

2. Use the personal magnetism technique to fill your aura with charismatic power.

3. Keep this aura clearly in mind as you encounter the person you wish to influence

4. Think of what you want. Project your thoughts silently out toward the person on a wave of your magnetic energy, such as, "You like me!" or "You want to know me!" If you are interested in communicating something you might say, "You will listen to me!" For overpowering someone you might want to say something like, "I am more powerful than you!" You will imagine your personal magnetic energy undulating into the person you wish to influence carrying the thoughts like an irresistible wave of force. Visualize, feel and hear the words emanating as a wave of power directly into the person.

5. You may repeat this as often as is necessary to get your psychic message to work. However, be subtle in these actions, because the forces you use are subtle, and the person will easily be able to resist them if he or she thinks you are creepy. This will quickly negate your work, so try not to stare fixedly at anyone, or to wave your hands dramatically or gesticulate with your head. Just seem natural, and project your will confidently.

6. Record your experience in your journal when you get home.

If the person that you would like to influence is not in front of you, you may either visualize the person as sitting before you, or else imagine a cord of energy extending out to where they are along which you can send your magnetism. Both seem to work fairly well some of the time, but there are more subtle ways to influence over a distance. There will be more on this in the section on telepathy.

Exercise 46 -Instant Rapport

Even if you get people's attention with either of the preceding techniques, in order to maintain it, you will need to establish a lasting rapport. The following suggestions are not strictly metaphysical, but they will have an almost magical effect if used correctly.

These must be done with a great deal subtlety, because if you do them awkwardly or obviously you can destroy rather than create rapport. We all do these things to a certain extent anyway, but by being conscious of them you can greatly increase your personal charisma and lasting magnetism.

1. Imitate the body language of the person you are wishing to establish rapport with. If they are sitting with legs crossed, mirror them. If their arms are folded, fold yours. If they are upright or rigid, do this too. If they are slumped, try slumping. This will instantly put you in sympathy.

2. Imitate the breathing patterns of the person you wish to establish rapport with. Some people breathe high in their chest, others in the belly. Some breathe quickly or shallowly or deeply or rhythmically. Match this, and you are well on your way to establishing rapport.

3. Try to determine the dominant sensory modality of the person you wish to establish rapport with. Listen to the language that they use, are they speaking visually, auditorily, kinesthetically? Match their usual predicates- I see, I hear, I feel etc. There are also several ways of spotting the dominant modality that a person uses just by their appearance and manner. Try to recognize these before you even engage the person. This way you can open up a conversation with them using their preferred sensory modality. Thus, if they are a kinesthetic person you could start a conversation with something like, "Don't you FEEL like this is a great party?" A list of these common characteristics of the modalities and matching common predicates follows in a moment.

4. Match the vocal tonality of the person that you are speaking to. Is their voice high, sharp, loud, soft, low, or smooth? Try to speak in a similar or congruent tonality.

5. Observe their verbal pace. Are they slow talking or fast talking? Do they speak rhythmically or are there many pauses in their speech. Try to match this as well.

6. How is their overall energy? Are they mellow, tense, enthusiastic? Be the same.

7. Are their movements graceful, clunky, clumsy, jerky, or fast? Make yours that way too.

Visible Signs of a Person's Dominant Modality:

Visual:

Well dressed
Upper chest breathing
Sharp breathing
Sharp tonality
Higher pitched voice
Fast talker
Tall, skinny- Ectomorph
Leads with chin
Stands Erect
Seems a bit snobby
Stiff movements

Kinesthetic:

Softer voice
Soft body- endomorphic
Slow, unrhythmic speech
Rounded shoulders
Stooped posture
Loose movements
Abdominal breathing
Lower tonality
Comfortable clothing

Auditory:

Pleasant voice
Arms folded
Medium weight
Rhythmic movement
Taps feet, as if hearing internal music
Taps fingers
Tends to tilt head, as if listening
Relaxed but not slumped
Rhythmic, "sing-song" speech
Full breathing in lower chest

Common Predicates of the Sensory Modalities:

Visual:

I see...
Picture this...
Take a look...
It seems a little hazy...
Things are looking...
It's crystal clear...
From my point of view...
Let's focus...
I need some perspective...
How colorful...

Kinesthetic:

I feel...
I can't get a grasp on this...
I need to get a handle...
I just want to get in touch...
It doesn't feel right...
I sense...
How firm is that...
That heats things up...
I'm cool to that...
I don't get a good vibe...

Auditory:

I hear...
That sounds right...
That rings a bell...
That doesn't resonate...
I'm listening...
What's the good word...
The tone seems a bit...
Everything is harmonious...
That's loud and clear...

Exercise 47 - Spreading Influence over Wide Areas

Time Required: 10 to 20 minutes

Sometimes you may want to influence a lot of people at once, particularly for the general purposes of attracting love, business opportunities, social reform, to influence society, or to start a trend of some sort. This is a challenging thing to accomplish, so you will need to raise your personal charisma level and general energy as high as possible. Timing is everything in this sort of an operation. If you time your influence at a time when the climate surrounding you is conducive, your work will be much more effective than if you time it when the general climate is against you. For instance, in the early eighties, wearing flair pants or bell bottom jeans was incredibly taboo, so if your intention was to create a trend of wearing bell bottoms at that time, everything would be against you. A few years ago, the seventies were being viewed as very cool, so bell bottoms made a huge comeback. If you time any kind of massive influence with outside conditions, you will find yourself accomplishing your will much more easily.

In order to accomplish something on a massive scale, you will need to raise as much energy as possible, so you will want to perform full opening rituals. You also must know exactly what you want, and make sure your subconscious and superconscious minds are completely on board.

1. Check in with you subconscious using the pendulum.

2. Do the Circle Casting exercise.

3. Do the Pentagram Ritual.

4. Purify and consecrate yourself.

5. Think about what you want to accomplish. Get really excited about it. You must raise a tremendous amount of power, so raise your emotions to a peak of excitement, arousing your Kundalini.

6. Build up your desired influence gloriously in you, feeling a surge of power from your superconscious entering you as a brilliant light, involving your whole body to a fevered pitch.

7. Send out a current of influence straight up through your body out of your head, visualizing it going out into the sky above you. Imagine that it is a powerful fire hose of energy bursting up continuously.

8. Imagine that this energy is starting to whirl slowly in a clockwise spiral outward, continuously expanding and blast up and out until it is whirling through the whole area you wish to affect.

9. See it entering the hearts and minds of those you are affecting.

10. Keep it whirling, telling your subconscious to continue powering it.

11. Visualize the results. See your success in the near future, feeling really good about it.

12. Do the pentagram ritual once again.

13. Come back to normal consciousness when you are ready, knowing that your influence will work.

14. Record your experience in your journal.

15. Take actions confidently in your life toward your goal, expecting results. As you encounter people that you have influenced in this way, be confident. Know that your work has been effective.

PSYCHIC HEALING

The main principle behind psychic healing is that all disease originates in energy and thus in consciousness. The physical symptoms of disease are the final manifestations of a problem in energy. By making changes in energy and consciousness, disease can be eliminated. Numerous diseases have been eliminated in people who have simply taken up the habit of meditation. By balancing and relaxing mind and energy, the physical manifestations have simply disappeared. Research has indicated that "peace of mind" can prevent or reduce the chances of quite a few degenerative diseases such as heart disease and hypertension. Many entire volumes have been written about energy healing, and I can only devote a few pages to the subject. Nonetheless, many of the fundamentals can be covered in just a few words.

First, I must caution you that if you are trying to heal yourself or someone who has some sort of serious illness, you should still seek out modern medical attention. Psychic healing should be used in addition to, not instead of, medical treatment. This being said, I have had the great privilege of being a part of a small healing circle that successfully participated in the healing of a woman suffering from lung cancer. She has been cancer free now for several years, thanks to her own faith, her medical team, and I'd like to think in some small way our healing work. I have also had the privilege of helping people come through depression, lose weight, recover from addiction and overcome traumas. The methods that I've used are extremely simple, and I will cover them fully in the next pages.

In order to be successful with psychic healing, you must believe in the healing power within, and your ability to share this power. You must believe in the possibility of perfect health. As you are doing healing work, don't think of the disease as much as think of health. Think about the person being balanced, whole and vibrantly healthy. As you are working, feel the reality of your healing, that you are really making an impact. Try to encourage anyone you are healing to feel this way too.

Above all, choose happiness! Desire happiness! Be happy! Nothing prevents happiness, it requires no outside stimulation. Simply smile, and encourage those who would be healed to adopt this same mindset. If you are truly happy, your happiness will be infectious, and will be an unstoppable healing force in the universe.

The Alpha State for Healing

If you are treating someone who is in the room with you, it may be a good idea to teach them the Alpha state exercise earlier in this book. This state is very healing in and of itself. It also will help you open the person up to the healing energies that you are going to be invoking.

If you are going to be putting someone into the Alpha state, simply guide them slowly through the steps, slowly and confidently, helping to guide them into relaxation and focus. You can also describe what you are doing throughout to your patient so that he or she can visualize it along with you.

Healing can also be just as effective at a distance. Simple prayer can be particularly useful for healing someone who is far away. You can also send healing colors at a distance.

Healing Colors

Some of the healing techniques you will use in a few moments involve the use of healing colors. The following list is meant to be suggestive. Research has proven a number of these colors to have some of these effects in laboratory conditions. Some of the other statements are merely traditional attributions. You may find yourself using various colors in any number of ways. You will find your own way in this with experience. These are traditional attributions that I have generally found effective myself. We have already discussed some of the meanings of these colors when we looked at the aura in previous chapters. Later, we will discuss these same colors in reference to elemental and planetary energies. You will notice many parallels and corollaries amongst these lists. Color has a powerful, automatic effect on consciousness, and these colors seem to have similar archetypal effect on all of us, regardless of culture or familiarity with any lists.

White Light – although this term often receives a smirk within the magical community, it is a powerful general healing energy that contains the properties of all the other colors. White light contains the full color spectrum. If you do not know which color to use, white light can always be useful. However, if possible you may want to try using specific colors. You wouldn't want to give a person every kind of medicine at once for their ailments. For colds you give cold medicine, for headaches, aspirin. The same is true for healing colors. Still, white light should not be ignored and is particularly useful in breaking up blockages in the energy system and the chakras.

Red - promotes energy, warmth, stimulates sexuality and reproductive systems, excites and warms the body, increases heart rate, blood pressure, brain activity, stimulates circulation of blood and flow of adrenaline and respiration, helps rapid tissue repair, sustains physical body, vitalizes blood, healing wounds, broken bones, allergies, weakened organs, relieves tiredness and weakness, paralysis, reviving unconscious or dying, draws poisons to a head on the surface, stimulates and builds liver, builds red corpuscles.

Orange - stimulates the appetite and reduces fatigue, lifts energy level, decongesting, cleansing, loosening, eliminating waste, germs, toxins, kidney and bladder ailments, constipation, arthritis, cysts, colds cough and lung issues, increases oxygen by stimulating lungs and thyroid, lung builder and respiratory stimulant, heals lung disorders, depresses parathyroid, stimulates milk production, eases indigestion, relieves gas, alleviates cramps and convulsions, ends hiccups, relieves spastic and sluggish colon and intestines, increases discharges and eliminations, , helps digestion in general, decreases menstrual cramps, menstrual problems, removing blood clots, promotes enthusiasm, has antibacterial properties, removes repression and inhibitions, broadens the mind.

Yellow - Stimulates memory, sensory stimulant, raises blood pressure and pulse rate, cheers you up, stimulating nerves, healing wounds, skin problems, cellular repairs, depresses the spleen and parathyroid gland, increases appetite, aids in assimilation to increase nutrition, stimulates lymphatic glands, motivates action in all kinds of paralysis such as strokes or sluggish organs, nerve stimulant and builder, stimulates and strengthens the heart for better circulation, stimulates

139

liver and gall bladder aiding eliminations, destroys body worms, stimulates and builds pancreas for better control of sugar balance, stimulates and builds eyes and ears, loosens and aids elimination of calcium and lime deposits that cause arthritis, heals nervous system, balances adrenal glands, diabetes.

Green - The color of natural growth, appeals to the aesthetic sense of balance and normality, soothing and relaxing to body and mind, helps the aging to feel more vibrant, detoxifying, disinfecting, antiseptic, germicide, breaking down blood clots, colds, fevers, stimulates the pituitary, raises body vibrations above vibrations of disease - a form of immunity from disease, destroys and heals all infections, destroys rotting material and builds cells and tissues, breaks up cancerous cells, wonderful on open sores, cuts bruises and damaged flesh, heals burns, ulcers.

Blue - calming and tranquilizing effect on body, lowers blood pressure, heart rate and respiration, has a profound cooling effect, disinfectant, soothing, mild anaesthetic, helps headaches, pain relief in general, heals ailments due to infection, relieves inflammation, slows motor action, induces rest and sleep, helps stop bleeding, reduces and breaks fevers, relieves itching and irritations, soothes burns.

Violet - powerful spiritual healing color that is useful on severe illnesses in general, soothes organs, relaxes muscles, calms the nervous system, antibiotic, spleen stimulant, builds white corpuscles, reduces anger, depresses lymphatic glands and heart, lowers appetite, relieves dysentary and diarrhea, promotes deep sleep, strong motor depressant, promotes enlightenment, revelation, and spiritual awakening

Exercise 48 – Laying on of Hands

Time Required: 15 to 20 minutes

For this practice you obviously need to have your patient present. You can also use this technique on yourself, although on yourself you do not need to use your hands unless it seems appropriate.

1. Consult your subconscious with the pendulum.

2. If possible, have your patient lie down, and put them into the Alpha state.

3. Go into the Alpha state yourself using your anchor.

4. Raise your personal energy levels, opening your chakras and arousing Kundalini.

5. Visualize the appropriate healing color energies as existing around and above you in a diluted and unconcentrated state. Begin to gather this color from all around you and see it collecting and swirling above your head.

6. Draw this energy down into you through your crown chakra, feeling the power and energy coming through from your superconscious, and send it down through your arms to your hands.

7. Place your hands on the patients, at the appropriate part of their bodies where possible, or else on their chests or backs.

8. See the energy flowing into them, healing them. Spend some time seeing this energy really doing its job, filling your patients with light, and clearing away the problem.

9. Finally, visualize your patients energetic, vibrant, and completely healed. See them enjoying their lives, free of any problems.

10. Come back to normal consciousness, and guide your patients slowly back to normal consciousness, regardless of whether you've put them into the alpha state or not.

11. Record your experience in your journal.

Exercise 49 – The Power of Prayer

Time Required: 15 to 20 minutes

Prayer is a very powerful healing technique in and of itself. Simply by asking the universe for its help, and wishing healing for the person, visualizing the person healthy can have truly magical results. This sort of simple technique can be particularly effective in groups. However, you may wish to use the formal format of the following tool, either alone or in a group, to empower your prayer even further.

1. Consult your subconscious with the pendulum.

2. If the person is not present, and you have a picture of them when they were healthy and well, take a few minutes to look at this picture and feel really loving toward them.

3. Go into the Alpha state yourself using your anchor.

4. Raise your personal energy levels, opening your chakras and arousing Kundalini.

5. Direct your attention up to your crown chakra, to the light of your superconscious mind.

6. Express your love for the ailing person, and your wish to see him or her healed. Visualize the patient energetic, vibrant, and completely healed. See him or her enjoying life, free of any problems. Send this picture up through your crown chakra, up into the light of your superconscious mind.

7. Return to normal consciousness.

8. Record your experience in your journal.

Exercise 50 – Aura Color Therapy

Time Required: 15 to 20 minutes

You can use this technique to heal energy problems directly in the aura of a patient.

1. Consult your subconscious with the pendulum.

2. If possible, have your patient sit or lie down, and put them into the Alpha state.

3. Go into the Alpha state yourself using your anchor.

4. Raise your personal energy levels, opening your chakras and arousing Kundalini.

5. View the aura of your patient, looking for blockages, ugly colors, or lines of energy draining off the life force of your patient.

142

6. Visualize appropriate healing color energies as existing around and above you in a diluted and unconcentrated state. You could also simply gather whatever healing energy your superconscious mind feels are appropriate. Begin to gather this color from all around you and see it collecting and swirling above your head.

7. Draw this energy down into you through your crown chakra, feeling the power and energy coming through from your superconscious, and send it down through your arms to your hands.

8. Direct your hands toward the energy problems of your patient. See the energy flowing into their aura. Spend some time seeing this energy really doing its job, clearing away the problem.

9. Finally, visualize the patient energetic, vibrant, and completely healed. See them enjoying life, free of any problems.

10. Come back to normal consciousness, and guide your patient slowly back to normal consciousness.

11. Record your experience in your journal.

Exercise 51 - Cleansing the Aura with Your Hands

Time Required: 15 to 20 minutes

This is similar to the last, except that you will be manipulating blockages in the energies of the aura directly with the energy channels in your hands and fingers. You can find these blocks using your third eye if you wish, but you can also simply feel for them, using your hands. The directions will indicate the latter, but you can use your third eye whenever you wish.

You will need a basin of water for this exercise. You will take any negative energy that you find and toss it into the basin of water. The magnetic power of water will absorb the negativity and you can dispose of the water later.

1. Consult your subconscious with the pendulum.

2. If possible, have your patient lie down, and put them into the Alpha state.

3. Go into the Alpha state yourself using your anchor.

4. Raise your personal energy levels, opening your chakras and arousing Kundalini.

5. Begin to stroke the aura of your patient slowly, using your fingers like combs, feeling for knots of energy that seem unhealthy, or lines of energy leading out which are draining the life force of your patient

6. When you find an area that seems to have bad energy, pull the knot out like a strand of rope, feel it sticking to your hand, and flick it into the nearby basin of water. Comb through the entire aura in this way.

7. When the aura seems clean, take a moment to view it with your third eye, trying to see if you've missed something. If you find anything, again clear it into the basin of water with your hands.

8. Once you are fairly certain you've cleared all you can find, take a few moments to fill yourself with light from your superconscious. Send it down through your arms to your hands and infuse your patient's aura with a gentle stream of this healing light until they are glowing brightly.

9. Finally, visualize the patient energetic, vibrant, and completely healed. See them enjoying life, free of any problems.

10. Come back to normal consciousness, and guide your patient slowly back to normal consciousness.

11. If possible, dispose of the negatively charged water into the earth, to ground it.

12. Record your experience in your journal.

INVISIBILITY AND INSTANTLY STANDING OUT

Becoming invisible was one of my personal childhood obsessions. I think many people have similar fantasies, so I am providing this simple and effective exercise. It should be kept in mind that invisibility is more a matter of distracting attention, or rather ceasing to attract attention, rather than absolutely disappearing. I would not recommend using this technique to try entering a bank vault or anything crazy like that. At the same time, you can easily avoid drawing attention to yourself, so that you can go about your business in relative secrecy. Drawing instant attention to yourself with your influence is also equally easy.

Exercise 52 - Invisibility

Time Required: varies

Accomplishing invisibility is a combination of metaphysical technique and common sense behavior. You will want to dress drably or in the typical clothes of the people around. Wear nothing that makes you stick out. This will be different kinds and varieties of clothing in different situations. If you wear dark gray in Miami, where everyone seems to be in pink and white, you will draw extra attention to yourself. But dark gray would be perfect in New York City. Don't create extra challenges to your energy work by doing anything at all that draws attention to you.

You will also want to slump your shoulders, focus inward, looking down as much as possible. Take on the characteristic posture of a depressed person. No one is more invisible in our culture than a depressed person.

1. Consult your subconscious with the pendulum.

2. Go into the Alpha state, using your anchor.

3. Visualize your aura around you.

4. Think to yourself, "I am becoming invisible."

5. Vividly visualize a barrier of darkness forming around your aura, a dark cloud of dull shadows. Let this darkness fill your aura.

6. Imagine vividly that your is body fading out of sight in this cloud of obscurity. Hold onto this image of invisibility. Focus on the darkness. Think only of yourself and your darkness no matter where you go or what you do. Pay no attention to anyone around you.

7. When you are through, visualize the obscurity of darkness completely dissipating. You do not want to stay in this state overlong, as it can actually become depressing.

8. Stand up straight and smile, feeling your aura lighten.

9. Record your experience in your journal.

145

Exercise 53 - Instantly Standing Out in a Crowd

Time Required: varies

This is essentially the opposite of invisibility. To accomplish it effectively you will want to dress sharply, colorfully, differently from others, and stand tall. Feel confident, lively, and vigorous.

1. Consult your subconscious with the pendulum.

2. Go into the Alpha state, using your anchor.

3. Visualize your aura around you.

4. Fill it with golden light from above until you feel you are positively radiantly glowing. You are the sun!

5. Be loud. Feel loud. Exude confidence.

6. When you are through, visualize the radiance dissipating. You do not want to stay in this state overlong, as it could lead to vanity and egotism.

7. Record your experience in your journal.

ANIMAL TRANSFORMATION

This is a challenging operation. Stories of animal transformation such as lycanthropy or animal warriors are relics of early civilization shamanism, and this practice was usually induced by psychotropic drugs and trance in which it was more of a dream or astral experience. These animal magicians were visible only to those who were sensitive and saw their astral forms, as they traveled and delivered their influence in the world. It may be a useful practice though, for learning the lessons that animal spirits can offer. I will give you three different techniques for doing this.

Before you begin any of these techniques, please choose an animal that you would like to work with. Spend some time researching as much as you can about this animal. Study the animal deeply, discover how it lives, where it lives, how it moves, what it eats. Discover all you can about it in as much detail as possible. Think about the animal as much as possible, obsessively.

Exercise 54 – Animal Transformation in Your Dreams

Time Required: n/a

This is essentially a variation on dream programming. You will most effectively be able to use this technique once you have perfected lucid dreaming.

1. Consult with your subconscious before you begin even researching your chosen animal, to make sure that it is ready to participate in this experience.

2. Once you have conducted your research, put an image of the animal by your bed or under your pillow.

3. When you are getting ready for bed, write at the top of a blank page of your journal, "Tonight I will become a (your animal) in my dreams."

4. Consult with your subconscious using the pendulum about whether it completely understands your intention, and is willing to play along.

5. As you are drifting off to sleep, continue thinking about your animal, letting images relating to this subject play through your mind until you fall asleep.

6. When you become lucid, imagine your body transforming, becoming the animal. It will happen easily. You also may simply find yourself lucidly dreaming of being the animal. If you wake up in the middle of the night, as you are returning to sleep imagine that you are transforming, and allow yourself to reenter your dreams in the animal form. Explore this state.

7. When you awaken, write down any dreams you have had, whether they relate to your animal or not.

Exercise 55 - Animal Transformation in Your Body of Light

Time Required: varies

This technique is essentially the same as the above except you will be performing this transformation during an astral projection rather than in your dreams. This will make it easier to travel through consensus reality to a certain extent. However, you also may find yourself in some other place, related to the energy of the animal you have chosen. This was the preferred technique of the ancient magicians, although they sometimes worked in their dreams as well. You will need to consult Chapter Seven to accomplish this technique, but I wanted to include it here amongst the other animal transformations.

1. Consult with your subconscious before you begin even researching your chosen animal, to make sure that it is ready to participate in this experience.

2. Once you have conducted your research, put an image of the animal in your temple or workroom. Spend some time looking at the image, really getting its energy fixed into your mind.

3. At this point, you may wish to conduct an opening ritual, how extensive is up to you.

4. Use your preferred method for astral projection.

5. Spend some time in your body of light, getting fully involved in your vision to the point that your physical body is far from your mind. You may wish to travel to the characteristic habitat of the animal.

6. Then imagine your body transforming, becoming the animal. It will happen easily, although it may seem imaginary, at least at first. Explore this state.

7. Before you return to body consciousness, reform your usual shape.

8. Return to your body, come back to normal consciousness and record your experiences in your journal.

Exercise 56 - Animal Transformation in Body Consciousness

Time Required: 40 to 60 minutes

This is probably the hardest technique, and the most likely to seem more like play-acting rather than a true transformation. However, it can be very powerful if you really let yourself go, involving yourself totally in the experience. This method will work best with animals that have a wild, powerful energy. You will probably not want to explore turtle consciousness using this technique. However, feel free to try. This practice will most likely remain subjective in any case, but who knows how far it could be taken if you really throw yourself into it. The only limits to our abilities are the ones that we set ourselves.

I will also add that this technique could also be explored using entheogenic enhancement. I will not go so far as to suggest this, for legal reasons, but this is most frequently the way in which shamans explored this phenomenon in our earliest cultures.

1. Consult with your subconscious before you begin even researching your chosen animal, to make sure that it is ready to participate in this experience.

2. Once you have conducted your research, if possible go to the natural habitat of the animal you will work with. Bring an image of the animal. Spend some time looking at the image, really getting its energy fixed into your mind.

3. At this point, you may wish to conduct an opening ritual, how extensive is up to you.

4. Once you are ready to begin the transformation, you should be in a very deep Alpha state. Bend your knees slightly, tucking your pelvis, leaning a bit forward. Begin arousing Kundalini until you feel yourself starting to shake. Sustain and increase this shaking until you feel yourself really twitching wildly all over.

5. As you do this, start hyperventilating so that you are breathing fast and shaking wildly. Allow yourself to get wild, beginning to move in a sort of dance resembling the way the animal you've chosen might move, continuing your breathing and shaking. Allow yourself to transform. At any point, this may become more of a vision than a physical experience. Explore whatever happens.

6. Once you have finished, it would probably be a good idea to perform the pentagram ritual to help in bringing yourself back to a sense of balance and normalcy.

7. Record your experience in your journal.

PSYCHIC PROTECTION

Before leaving the subject of influence, I want to give you a few simple techniques for resisting negative psychic influence from others. Most so-called

149

psychic attacks are actually produced in our own minds due to fears and un-balanced energy in ourselves. It is important to avoid becoming obsessed with the idea that people are "out to get you," because in all likelihood this not the case. These sorts of paranoid thoughts will cause you much greater harm than any attack from outside you.

However, occasionally people do try to use techniques like the ones in this chapter for negative purposes. Also, some people emanate a sort of negative psychic influence unconsciously, just by their very presence. Some people just seem to exude a sort of psychic vampirism of negativity, draining you of energy when they are around. The following techniques should help you to resist these attacks whether they are intentional or not.

If you believe yourself to be under magical or psychic attack, it is a good idea to consult your subconscious using the pendulum. Your subconscious will be very able to discern the validity of your fears. But it should be kept in mind that your subconscious wants to please you. So, if you have it fixed in your mind that all of your enemies are out to get you with evil magick, your subconscious may confirm this whether or not it is true. Be sure to emphasize that you really want to know the truth when consulting your subconscious.

Exercise 57 - Personal Globe of Light

Time Required: 2 to 10 minutes

The very easiest thing you can do is to simply fill your aura with the light you draw down from your superconscious. This can be done at a moment's no-tice in any situation. It is a simple variation on the circle casting exercise you performed earlier in the chapter. It's advantage is that it can be used quickly and easily in any situation without drawing undue attention to yourself. It should be sufficient to clear away any negative influences from your aura.

1. If possible, consult your subconscious with the pendulum.

2. Go into the Alpha state, using your anchor.

3. Continue to allow the light from your superconscious to flow into you, imagine that it is beginning to accumulate in your heart. Visualize it as a bright ball. Let it continue growing and expanding until it is expanding past your body.

4. Send this light turning in a counter-clockwise direction, as it continues to grow, imagining that the turning light is sweeping away all outside energies.

150

5. Continue this growing and sweeping light until the globe of light fills the whole circumference of your aura, an egg shape surrounding you about a foot to a foot and a half around you in all directions.

6. All outside energies have now been dispelled from your personal space.

7. Tell your subconscious to maintain this swirling light, and return to normal consciousness.

8. Record your experience in your journal when you can.

Exercise 58 - Psychic Barrier

Time Required: 2 to 10 minutes

This following technique can be used in addition to the preceding whenever you are in a situation in which you wish to avoid the negative energy of someone who is nearby. We have all been in situations where people have aggravated and drained us with their negativity. You will be surprised at how easily this technique will repel negative people. You may even do it in the midst of a conversation, and you will find that the negative person will find a polite excuse to leave you.

1. Go into the Alpha state, using your anchor.

2. Do the preceding exercise quickly and simply visualizing the white light from your superconsciousness filling your aura.

3. Visualize this light accumulating at the outer edges of your aura, and becoming a solid clear barrier, like a force field around you or a crystalline, impenetrable egg.

4. Ask your subconscious to maintain this barrier as you continue to go about your business.

5. Record your experience in your journal when you can.

These two simple exercises should easily neutralize any negative influence, particularly when you are out and about in public and need a quick solution. However, if you are at home or in your workspace, you may also use the pentagram ritual or the circle casting procedures to achieve a similar effect. Regular use of all of these practices will render your personal psychic vehicle impervious to all negativity whether from within or without.

If you should ever find yourself in magical battle, which I strongly suggest you avoid, or under magical attack from someone who really wishes you harm, you might also want to consider creating a magical guardian servitor. General instructions on creating artificial servitor spirits will be explained in chapter 8. You can easily adapt these instructions to create a sort of psychic warden, whose job it will be to block or extinguish any negative currents that are directed your way. Traditionally, magicians have created such astral guardians in the forms of dogs, cats, or birds of pray such as hawks or eagles. You may of course design a guardian in whatever form suits your needs.

Exercise 59 - Binding

Time Required: 20 to 30 minutes

Hopefully you will never experience this, but if you absolutely know some-one is out to get you, and they are sending bad energy toward you relentlessly you can bind them away from you psychically. You may also use this technique if someone is dangerously bothering you or threatening you with physical violence. This should only ever be used on people who are actively threatening you. Don't simply use this idly. You must not do this with the intent to harm, or you will bring harm upon yourself. The only purpose of this is to keep the person away from you, to protect yourself from harm.

It is traditional to perform a binding operation when the moon is waning, but your own experience will be the best judge in this matter.

If you have a photograph of the person or something that belongs to them, you can physically bind this object with a black ribbon while you are doing this, creating a physical talisman of your operation. In this case you will also need a piece of black cloth to contain these things. You will then bury this ritualized object in the ground somewhere far from your home. However, if you do not have such an object, the whole operation can be performed simply through the visualizations that follow. The instructions will contain the physical actions of working with the picture and the black ribbon and cloth, but you may omit them, concentrating very vividly on the visualization portion.

1. Consult your subconscious with the pendulum, to make sure that this operation is really necessary and advisable.

2. If you have a picture or some object, and a piece of black ribbon about two to three feet long, and a piece of black cloth, you will need to place it on a table or altar in the center of your work room.

152

3. Go into the Alpha state, using your anchor, and perform a purification, circle casting and pentagram ritual if you wish.

4. Do some Kundalini arousing breaths to increase your accessible power.

5. Look at the photograph of the person you wish to bind. Remind yourself of why you need to keep this person away from you. With your third eye, begin to visualize the person as standing just outside the barrier of your circle. This visualization should be of the person exhibiting their negative behaviors or bad energy. You are only attempting to bind up this bad energy.

6. Pick up the length of black ribbon, and tell your subconscious that this black cord has the ability to bind the person's negativity away from you. Your subconscious will respond with some sort of emotion. At first this emotion may be fear or doubt, Keep telling your subconscious that their negativity will be bound away from you over and over again, until the emotion that you feel is strength and empowerment.

7. Once you are feeling strong, begin to visualize black tendrils of energy coming up from the earth around your visualization of the person right outside your circle. Take the photograph in your hand, rolling it tightly into a tube, and begin to wrap the black ribbon around it. As you wrap the ribbon, visualize the black tendril wrapping around your visualization of the person too. At this point you could also include a rhyming spell if you wish. See Chapter Eight for an explanation and instruction in writing these simple sorts of spells.

8. When you have fully wrapped the object with the whole ribbon, tie it off in a knot, at the same time visualizing the person completely surrounded by the black tendrils of energy, so they are completely obscured from view.

9. Take the wrapped object and placed it onto the black cloth. Enfold it slowly in the cloth, at the same time visualizing the tendrils of black energy, sucking the person deep into the earth, to absorb their negativity. You do not wish to destroy them with this, simply to suck away their negativity. Be sure not to think of killing or hurting them, as this will cause you psychic and spiritual harm. Fold the cloth over a few times, until the picture is fully wrapped up in the cloth, and your visualization has been sucked completely into the earth.

153

10. Feel safe and accomplished. You have bound the person's negativity, and it can no longer harm you in any way.

11. At this point you may wish to do the pentagram ritual to balance your own equilibrium, and release any negativity that may have accumulated in you.

12. Come back to normal consciousness when you are ready, knowing that your influence will work.

13. Record your experience in your journal.

14. Take the black cloth somewhere at least a mile away from your home, and bury it in the earth. This will ground the energy, and assure your success.

CHAPTER SIX
Psychic Communication

"When two friends, or two members of a family, understand how the low self [subconscious] works, they may profitably begin the practice of sending telepathic messages to each other."

-Max Freedom Long[1]

Telepathy is the power to communicate information or to receive information from one mind to another by paranormal means. In this chapter we will explore several techniques and exercises are provided for establishing telepathic communication, both as a receiver and a telepathic sender. There are a number of different kinds and qualities of telepathic communication. We will cover most of the simple and effective techniques for these abilities in the next few pages.

In truth, you have already had some experience in a certain sort of telepathy in the last chapter through psychic influence. However, now you will attempt to send and receive meaningful information between two or more people. You should also keep in mind the instructions you've learned for reading body language and other nonverbal communication, because these sorts of communication form an integral part of telepathy as well.

For many of these exercises you will need a partner. Hopefully your growing psychic influence has attracted one to you by now. These exercises can also easily be adapted to group work. It seems that some people naturally gravitate toward either telepathic receiving or telepathic sending. With these exercises, try to build up your skills on both sides of the communication.

---

[1] *The Secret Science at Work*, p. 61

Exercise 60 - Establishing Telepathic Rapport

Time Required: 5 to 10 minutes

When you are conducting any telepathic experiment with someone who is in the same room as you, you will want to be in deep sympathy with your telepathic contact as much as possible to establish the necessary psychic link. Take a few minutes to establish rapport with the following exercise.

1. Both participants should enter the alpha state.

2. You may want to hold hands, at least at first, to establish a link.

3. Look into each other's eyes.

4. Take a few long deep breaths together. Begin and end your exhales simultaneously. This will connect you very well.

5. Then chant together, saying AUM slowly or something similar, three to five times. Feel yourselves really getting in tune with one another.

6. Then take a few minutes to specifically set up the telepathic link. For instance, if you are going to be generating images, choose a limited set number of these in advance, and go through a pre-selected series of these images. In other words, let us say you are going to be communicating colored shapes to each other telepathically. Decide in advance the shapes you are going to be using. Let's suppose you've chosen a red triangle, a blue circle and a yellow square. The sender will then go through these one at a time to set them up. "I am sending the red triangle." The sender then visualizes it, and the receiver empties their mind to receive it. You will go through each of your images in this way. By doing this you are establishing the "animal magnetic" telepathic link between each other. Once you are familiar with each other and telepathy in general this last step will become unnecessary.

These steps are only absolutely necessary for certain exercises. Obviously when you are trying to communicate to someone at a distance they will not be possible. However, when you are first learning these skills, try to use these opening steps as much as possible.

Exercise 61 - Contact Telepathy

Time Required: 15 to 20 minutes

This was a popular sort of parlor trick around the turn of the twentieth century. A lot of people used it as an example to "prove" the existence of telepathy and mind reading. However, it is possible to achieve this effect without any metaphysical abilities, so I think it went rather out of fashion in paranormal circles. The fake way of doing this is sometimes called "muscle reading." Since you are going to be holding on to the person who is "psychically guiding" you to an unknown object in the room, it is possible to let them unconsciously guide you with muscle resistance exactly to the right place.

Try to avoid doing this, because you are attempting to really develop your telepathic abilities. The reason for the contact is really so that the sender and the receiver can be wired directly to one another, facilitating greater telepathic connection.

To a certain extent, at least at first, it is probably okay to let the muscle reading guide you a little bit. After all, we are supposed to be using all of our senses in our psychic development. But try not to cheat too much.

You will need a partner, and to do this in a room that has a number of small objects in it. One of you will be the sender, and one the receiver, then you can switch if you like. This exercise works especially well in groups, where everyone is acting as the sender, and the main sender acting as a radio tower for all that energy.

1. The sender must choose an object, and keep it to themselves (or tell the rest of the group excluding the receiver). This can be any randomly selected small object in the room.

2. The sender and the receiver should get into the Alpha state and establish telepathic rapport.

3. The sender will then hold out their arm, powerfully visualizing the selected object, and powerfully willing the receiver toward it. All of the sender's effort should be spent in propelling that telepathic instruction down into their extended arm.

4. The receiver should grab hold of the arm sender's arm at the wrist and clear their mind, passively receiving the telepathic communication from the sender.

157

5. The receiver should allow themselves to receive any impressions that come, but also simply allow their subconscious to guide their movements. When they feel, see or otherwise experience any urge, the receiver should move wherever the feeling urges.

6. The sender should continue at all times to powerfully focus on sending the receiver to the correct location.

7. The receiver should move toward the object until they've found it. This will in most cases be relatively easy.

8. Record the experience in your journal.

Exercise 62 - Empathic Telepathy

Time Required: 15 to 20 minutes

The purpose of this technique is to receive telepathic information on an emotional level. Sometimes you will just receive emotions in this exercise. Other times, you may find yourself vividly entering the consciousness experience of the person you are in rapport with.

This technique is really a corollary of the establishing rapport technique from the last chapter on influence. When we imitate the body language and breathing of someone exactly, we are not only establishing a connection with them, we are also creating the same emotional state that they are in within ourselves. This is because some of the most powerful ways in which we create emotions in ourselves are through our body posture and our breathing. So, by imitating the body language and breathing of someone who is in an acute emotional state, we can enter into that exact state with them. By doing this, we can connect with the person on a very deep and powerful level.

You will obviously need a partner for this exercise.

1. The sender must choose an experience from their past in which they felt a very strong and powerful emotion. This must be a specific experience that they can clearly recall. It can either be a positive or negative emotional state, but it must not be an ambiguous or insignificant state, particularly at first.

2. The sender and the receiver should get into the Alpha state and establish telepathic rapport, omitting the last step.

3.   The sender will then go back to that experience from the past vividly in their imagination, powerfully returning to that specific time when they were experiencing a distinct emotional state. The sender should get into the exact bodily position that they were in when they were experiencing that state, so that they can become totally immersed.

4.   Once the sender is totally and deeply experiencing the emotional state, they should nod their head or say that they are there, remaining totally in this powerful emotional place. The receiver should endeavor to imitate the posture and breathing of the sender, right down to minutia such as facial expression, head position and the exact breathing rate and location of the breath in the body.

5.   Once the receiver has completely imitated the sender's physical expressions, the receiver will begin to feel exactly what the sender is feeling, and can describe it to them, sometimes including exactly what is going on in the imagined scenario. The important thing however is the feelings. The receiver should endeavor to describe what they are experiencing, keeping it as much as possible in sensory terms, rather than passing any judgment or complex labels to it.

6.   Record the experience in your journal.

Once you have become adept at this practice, you can use it with subtlety in other situations, to really understand what someone is going through emotionally.

Exercise 63 - Projecting Images

Time Required: 15 to 20 minutes

You can try this exercise with sending alphabet letters, shapes, colors, emotions, numbers or anything else that you can imagine. As I mentioned above, you should probably confine this exercise to a set number of possibilities that you decide in advance, at least at first. You could also simply decide with your partner that you may be sending a shape, a letter, a number or a color, and have your partner simply try to receive what category of image is being sent. You will of course need a partner for this exercise.

1.   The sender must choose an image to project, and keep it to themselves. At first it should be from a pre-selected limited set. Once you are experienced and successful it can be random.

2. The sender and the receiver should get into the Alpha state and establish telepathic rapport.

3. The sender will then powerfully visualize the selected image, projecting it toward the receiver's brain.

4. The receiver should allow themselves to receive any impressions that come, and say the first thing that pops into their head from their subconscious.

5. At first, the sender should allow the receiver to try a few times until they get it right. Eventually, this can be eliminated.

6. Try it several times, then switch roles and try it the other way.

7. Record the experience in your journal.

Exercise 64 – Psychic Wall Drawing

This is essentially the same as the last exercise, except instead of projecting into the mind of the receiver, the sender will "draw" the image on a wall using the "astral light." Again, you will need a partner for this exercise. You will also need a blank wall, on which to project the image.

1. The sender must choose an image to project onto a wall, and keep it to themselves. At first it should be from a pre-selected limited set. Once you are experienced and successful it can be random.

2. The sender and the receiver should get into the Alpha state and establish telepathic rapport.

3. The sender will then begin to "draw" the image on a specific spot on the wall that both participants have agreed upon, using their imagination to powerfully visualize the selected image projected in front of them. Every effort should be made to picture it so powerfully that it is actually visible to the eye. The sender can draw and redraw it over and over again if this helps maintain the image.

4. The receiver should look at the wall, focusing with their third eye, and receiving any impressions that come. The first thing that they see will most likely be the correct one.

160

5. At first, the sender should allow the receiver to try a few times until they get it right. Eventually, this can be eliminated.

6. Try it several times, then switch roles and try it the other way.

7. Record the experience in your journal.

Exercise 65 - Distance Telepathy

Time Required: 15 to 20 minutes

This technique can be used with a partner, in which case the receiver should go to some remote location, and attempt to receive the message of the sender. However, this technique is really most useful for those occasions that you really just want to get a message across to someone who is not around. In either case, it will work best if you have had some success between the two people using earlier techniques in this chapter.

You will also be surprised how often this technique works with a person who you've never had a telepathic experience with, as long as you have an emotional connection. Telepathy really works best with people that you know. You can try sending a telepathic message to Britney Spears, but keep in mind that you are not alone in doing so, and may have some real trouble getting her attention.

The receiver may or may not realize that a message is being sent, very often thinking the idea has just "popped into their head." It is best to have a recent photo of the person you will be sending a message to, so that you can really build up a vivid image of them.

1. Consult with your subconscious using the pendulum, if possible.

2. Get into the alpha state.

3. Picture the person you wish to send a message to as vividly as possible. Imagine that they are right in front of you, either sitting or standing. Picture this until you get the sense, a sort of odd internal feeling that you are actually connecting with the person. This may just be an inner knowing that you have made contact.

4. Powerfully send the message to them, using the full energy of your consciousness. If you know the preferred sensory modality of the person you are sending the message to, send thoughts in that way. If they are a

161

visual person, send pictures. If they are auditory, send words. If they are kinesthetic, send your message as much as possible through emotions or feelings. Imagine that your message is entering their mind and body until the imagined figure nods their head in recognition or otherwise seems to have received your message.

5.   Return to normal consciousness and record your experience in your journal.

You can also adapt this same technique or the one that follows for healing, or reverse the process to receive a sense of what the other person is currently experiencing.

Exercise 66 – Distance Telepathy Cord

Time Required: 15 to 20 minutes

This is just a variation on the previous exercise using a slightly different technique. You can use either. Try them both, and see which one works better for you. You may want to use different techniques for different people, different types of messages or different circumstances.

1.   Consult with your subconscious using the pendulum, if possible.

2.   Get into the alpha state.

3.   Imagine a cord or tube of energy beginning to protrude from your belly area. Picture and feel it vividly as an extension of your energy. Send this cord traveling out into the universe to the place where the person is, looking for them psychically. Imagine the psychic cord attaching to the person you're trying to reach. Picture this until you get the sense, a sort of odd internal feeling that you are actually connecting with the person. This may just be an inner knowing that you have made contact.

4.   Powerfully send the message to them. If you know the preferred sensory modality of the person you are sending the message to, send thoughts in that way. If they are a visual person, send pictures. If they are auditory, send words. If they are kinesthetic, you're your message as much as possible through emotions or feelings. Imagine that your message is entering their mind and body until the imagined figure nods their head in recognition or otherwise seems to have received your message.

162

5. Return to normal consciousness and record your experience in your journal.

Exercise 67 - Sending Telepathic Messages to Long Lost Friends

Time Required: 15 to 20 minutes

For this exercise, you can use either of the preceding techniques, but you must spend a little time in preparation to reestablish that psychic link. If you have lost contact with someone and really wish to find them again, this technique may help to open the door. You may find yourself asking a mutual friend if they know where the person is, and discover that they've just "coincidentally" gotten their number. Or you may get a phone call from them, and discover that they've done the same for you.

1. Consult with your subconscious using the pendulum, if possible.

2. Think about the old times. If possible, gather together some pictures, or souvenirs, anything that was a memory of good times spent together. Really try to deeply reconnect with the person you wish to reach. Spend a while really recalling the friend and time spent together.

3. Place whatever memorabilia you've managed to find around you in your working area.

4. Get into the alpha state.

5. Use whichever technique from above you'd prefer to send your message, but be sure to load it with as much nostalgic good feeling as possible. Spend a good deal of time really powerfully sending the message.

6. Return to normal consciousness and record your experience in your journal.

7. You may wish to repeat this several times, for a week or so.

Exercise 68 - Telepathic Advertising

I have personally found this technique to be very useful, because it essentially opens up communication directly between your subconscious mind and

163

the subconscious of others. It does this by establishing the communication at a time when both parties are most open, in the middle of the night when we are sleeping. The superconscious mind is also directly involved because it is through the superconscious that we discover the best time for the communication. This technique can be used either to send a message to someone, to powerfully influence someone's subconscious, or used as a sort of psychic advertising to attract love, business, to locate lost friend, or anything else you can imagine. It works surprisingly effectively, though the person will almost never realize that you've sent a message. At most, they will feel that they've dreamed about you, but this probably won't happen either. Please do not try to use this technique to do anything malicious or negatively manipulative to another person. It may work in the short term or not, but it will wreak long term havoc in your life. It is acceptable to use this technique to help someone, such as improving someone's mood, increasing motivation, study habits, focus or something like that. But even this borders on overly manipulative behavior.

1. Choose a message that you would like to send, either to an individual or a larger group of people (for instance if you are advertising a product or service, or seeking a new mate). Always choose a positively rather than a negatively worded message. Avoid using words like "not" or "don't" in whatever you are communicating.

2. Use your pendulum to make sure your subconscious is willing to work on this, and to discover if your subconscious and superconscious feel it is an appropriate project.

3. As you are going to bed, use your anchor to go into the Alpha state. Tell your subconscious mind to awaken you in the night when the person or people you are sending the message to are most open to psychic communication in their nightly dreaming.

4. Go to sleep.

5. In the middle of the night when you awaken, you will know that this is the perfect time to send a psychic message. Stay in the alpha state, and repeat your message several times, feeling that you are communicating directly to whomever you are trying to reach. Know that this message is directly entering their subconscious.

6. Allow yourself to drift back to sleep, repeating the message over and over again. Remember, this message is going to affect your subcon-

scious as well, so don't use this technique for any kind of negativity, or you will bring it to yourself as well.

7.   In the morning, record your experience in your journal.

You may repeat this nightly for a week or so, but don't do it indefinitely, or it could start to backfire. Your message will get across. Be prepared for amazement.

You can use on this technique on large groups of people, telling your subconscious to awaken you when the largest number of people are most open for psychic communication. You can advertise your business, product or send out a meme or new cultural idea in this way. This simple technique can be surprisingly powerful.

CHAPTER SEVEN
Moving Beyond the Body

"The essence of the technique of Magick is the development of this Body of Light, which must be extended to include all members of the organism, and indeed of the Cosmos."

-Aleister Crowley[1]

Many names have been attached to the phenomenon: astral projection, the out-of-body experience (OOBE or OBE), spirit vision, traveling in the body of light, skrying in the æther, mental wandering, traveling in the spiritual body among others. In essence, all of these names describe the same thing. There are a few differences in the level of expectation and the kinds of things that are traditionally done when conducting the practices associated with these various epithets, but they are really the same in the end. It is just a matter of how deeply involved in the experience we get. If you have ever vividly daydreamed, then you have experienced a certain kind of astral projection. This is really all there is to it. The only difference is that we become so involved in our vision that we lose track of our body, and associate most or all of our consciousness into our imagined body or body of light.

Many scientists are starting to acknowledge Astral Projection as a valid form of perception and that it is something different from mere fantasy or nocturnal dreaming. Scientists have even determined the section of the brain where Astral Projection and other mystical phenomena such as Unity with God and Near Death Experiences seem to take place. It is in the right hemisphere's temporal lobe in an area of the Sylvan Fissure above the ear. By directly stimulating this area, as in the case of brain surgery, these consciousness phenomena occur. However, it is not necessary to open up your skull and poke your brain to experience the subtle planes.

---

[1] *Magick: Book 4 Liber ABA*, p. 284

Astral Projection is a natural experience that is safe, educational and life transforming. Astral Projection is possible when you become aware of your own consciousness, and realize to your delight that your consciousness has nothing to do with your body. Your body is merely the end result of your process of consciousness. You could close your eyes right now and place your consciousness in the top of your head, in your toes, in your television set, into the middle of a village in China, right into the lap of God or the Buddha, or onto the planet Mars. Of course these are just subjective experiences, but the idea that your consciousness resides in your physical body is just a habitual subjective experience too. Your consciousness can go anywhere and be anything.

There will also be times, perhaps most, when you will retain a certain awareness of your body while you are conducting astral projection exercises. This is not a sign of failure. It is just something that happens. As I told you earlier, I have had numerous fairly subjective seeming astral projection experiences in which I have perceived things at least somewhat accurately in consensus reality. There is actually an advantage to maintaining some of your awareness in your body while you are having an astral experience. This will allow you to tell people around you what you are seeing, and it can be recorded as you are experiencing it. This is particularly useful if you want to communicate with some sort of non-human intelligence on a higher plane, because you can report what it is saying to a partner or assistant, and it can be recorded exactly as it is happening. I have conducted many dozens of such workings and frequently obtained quite amazing results.

There will also be times when you seem absolutely disconnected from your body. These should not necessarily be regarded as in any way superior to the others. They will give you a powerful spiritual charge and a sense of accomplishment, but they are not necessarily in any way more advanced or better than your experiences that seem at first glance to be more subjective. Experiences that seem very subjective at first can easily be transformed into the fully projected state, simply by fully involving all your senses into your astral experience. If you involve yourself fully in your visions, you will swiftly find that as you are returning to your body it is indeed far away. The best thing to do is to ignore your body once you have begun your vision, because by doing so your consciousness shifts completely into the place where you are focusing it. So, as you are conducting your exercises, don't worry about whether or not you can "still feel" your body. If you keep checking in on whether you are experiencing body sensations, you will keep moving your consciousness back to your body. If you just forget about your body, soon you won't feel it any longer.

There is only one real danger in Astral Projection, and that is getting too enthusiastic about it and not paying enough attention to your life in the physical world. Astral Projection is very pleasurable and seductive and you can easily retreat into your inner world to avoid real life issues. The best way to avoid this is to make sure that your inner world work is an extension of and a healing for your outer world. There is no danger of dying or becoming injured during any astral projection work. The worst thing that could possibly happen is that you will lose consciousness, in which case you will naturally be back in your body when you awaken.

There is a lot of speculation about whether or not lucid dreaming is a form of astral projection, and a lot of people have written extensive lists of the differences between these experiences, trying to assert that they are not one and the same. It is my feeling that these people have for the most part had little practical experience with either, because from within the experience there is absolutely no discernable difference. Both astral projection and lucid dreaming are out of body consciousness experiences. When you are astrally projecting, you may see things which correspond to consensus reality, or you may see things which exist in various spiritual planes and alternate realities, or you may experience things that are entirely imaginary. The same holds exactly true for lucid dreaming and I must beg you not to waste your time trying to discern a difference between them. Instead, try to experience both, and enjoy the new knowledge and possibilities that await you. Consider your lucid dreaming and your astral projection work to be equally important components in your psychic development. They are both opportunities for power and transformation.

In order to do Astral Projection, it is best to be in a deeply altered state of consciousness. Ideally you should be at least bordering on the Theta state, but you must hold onto as much of your awareness as possible, so a very deep Alpha may be more appropriate. You will want to keep your focus, so that the experience stays in your control. As you get deeper and deeper, you will notice changes in your body and consciousness. You will know that you are ready to project when the following things start to occur:

- Your body feels very heavy as your relaxation deepens. It may feel immobilized, paralyzed.

- You will feel a sense of slipping, falling, floating, tingles or vibrations in your body, and you may blackout for a moment or two.

- You will see at least a few hypnagogic images, or mini-dreams.

When you experience these things, you will know that you could move your consciousness away from your body if you wanted.

Many different techniques have been expounded for doing astral projection over the years, but there are three essential methods for achieving Astral Projection upon which all specific methods are just variations. These are:

1. Using your Imagination, in which you visualize an astral body or scene, and project yourself into it with your imagination.

2. Will (Dynamic or Passive), in which you try to push yourself out of your body, or wish yourself to have an experience of leaving your body.

3. Holding on to Hypnagogic Images, in which you relax yourself to the very border of sleep, grabbing hold of subconsciously created images or energy phenomena to gain freedom from your body.

All three are interrelated, but distinct from each other. Each has its value and its drawbacks. Each one also requires greater and greater depths of trance in descending order. The first is obviously the most subjective, the second often results in feelings of failure, and the last is by far the most difficult to control. However, the first is very easy, and makes it possible to travel far and wide, and easily allows you to be entirely in control of the experience. The first method is really the best for traveling on higher planes, and communicating with their residents. When you do this, you will often get so completely involved in the vision that you do lose all sense of your body. The second gives you a very profound sense of accomplishment when you succeed, and still allows you a fair amount of control and ability to explore. The third is relatively easy to accomplish, and gives you a strong sense of detachment from your body. It is an excellent way to explore learning from the lessons of your subconscious and superconscious. It is really a variation on lucid dreaming. Now we will explore a few simple methods for achieving all three.

For all three of the following exercises, I do not specifically note it in the instructions, but you may wish to perform these exercises in the protective sphere of your magical circle. This is not necessary for success, but it will help to prevent too much interference from outside energies. This is of particular importance if you plan to visit other planes to contact non-human entities such as elementals or other spirits. In this case, it is highly suggested that you cast a circle, perform the pentagram ritual, and then use the techniques you will learn in the next chapter to invoke the proper energies. When you return to your body, you will also want to properly banish those energies and perform another pentagram ritual.

Exercise 69 – The Body of Light (Using Imagination)

Time Required: 30 to 40 minutes

With this technique you are basically just going to be imagining yourself into your Astral body. You will be creating an imaginary body and moving your consciousness into it. Although it may all seem to be totally subjective, you must remember what I said earlier about your consciousness. What you pretend is real to all parts of your consciousness except for your waking mind. If you use this technique enough times you will eventually lose all sense of your body, becoming completely involved in your visions.

1. Use your pendulum to make sure your subconscious is willing to work on this right now.

2. Go into the Alpha state using your anchor.

3. Relax yourself even more deeply using the Theta state technique until you feel a sense of lightness or floating. This is unmistakable and you will be able to get there quite easily, if you just relax and let yourself go.

4. Imagine the focal point of your consciousness shrinking so that you're whole consciousness is in the center of your being. You may associate this center at your belly, your heart, or in your forehead. Just use what is easiest for you to imagine. Don't worry if it seems like you're just pretending.

5. Imagine a shape made out of light resembling your body, and floating a few feet above you. Allow this shape to become just like you, an image of yourself made of light.

6. Move your point of consciousness into the Body of Light.

7. Fully associate yourself in this new body.

8. Look around the room from the vantage point of this new body. See your body sitting or laying immobile a few feet away from you. Look at your body of light, seeing your hands and feet made out of light particles.

9. Move away from your body and start examining the objects in the room around you. Again, this may seem like a mere daydream, but continue pretending.

10. Go out of the room and look around the rest of the building you are in.

11. You can now go anywhere you wish, simply by willing yourself to move there. Again, it may seem imaginary, but you will discover things that

171

you could not otherwise know some of the time. Other times you will experience things that are not actually real in the physical world. This is the nature of the astral plane. It is not reality, but the place where all possibilities reside. The more often you practice this pattern the more real your experiences will seem and the more really out of your body you will seem to become.

12. Return to your body and slowly re-associate, imagining your body of light re-entering your body, even if this just seems imaginary. It is still important to go through the whole motion.

13. Record your experience in your journal.

Later, you may want to use ritual techniques to invoke specific energies, and try using this technique to explore other planes associated with these energies. You will create the appropriate atmosphere, then imagine that you are rising up into this atmosphere until you encounter beings or a landscape. You could also imagine a doorway with appropriate colors or symbols on it and travel through the doorway to experience other planes. In other words, if you are interested in exploring the Venusian plane, you would imagine a green doorway with the symbol for Venus on it. Travelling through this doorway will give you access to the psychic plane of Venus. There will be more about the colors and energies associated with the planets and the elements in the next chapter.

Exercise 70 – The Pineal Gateway (Using your will)

Time Required: 40 to 60 minutes

In this technique you will exit your body directly through your third eye. It too may remain somewhat subjective at first, but you will endeavor to be deep enough in trance and focused so single-pointedly that you really experience this as a separation. If it seems impossible, simply use your imagination as in the previous technique to pretend your way out. Don't allow yourself to become frustrated or tense. This will only make things harder for you into the future.

1. Use your pendulum to make sure your subconscious is willing to work on this right now.

2. Go into the Alpha state using your anchor.

3. Go into the Theta state.

172

4. Move your point of consciousness upward until you are entirely focused on your Ajna chakra, the third eye.

5. Imagine that your third eye is a trap door and start to push this door open. Make sure that this is not a physical pressure, don't tense up your body in any way. Push on this doorway with your energy. This may cause some strange perceptions and sensations, including hallucinatory voices and images. Just keep willing yourself through, remaining totally relaxed.

6. Move out of your head and "look at" the room that you're in. You may be in the room with your body or some other place.

7. Go out of the room and look around the rest of the building you are in.

8. You can now go anywhere you wish, simply by willing yourself to move there.

9. Return to your body and slowly re-associate.

10. Record your experience in your journal.

Exercise 72 - Holding on to Hypnagogic Imagery

Time Required: 40 minutes or longer

In this exercise you will allow yourself to drift toward the very edge of sleep, remaining aware so that you can use this transitional moment to slip out of your body.

1. Use your pendulum to make sure your subconscious is willing to work on this right now.

2. Go into the Alpha state using your anchor.

3. Go into the Theta state.

4. Stay aware of the sensations in your body and the images popping into your mind.

5. Allow yourself to relax even more deeply.

6. Begin holding on to the images that are coming to mind, while letting your body relax even more. Become involved with them, allowing yourself to move into them and interact with whatever you are seeing, hearing and touching.

7. You will experience a falling or slipping sensation and then you will be out of body, in some place. You may also momentarily black out, but as soon as you become aware again you will be out on the astral

8. To change locations you may will yourself there or look at your hands.

9. You can now go anywhere you wish.

10. Return to your body and slowly re-associate.

11. Record your experience in your journal.

All of these techniques are really just meant to be guidelines. Eventually you will find your most productive method for accomplishing astral projection. It may combine elements of all of these exercises, or you may adjust certain parts of these exercises to suit your particular needs. Astral projection need not be hard. You can succeed the first time you try, as long as you just let yourself go, and experience what you experience, rather than trying to fit your experience into a preconceived idea about how it should be. Set yourself free.

CHAPTER EIGHT
Manifesting Your Will

"We have, therefore, to treat in this place of the grand and terrific question of magical works; we are concerned no longer with theories and abstractions; we approach realities, and we are about to place the wand of miracles in the hand of the adept, saying to him at the same time: 'Be not satisfied with what we tell you; act for yourself.' We have to deal here with works of relative omnipotence, with the means of laying hold upon the greatest secrets of Nature and compelling them into the service of an enlightened and inflexible will."

-Eliphas Levi Zahed[1]

In this chapter you will learn how to use your growing magick power to manifest anything into your life including prosperity, love, health, and everything else you could ever need. Miracles can and will happen in your life. Miracles already happen to you all the time, if you would but observe them. By miracles I mean manifestations or occurrences in your life that seem to be meaningfully connected with practical metaphysical work, or even with just positive thinking. You will experience synchronicities and serendipities more and more regularly the longer you work with the powers of your mind. I have been keeping a list of miracles in my journal for the last few months, and on average I experience 15-20 miracles per month. Most of these miracles occur in fairly mundane ways, traveling through the normal channels of manifestation.

To choose one at random, a while back I broke up with a girlfriend, and found myself without a car, because we'd both been using her car. Looking at my finances, I realized that I really couldn't afford a new car on my budget at

---

[1] *Transcendental Magic*, p. 249

that time. I realized that the only way I could have another car would be if someone literally gave me one for free. I closed my eyes and briefly expressed this to my own superconscious mind. Literally less than an hour later my dad called and offered me his car as a gift, because he was moving to another state. Manifesting your desires can be this easy.

This does not however mean that everything that you wish for will come true. There are dozens of mediating factors that will determine your success in creating miracles in your life. You must have, create or discover some causal way for any manifestation to occur. If you attempt to manifest money, but have no friends, no relatives, no job, no plan to get a job and no way for income to flow in, money will not manifest. If you have some sort of internal block to something, a fear, neurosis or other complex, you will inhibit or prevent its manifestation. The universe will not give you something you can't handle. This is why personal development goes hand in hand with psychic and magical development, and why I so highly encourage you to explore the empowering techniques of *The New Hermetics* alongside those found in this book.

I am not going to cover the use of herbs, poppets, sachets and other folk magick in this chapter. These things have been written about exhaustively by a multitude of other writers, and I don't really use these techniques myself, so I don't feel I would do them justice. The basic principles that you are learning in this book could easily be applied to these techniques, but I think you will find the exercises in this book just as powerful, perhaps more so, than any other kind of practical magick. You will occasionally want to use various implements in your work, but for the most part these techniques are clean and easy, and you will be able to accomplish your work quickly and effectively. The magical techniques in this chapter are by no means traditional, in any sense of the word. Elements from traditional magick have been incorporated, along with bits of modern ideas such as Chaos magick, and a few of my own personal techniques and modifications that I've found to be effective myself. At all times, use your own judgment and feel free to try your own experiments and modifications.

Many of the techniques in this chapter are fairly similar to techniques in *The New Hermetics*, but I have attempted to provide alternate approaches in most instances, sometimes simplifying these techniques even further than I did in *The New Hermetics*, sometimes adding a few more ritual elements for the practical magician. In all cases I have kept these techniques simple enough that anyone could use them quickly, easily, and painlessly.

GENERAL OBSERVATIONS FOR MANIFESTING

A positive, hopeful and relaxed attitude is the most important thing to develop if you expect to manifest anything in your life. Too much effort shows anxiety and fear. A fearful attitude, or a great sense of need or lack, will block your subconscious mind from working properly to manifest your desire. Be relaxed and accept the idea that you will succeed with confidence so your subconscious will be comfortable. Sometimes, your subconscious will be irrationally fearful about something that you really need. If necessary, help your subconscious to feel appropriate emotions toward what you want. Avoid conflicting with your subconscious if it is overly resistant during the pendulum consultation. Instead, try programming your subconscious with positive affirmations as you are going off to sleep, or regularly throughout your day, until all parts of you are feeling congruently positive toward your desires.

Wish success upon everybody. Generosity of spirit will create an atmosphere of success and prosperity in your life. The universe is infinitely abundant. Particularly wish success upon people you feel may be in competition with you. This will show your subconscious that you believe in abundance, generosity, and will pave the way for success. Never hate or resent anybody. Never be cruel or wish cruelty upon others. Having any kind of negative attitude brings more negativity into your life. What you are habitually thinking is what your life will be.

Imagine your desires vividly and joyfully. If you think negative thoughts about your manifestation, your subconscious will swiftly take those up and negate your work. For this reason, it might be smart to start with manifesting small things at first, things that you believe you could receive easily. Then, when you are more confident, you can work on the big stuff.

Keep in mind that your manifestations may come to you in different ways than you anticipated. You may not get exactly what you've asked for, but instead the universe will provide with something even better that more appropriately fits your needs. Always attempt to notice how your magick has affected things, looking for ways to feel successful in your operation even if the results seem tangential from your original intent. The more you can feel successful, the better you will feel about your magick, and the better you will succeed in the future.

One of my magical teachers recently told me that he has a 90% or better success rate with his magical operations, and I wondered what his secret was. So, I've observed his attitudes and his work and I realized that his secret is very simple. When he casts a spell, he looks for any tiny little part of it that succeeds, and considers his work successful. If he does a prosperity spell, and finds a ten dollar bill on the ground, he considers that a success. Or he might simply have someone forgive a debt, and considers that a success. In other words, he's an optimist, and he places meaning on his actions that make him feel successful in everything that he does. This improves the quality of his life, and his magick is often quite amazingly successful as a result. So, whether your results are dramatic or tiny, consider yourself a success at magick. Always have fun.

Gratitude is one of the most important emotions for you to experience if you want to manifest new things in your life. Have gratitude for all that you have. You may find it useful to think regularly, daily or even hourly, about the things in your life that you are grateful about. Be grateful often, and you will be rewarded with more.

Exercise 72 - Setting Personal Goals

Time Required: 45 to 60 minutes

Before you can really begin to manifest your desires, you need to know exactly what it is that you want. To get what you want, you need to know what that is. I am a huge proponent of goal setting, and of putting your goals in writing. Often just this action is enough to set the wheels of manifestation into motion.

In *The New Hermetics* I basically created a whole goal setting workshop for you, and I don't want to simply repeat that here. Rather, I will just give you some categories of goals that you might find helpful in creating your ideal life.

Categories:

Love Relationships - Whether you are in one or not, you should set goals for what you'd like your ideal love relationship to be like, and what role you see this relationship playing in your life into the future. What would your ideal partner be like? Are you with this partner now?

Friend Relationships - Do you have enough friends? We could all stand to improve our relationships with our fellow human beings. How do you see your friendships manifesting and improving over your life?

Work/Career - What do you want to do for money? Are you currently working toward your ideal career, or involved in it? Are you satisfied with your job? In what ways could you improve this very important part of your life?

Spirituality - Are you involved in some sort of spiritual community or practice? Are there ways in which you could improve your relationship with your spiritual source?

Lifestyle - Where would you like to be living? Do you like where you are now, or would you like to be somewhere different or better? What is your ideal kind of house? What is you're your ideal neighborhood, community, city, state?

178

Creativity - We are creative, whether we are actively involved in the arts or not. We all have ideas, thoughts and dreams. It is part of being human. Are there things you want to make? Innovations? Work projects? Are you allowing your own creativity to be fully expressed?

Education - Are there new things you'd like to learn? Continuing to learn throughout our lives is essential to really getting the most out of life.

Travel - Are there places you'd like to see, go and experience?

Internal/Feelings - Are there ways in which you think, feel or behave that you'd like to change?

Before you begin to set goals, please keep the following things in mind:

- Set only positive goals. Don't set goals about things you want to get rid of, or stop doing. Instead, imagine where you would like to go and set goals that inspire your imagination forward, using words such as "I will," or "I'm going to" rather than "I won't," or "I'll stop" or "I'll quit." Setting goals in the present tense ("I am...") may also be useful.

- Make sure your goals are things that have to do with you. Don't set goals that require other people to change before they can be accomplished. Focus your goals on yourself, on how you can change and improve your life.

- State your goals in detailed, sensory-based terms. Imagine what it will be like when you have your goals and describe the specific, positive sensations that you will experience. State specifically what you desire. How much do you want? What environment will it take place in? What is the time-frame until you get it? Establish it exactly. Whether or not this is the way your manifestation comes about, knowing what you want to happen will help steer you specifically toward your actual desire.

- Make your goals in small increments or chunks that you can really accept and believe are possible. Make your goals in stages rather than just, "I will have a beautiful body." Instead, create a plan within your goals to get there by taking it one step at a time. "I will eat more healthfully, exercise three times a week and actively visualize my ideal body. I will work toward my goal slowly and diligently until I reach my ideal body, which will look like etc."

- Be specific about what these goals will be like when you have them, so that you can congratulate yourself when you succeed. If you want more money, how much will you have before you know that you've succeeded? By setting up your rules for success in advance, you will be able to fully enjoy your success. Try to make these rules easy, so you'll find it easy to feel good.

1. Now please take a little time as soon as possible and create some goals for yourself in your journal. Just write out whatever comes to mind from the above categories. You can always change your goals, so don't be afraid to get really creative. What do you really want in your life? If you could have any kind of life that you could imagine, what would it be like?

2. After you've set some goals, use your pendulum to check in with yourself. What does your subconscious think of your goals?

3. If they are not approved by your subconscious, discover why, and make any necessary changes in your personal outlook or your goals so that you can really create the life you want!

MONEY, LOVE AND HEALTH

These are the three biggest things that people want to generally get out of practical magick. We have already extensively covered the topic of healing else-where, but here are some general observations to help manifest wealth and love in your life.

Prosperity Consciousness

The key to having abundance flowing into your life is to think abundantly. Wish success upon yourself and everybody around you. Don't be jealous of other people's success. There's plenty to go around. Rejoice in the success of others. This will show your subconscious that you are positive about wealth and it will be possible for you to manifest it. Misers have nothing, even if they end up with a lot of cash.

180

Make friends with money. If you see money as something that is negative or evil, you will never have any. Your subconscious will keep you away from money if it thinks money will cause you harm. Know that poverty is not a virtue.

Think really big. All that you need is available to you. Even if you don't have a dime in your pocket, think of money like the ebb and flow of the sea. Right now it may be low tide, but it will assuredly flow back to you with time and patience. Don't fear spending money. This will lock you into poverty. Know confidently that you will always be supplied with what you need.

Spend money if you wish receive it. Support the economy, particularly those parts that you feel are worthy of your support such as the arts and humanitarian causes. Seek new opportunities to give as well as receive. Remember, it is not really money that you want or need. It is abundance that you desire. Seek more than money. You may already have emotional, spiritual and mental wealth. Be forever grateful for what you already have. Seek peace, joy, and happiness above all monetary concerns.

Seek wealth in what you love to do. As long as you are happy with what you are doing, you are abundant, and more abundance will come to you. Teach yourself to know that the world is infinitely abundant. Picture yourself regularly with all that you want. You will have it, if you really desire it and need it. Work with Jupiterean, Solar and Earth energies regularly to really begin to feel and be abundant.

Love Consciousness

There is someone out there for everyone. Don't be desperate for a relationship if you're not in one, because this may cause you to make poor choices, and it will block your subconscious from allowing the manifestation of what you really want. Instead, concentrate on loving yourself, and try to get closer to your own superconscious and "the All" or whatever you'd like to call the ultimate animating principle of the universe.

Be loving to everyone in your life, and love will manifest all around you. Like attracts like, so whatever you are putting out into the universe will be what comes to you. Try to be your best in whatever you do, because success is the most powerful aphrodisiac.

Make a list of the qualities you want in a mate, and be as specific as you'd like. Try to come up with exactly what you need in a mate to fulfill all your needs. Check in with your subconscious to establish your real desires and needs. Often what we think we want is not what will really make us happy.

When you begin to work actively to attract love with magick, don't do love spells on a specific person. Even if you think you've found the person who fulfills all of your needs, it is still inappropriate to try to force them into anything.

181

Instead, you could use the techniques in the chapter on influence to be as charming and magnetic as possible. Love spells on specific people do not tend to work well, and are not a loving behavior. Work with Water, Fire, Venusian, and even Lunar energies to really begin to manifest the energies of love in your life.

Instead, use love magick to put out a general call to the universe, attracting appropriate mates to you at the discretion of the universe. This will prevent you from making poor choices as well. Don't seek lust fulfillment through love magick. If you want to dally with one night stands, create some personal magnetism and go get it.

Exercise 73 - Manifesting Synchronicity

Time Required: 20 to 40 minutes

This is a simple but extremely powerful creative visualization exercise that can help you to create any manifestation in your life that you can come up with. It is very similar to a New Hermetics tool, but I have attempted to further streamline and improve it to give you an incredibly simple but powerful technique for manifesting whatever you desire. This is an extremely flexible tool that you can use for almost anything.

However, in order for this tool to work correctly, you must believe it will work, and make sure that your subconscious and superconscious really approve of the things that you desire. If you have any doubt about this technique, it will not work, because your subconscious will take up that doubt and undo your work. Also, if you try to manifest things that are not in your best interest, or things that your subconscious believes might be too much for you, this technique will not work well. So, you may wish to begin with a few smaller manifestations before you jump into the really big and important things.

1. Before you begin, choose something that you would like to manifest in your life. Take a look at your goals. We all have things that we want and need. This does not have to be something huge at first, but it must be something that you really want.

2. Consult with your subconscious using the pendulum. Check in to make sure this is something that all parts of you really want to experience in your life. Make any necessary adjustments to your desire.

3. Sit down and go into the Alpha state using your anchor.

4. You may purify, consecrate, and cast a circle if you wish. If you do so, you may sit or stand for the rest of this procedure.

5. Open your chakras, and do some Kundalini arousing breaths to increase your personal dynamic power.

6. In your mind, begin to make a detailed movie or series of images of your desire in the region of your third eye, as if on a movie screen, watching yourself from the outside, experiencing your desire exactly the way that you'd like it to manifest. You can bring into your mind past times when you have experienced the desired manifestation, or some part of it, or think of someone who has experienced what you want. By doing this, you will be actively involving your subconscious, and you can further arouse your inner energies to accomplish your desire. Make this as exciting and dramatic as you like, seeing the images, feeling the feelings and hearing the sounds.

7. Play through these images a few times until you really have a coherent story of what you would like to have happen.

8. Now, step into your movie, experiencing it in your body, as if you were really there, seeing, feeling and hearing all of the content that you would like to occur. If you are standing in your circle, you can actually step forward into your movie physically, trying it on in as much detail as you can imagine.

9. Step out of the movie, keeping it frozen at the most exciting part, and direct your attention up to the light of your superconscious above you. See and feel yourself filling with this light again, feeling love and power passing between you and your superconscious.

10. Tell your subconscious and your superconscious, both of which you are now intimately connected with, that you would like this desire to manifest, or something even better.

11. Again arouse Kundalini, imagining that the movie screen is floating upwards on a wave of energy into the light of your superconscious, knowing that your superconscious is going to handle the details of this manifestation. You can travel up with the movie experiencing an ecstatic "gnosis" experience at this point if you wish.

183

12. Now, travel in your mind to the near future, and imagine what it will be like to have this manifestation in your life. Really feel like you are already there, and feel totally excited and happy about it.

13. Return to normal consciousness.

14. Record your experience in your journal.

15. Take some real outward actions toward getting what you have just projected, knowing that you are going to succeed. Don't omit this last step.

For many things, this simple technique will be sufficient. However, you may wish to use the energies of the higher spiritual planes and other techniques to enhance you powers further, effecting change on a higher level.

ENERGIES OF THE ELEMENTS AND THE PLANETS

The vast majority of magical work involving specific subtle energies and non-human intelligences generally falls under the categories of elemental magick and planetary magick. I have written about these topics extensively in my previous works, and most of us are at least vaguely familiar with these ideas. But here is a brief recap, nonetheless.

The Four Elements

The ancient Greeks conceived of the world as consisting of four basic root elements- Fire, Air, Water, and Earth, and these ideas have stayed in the magical tradition for thousands of years. Nearly everything can be classified by its relationship to the four elements. Today, we no longer conceive of the world as being literally constructed by these four elements, but we can still see these four elements as parts of our psyches and character makeup. The element of earth is the animal needs of the human mind, the element of water the emotions, the element of air the intellect and the element of fire the will. The four elements also continue to exist in a spiritual sense as the building blocks of reality. Sunlight and fire still warm us and fuel our machines. Water still cleanses us and nourishes the land and our bodies. We still breathe the air, and our voices are carried through it as a medium of communication. We still tread upon the earth, and return to it as dust and decay when we die. The four elements are still a constant part of our lives. The basic qualities that define the four elements are the following:

184

FIRE: warmness and dryness, and the quality of expansion
WATER: coldness and wetness, and the quality of contraction or shrinking
AIR: warmness and moistness, and the quality of lightness
EARTH: coldness and dryness, and the quality of heaviness

The lesser pentagram ritual that you have worked on has given you the beginnings of working with the elements, but you can also use these subtle forces to create changes in yourself and the world around you. You can use the element of fire to energize you or someone else, to raise tempers or to cause creativity. The element of water can bring you tranquility, sensuality and dreams. The element of air can bring you joy, inspiration and eloquence. The element of earth can bring prosperity, organization, and love of work. You can also literally warm yourself up by invoking fire, cool down with water, lighten your spirits with air, and ground yourself with earth. The elements are also necessary for the creation of weather magick.

Here are a few of the practical ways in which the four elements can be used in your magick:

FIRE: inspiring success, creating passion, obtaining and improving sex, creating sexual love, enhancing creativity, developing strength, strengthening will

WATER: creating friendship, attracting and understanding love, increasing tranquility, assisting with emotional and spiritual healing, calming or changing emotions, getting needed rest, improving understanding

AIR: increasing education, improving memory, enhancing intellect, learning and teaching, improving communication, encouraging travel, inspiring writing, developing new theories, organizing your things

EARTH: attracting money, obtaining jobs, getting promotions, improving investments, building your physical health, increasing business, building and enhancing your physical body, material construction of buildings and plans, improving physical appearance, understanding and making peace with materialism

The four elements also have four sets of elemental beings associated with them which we will discuss more later:

Salamanders are fiery.
Undines are watery.
Sylphs are airy.
Gnomes are earthy.

The Seven Ancient Planets

The magicians of the past conceived of the heavens above us as consisting of ever expanding onion skin-like spheres of energy or spiritual substance, each occupied by the forces of the seven ancient planets, expanding outward until you eventually entered the highest heavens where the ultimate god exists. All of these interpenetrating spheres contained myriads of beings: angels, gods and demons who controlled various aspects of nature. Again, we obviously no longer believe this to literally be true in physical reality, but there is still a spiritual and energetic validity to the concept. All of these energies make up our conscious, subconscious and superconscious minds. The separations based on the formulae of the planets are of course synthetic, but they are a convenient way of classifying things so that we may meaningfully deal with them. There are also now known to be more than the seven ancient planets in our solar system, but we will just concern ourselves in this work with the seven. These are some general attributions for the ancient planets, as in The New Hermetics:

Moon: Imagination, Instinct, Subconscious, Emotion
Mercury: Reason, Communication, Logic, Knowledge
Venus: Love, Passion, Aesthetics, Nurture
Sun: Beauty, Harmony, Balance, Wholeness
Mars: Justice, Strength, Force, Violence
Jupiter: Generosity, Abundance, Leadership, Vision
Saturn: Structure, Limitation, Seriousness, Responsibility

For magical purposes, these energies can be used for the following things as well as much more:

Moon: increasing imagination, improving instinct, connecting with the subconscious, altering and developing emotion, connecting with the astral world, developing clairvoyance, enhancing dreams, getting sound sleep, working with the sea.

Mercury: developing reason, improving communication, becoming more logical, gaining hidden knowledge, success in examinations and tests, safety and speed in travel, success in business, improving writing, getting into and succeeding in school, learning science or medicine or mathematics, developing the mind, self-improvement in general, understanding statistics or calculations or systems

Venus: gaining love, creating desire, improving and developing aesthetics, becoming more nurturing, enhancing beauty, increasing pleasure, appreciating and creating art, creating luxury, enhancing femininity

Sun: Creating harmony, improving balance, establishing and/or understanding wholeness, developing friendships, improving health and vitality, regaining youth and beauty, finding peace, experiencing illumination, obtaining windfalls of money, divine power

Mars: bringing justice to a situation, developing strength and passion, applying force, understanding and directing violent urges, enhancing energy, creating or stopping war or warlike thoughts, using aggression, developing courage, winning in competitions, improving in athletics, enhancing masculinity

Jupiter: Increasing generosity, creating and understanding abundance, developing leadership skills, becoming a visionary thinker, receiving favors, acquiring influence and prestige, acquiring wealth, solving legal issues, getting good luck, personal expansion

Saturn: understanding and creating structures, overcoming or creating limitations, developing responsibility, becoming more serious, understanding reincarnation, understanding death, receiving inheritances, extending life

In doing your spell work with the planetary and elemental energies, you will want to create an appropriate atmosphere. The best way to do this is by using objects and visualizations that are congruent with the energies. There are hundreds of traditional correspondences. You can research and find appropriate incense, geometric shapes, gemstones, plants, names of gods, and a multitude of other things. Here are a couple of correspondences that you might find useful, particularly in the case of incense:

Planet	Shape	Incense
Saturn	Triangle	Myrrh
Jupiter	Square	Cedar
Mars	Pentagram	Tobacco (Red Pepper or hot scents)
Sun	Hexagram	Frankincense
Venus	Septagram	Benzoin
Mercury	Octagram	Sandalwood
Moon	Enneagram	Camphor

Element	Shape	Incense
Fire	Red Triangle	Cinnamon
Water	Silver Crescent	Cedar
Air	Blue Circle	Sandalwood
Earth	Yellow Square	Myrrh

I'm not going to spend more time on these things, because one of the easiest and most effective ways to create an appropriate atmosphere for working with these energies is through the use of color. But feel free to use any you desire, or add more from other correspondences you find on your own.

The effect of color on consciousness is instant and automatic. You have doubtless already experienced this from your work in other chapters. But by building up the colors in your imagination, along with the appropriate archetypal idea behind the energies of the planets or the elements, you will be instantly bringing its power into your consciousness and your magical circle. In other words, if you imagine a red glow filling your circle, while you also imagine the qualities of heat, dryness and expansion, you will be tapping into the spiritual energies of fire. It's that simple. Once you have established this connection, you will be able to direct that energy however you like, or contact the spiritual entities of fire.

When working with the four elements, the following colors are the traditional ones used by most magicians:

Fire: red or red-orange
Water: blue or blue-green
Air: yellow or blue
Earth: green, black or brown

When working with the planets, these colors are traditional:

Saturn: black or violet
Jupiter: blue or violet
Mars: red
Sun: yellow or gold
Venus: green
Mercury: orange or mixed colors
Moon: violet, blue or silver

You can of course use whatever colors you like in your practice, but these are the traditional colors that have been used for centuries. These colors should be built up powerfully in your imagination to form the general atmosphere of your working, but you can also use appropriately colored cloths and candles in your work area, if you have these things available. You will certainly not want to have a lot of unrelated colors in your working space, as these will be distracting.

Exercise 74 – Creating Magical Atmospheres

Time Required: 15 to 20 minutes

This simple exercise will allow you to easily tap into the forces of the elements and the planets from deep in your unconscious and thus from the universe. In this exercise, you will draw the appropriate energy into your circle, but you could also use this technique to charge a room or your house with the energy, so that its force permeates the area for whatever purpose you like. You can also use a generalized energy such as vital power, or general magick force, simply using white light or blue-white light instead of one of the planetary or elemental forces.

Again, this is rather similar to a New Hermetics technique, but I have attempted to simplify it even further, so that you can use it easily within your magical work in this book. This also shows an example of how to apply New Hermetics techniques in a ritual setting.

If you are using elemental energies, you can face the appropriate direction in your workroom or temple. Air would be the East, Fire the South, Water the West, and Earth the North. For the planetary energies, you may direct yourself toward the area in the heavens where the planets currently are, or you could simply orient yourself toward the east, where the planets rise, or else generally above your head.

1. Consult with your subconscious using the pendulum.

2. Get into the Alpha state using your anchor.

3. Do opening preparations, including any combination of purification, consecration, chakra opening, Kundalini arousing breaths, circle casting and the pentagram ritual.

4. Imagine the energy you will be invoking as being all around the protective sphere of your circle in a diluted but all encompassing form. In this form it is mixed with all other energies. However, isolate this particular energy by imagining an appropriate color.

5. Begin to concentrate this energy before you, or above your head being drawn into the light of your superconscious area. See it accumulating as a cloud of appropriate color, focusing on the specific nature of the force you are accumulating. (In other words, if you are drawing in Water energy, focus on Coldness, Wetness, and Contraction, while if

you are drawing in Jupiterean energy, focus on Generosity, Abundance, Leadership, and Vision)

6. Create an opening in your protective sphere, and imagine the appropriate energy filling this opening. (This can be done with the pentagrams or hexagrams that we will discuss shortly).

7. As you breathe, begin to draw this energy into you, feeling and visualizing the energy moving into your body from above. Fill yourself with this energy until you feel you could nearly burst. Experience this energy palpably, visibly in the appropriate color inside your physical body.

8. Express to this energy what specific purpose it will serve, and how long it will remain in effect.

9. Send the energy out of your solar plexus beginning to turn in a clockwise spiral through your personal circle and sphere.

10. Continue to repeat this process until you experience that the space is fully charged. You will know when you have fully charged the area, because you will feel the power and see it clearly with your third eye, ands perhaps somewhat with your physical eyes as well.

11. Close the opening in your protective sphere.

12. You can now conduct whatever work you will.

13. Return to normal awareness.

14. Take some real outward actions toward getting results in whatever you have just projected, knowing that you are going to succeed. Don't omit this last step.

You can also charge spaces at a distance. You would simply draw in the appropriate energy as above, and then send it all to the distant location, visualizing this location becoming permeated with this energy. You could use this to positively influence your work environment, a room, a house, a town, or cause change anywhere you desire. Of course the larger the effect, the larger the amount of energy you will need to collect.

PENTAGRAMS, HEXAGRAMS AND SACRED GEOMETRY

The "Greater Rituals" of the Pentagram and Hexagram are part of our magical inheritance from the 19th century occult group The Hermetic Order of the Golden Dawn. They have been reprinted in so many books that I was almost going to skip them as a topic in this already crowded manual. However, they have a useful function within your magical work, so I thought I had better give them a little space. Besides, I have a few unique viewpoints that you will hopefully find helpful in understanding and using these techniques.

In the Order instructions given out by the Golden Dawn, pentagrams are supposed to be drawn in a specific way to invoke and banish elemental energies, and hexagrams to invoke and banish the energies of the planets. It is said that when you trace the symbols carefully in the air, "From each re-entering angle... issueth a ray, representing a radiation from the Divine."[1] This is the only explanation offered by the Order for exactly what these symbols are for, and why you should use them. This has always seemed a strange statement, and one that explains very little.

The pentagram is generally considered a symbol representing the microcosm, or humankind, and that the upright pentagram shows the triumph in humans of spirit over the elements. Humans can control the elements through spirit, and this symbol is a representation of that. If you look at Diagram Twelve you will see the attribution of an element to each of the points of the pentagram, with the element of spirit at the topmost point. However it is still unclear exactly what is meant by the ray that "issueth forth," from each re-entering angle.

However, when you begin to explore sacred geometry, you quickly discover that within the geometry of the pentagram there is an interesting ratio known as "phi" or "the golden mean." This is depicted in Diagram Nine.

A rectangle created with this ratio, called a "golden rectangle" can infinitely reproduce itself, larger or smaller, making the geometry for a "golden spiral." This is depicted in Diagram Ten. This spiral measurement can be found all through nature, creating seashells, weather patterns, air resistance and the spiral form of galaxies. This geometry also plays out in the growth of plants and the expansive reproduction in all life forms.[2]

So, the pentagram is representative on a symbolic level with the dynamic forces that create the universe. This is very congruent with its nature as ruler of the elemental forces. But looking at geometry, we can also understand the pow-

---

[1] Regardie, Israel, *The Complete Golden Dawn System of Magic*, Volume 4, p. 10
[2] Schneider, Michael S., *A Beginner's Guide to Constructing the Universe*, pp. 109-177

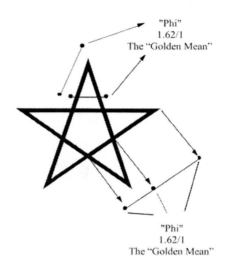

Diagram 9 - Pentagram with "Phi Ratio" or the "Golden Mean"

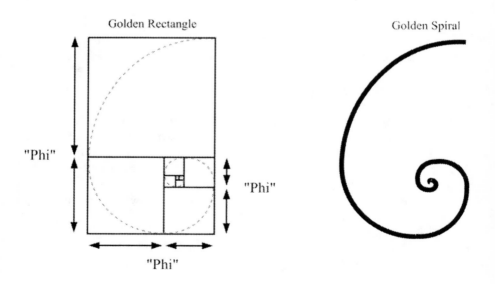

Diagram 10 - The Golden Rectangle and the Golden Spiral

er of the pentagram in a whole new way. I'm not sure if this was on the minds of the magicians who began to use it, but it immensely helps me to empower the pentagram with a whole new level of influence. When we trace a pentagram in the air, with the intention of making use of a force, we are creating a massive geometric progression of power and manifestation that can dramatically influence the universe through our spirit. This power expands outward or inward with the force of all of nature's expansive and contractive processes. Perhaps this is after all what the Golden Dawn document is referring to by this "ray" from the divine.

The hexagram on the other hand, consists of two separate equilateral triangles, facing opposite directions. This is said to represent the macrocosm, or greater universe, as opposed to the microcosm of mankind. It also shows our relationship to the universe, the upward pointing triangle representing our aspiration to understanding, and the downward pointing triangle representing the flow of understanding from the divine.

Geometrically, the hexagram represents perfection in form and structure. It is stable and economically uses space to perfection. The structure of honeycombs uses this geometry to maximize the amount of available spots for honey storage without wasting any space. If you place equally sized spheres next to one another they will naturally take on hexagram patterns.

Diagram 11 - Spheres in a Hexagram

So, in using this shape in our rituals to invoke planetary energies, we are emphasizing perfect harmony, balance and structure, the very laws through which the universe maintains equilibrium.[1]

---

[1] Ibid., pp. 187-196

Each of the points on the pentagram and the hexagram are assigned corres-pondences from Hermetic and Qabalistic tradition, and it is through the rela-tions of these correspondences when we trace the shapes that the specific ener-gies are invoked. Further symbols of the elements and planets, as well as holy names have been assigned for invoking each of the forces as well. We will get more into this as we discuss each ritual in turn.

Diagram 12 - Elemental Pentagram and Planetary Hexagram

These rituals are of course not strictly necessary for basic magical work, the simple exercise for accumulating magical atmospheres will work just fine in most cases. However, these special, ritualized shapes form an excellent method of testing the validity of contacts with spiritual entities that you will learn about in a later chapter. This testing method works best when you are familiar with these techniques, and have already used them a few times. It is for this reason that I am providing these techniques to you now, and suggest that you use them regularly in your magical work.

In the following exercises, you are going to be asked to "vibrate" appropriate divine names in portions of the rituals. This is really a simple matter, and you have already done it in the previous pentagram ritual. You ima-gine the name in shimmering white letters in your heart from the white light above you as you inhale, and as you exhale, you say the name slowly and melodiously causing a vibration as you imagine the white light letters going out with your breath. This creates a powerful magical effect, transforming your speech into magical projection. If you are going to be using the Hebrew formulae, imagining the Hebrew letters themselves would be ideal.

There are also signs or gestures associated with each of the elements. These are not strictly necessary and I'm not going to go into their use. If you are familiar with them you can add them to these exercises if you wish.

Exercise 75 - Greater Pentagram Ritual for Invoking Elemental Energy

Time Required: 2 to 5 minutes

This ritual is extremely easy to perform, and really can be done in a manner very similar to the Creating Magical Atmospheres technique. Here are the directions for which point you begin to trace each of the pentagrams in invoking the elements, along with the appropriate symbols to place in the middle of your pentagrams, and the associated divine names:

Air — YHVH (Yehowau)

Water — AL (El)

Earth — ADNI (Adonai)

Fire — ALHIM (Elohim)

Diagram 13 - Invoking Elemental Pentagrams

195

With all of the divine names, you could also simply state the name of the element, or the purpose you are calling it for, in other words:

Diagram 14 - Modern Elemental Pentagrams

At the end of your ritual, you will need to banish the energies, reversing the energy. These are the banishing pentagrams:

Diagram 15 - Banishing Pentagrams

However, before tracing the elemental pentagrams, you are supposed to invoke the ruling element of Spirit, using the following pentagrams:

Diagram 16 - Invoking Spirit Pentagrams

197

When invoking Water or Earth, you use the Passive spirit pentagram. When invoking Fire or Air you use the Active Spirit Pentagrams. At the end of your Ritual, you will use the banishing Spirit pentagrams, which are:

AHIH (Eheieh)   AGLA (Agla)

Active Spirit   Passive Spirit

Diagram 17 - Banishing Spirit Pentagrams

1. Consult with your subconscious using the pendulum.

2. Get into the Alpha state using your anchor.

3. Do opening preparations, including any combination of purification, consecration, chakra opening, Kundalini arousing breaths, circle casting and the pentagram ritual.

4. Face the appropriate direction in your workspace, and trace the corresponding Invoking Spirit Pentagram, drawing it in the air largely and clearly, using the same technique as in the earlier pentagram ritual, while vibrating the appropriate magick word. As you trace the wheel of spirit in the center of the pentagram, you vibrate the second magick word.

5. Imagine the energy you will be invoking as you face the appropriate direction in your workspace. (If you have used the earlier pentagram ritual, you will already have visualized the element in its appropriate direction.

6. Begin to concentrate this energy before you, See it accumulating as a cloud of appropriate color, focusing on the specific nature of the force

you are accumulating. (In other words, if you are drawing in Water energy, focus on Coldness, Wetness, and Contraction etc.)

7. Trace the Invoking Pentagram of the element, drawing it in the air largely and clearly, using the same technique as in the earlier pentagram ritual, while vibrating the appropriate magick word. As you trace the appropriate symbol in the center of the pentagram, you vibrate the second magick word.

8. Visualize and feel the energy rushing through the pentagram into your circle. Experience this energy palpably, visibly in the appropriate color, feeling it whirling past you, turning in a clockwise spiral through your circle and sphere. Continue experiencing the energy rushing into your circle until you experience that the space is fully charged. You will know when you have fully charged the area, because you will feel the power and see it clearly with your third eye, and perhaps somewhat with your physical eyes as well.

9. Express to this energy what specific purpose it will serve, and how long it will remain in effect.

10. You can now conduct whatever work you will.

11. When you are finished, simply reverse the process, using the banishing pentagrams.

12. Return to normal awareness.

13. Take some real outward actions toward getting results in whatever you have just projected, knowing that you are going to succeed. Don't omit this last step.

Exercise 76 - Greater Hexagram Ritual for Invoking Planetary Energy

Time Required: 2 to 5 minutes

This again is easily performed, and is in fact in many ways more simple than the Greater Ritual of the Pentagram, because you do not need to invoke Spirit first. Here are the hexagrams of the planets, with their divine names. You trace each of these hexagrams as two separate triangles:

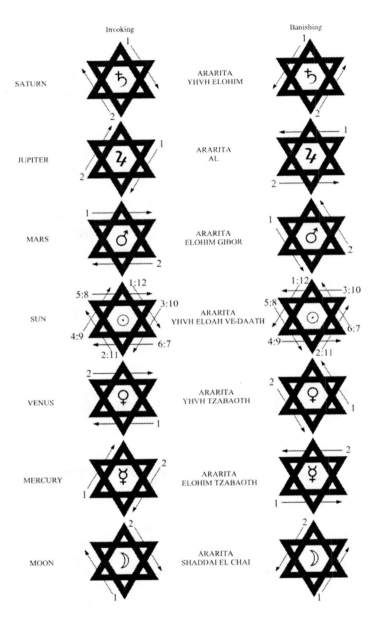

Diagram 18 - Hexagrams of the Planets

For the sun, you must trace all of the other planetary hexagrams one at a time, one on top of the other.

You could also simply use the name of the planet instead of the Hebrew name of God. I have noticed no discernible difference in my own personal practice. I also tend to prefer using the unicursal hexagram because it is easier and allows you to make the hexagrams in one motion rather than two, and the solar hexagram in one motion rather than twelve! If you would like to be able to trace hexagrams in one motion, you can use a unicursal hexagram instead of two triangles. Two versions of these hexagrams can be found in Appendix 3. You can experiment yourself, and see which ones you prefer.

1. Consult with your subconscious using the pendulum.

2. Get into the Alpha state using your anchor.

3. Do opening preparations, including any combination of purification, consecration, chakra opening, Kundalini arousing breaths, circle casting and the pentagram ritual.

4. Imagine the energy you will be invoking as being all around the protective sphere of your circle in a diluted but all encompassing form. In this form it is mixed with all other energies. However, isolate this particular energy by imagining an appropriate color.

5. Begin to concentrate this energy before you, or above you. See it accumulating as a cloud of appropriate color, focusing on the specific nature of the force you are accumulating. (In other words, if you are drawing in Jupiterean energy, focus on Generosity, Abundance, Leadership, and Vision)

6. Trace the invoking hexagram of the planet, drawing it in the air largely and clearly, while vibrating the appropriate magick word. As you trace the appropriate symbol in the center of the hexagram, you vibrate the second magick word.

7. Visualize and feel the energy rushing through the hexagram into your circle. Experience this energy palpably, visibly in the appropriate color, feeling it whirling past you, turning in a clockwise spiral through your circle and sphere. Continue experiencing the energy rushing into your circle until you experience that the space is fully charged. You will know when you have fully charged the area, because you will feel the power and see it clearly with your third eye, and perhaps somewhat with your physical eyes as well.

8. Express to this energy what specific purpose it will serve, and how long it will remain in effect.

9. You can now conduct whatever work you will.

10. When you are finished, simply reverse the process, using the appropriate banishing hexagrams.

11. Return to normal awareness.

12. Take some real outward actions toward getting results in whatever you have just projected, knowing that you are going to succeed. Don't omit this last step.

Exercise 77 – Writing Spells

Time Required: 20 to 50 minutes

Spells need not be complicated, nor long, nor in barbarous syllables or some ancient forgotten language. Spells are simply the expression in words of our magical intent, and they are often most effective when they are very simple. The reason to use spells is to activate your mind creatively both in the process of creating the spell, and then in the process expressing it in the ritual. If you are powerfully thinking about the manifestation you are trying to create as you write your spell, it will become an anchor just like the anchor that you use to get into the Alpha state.

When you write a spell, you will want to check in with your subconscious with the pendulum to make sure it approves. Truthfully, just writing it will activate your connection with your subconscious (energy) and superconscious (inspiration), so doing the ritual will simply activate the conscious mind's (image) desire, sealing the spell in the power of three.

Rhyming Couplets are often very pleasing to the subconscious mind. They are playful and evocative, while giving your spells a sort of songlike quality that will help to evoke the appropriate energy. I highly recommend that you try writing some rhyming spells and see how they feel to you when you use them in a ritual space.

Here are a couple of rhyming spells for wealth and love that I've just dashed off simply as examples. I suggest you write your own, rather than using these silly things, but as you can see, no great poetry is required. You could make your spells shorter or longer, but I would suggest no more than six or seven couplets or you will have to spend too much energy trying to remember them.

Love Spell

I beseech the powers above.
To bring me what I seek in Love.
Let her be both fair and mild,
Funny, lovely, sometimes wild.
May she be both smart and wise
Shining hair and haunting eyes.

Wealth Spell

I seek the riches that I need
Successful thoughts success will breed
Currents of wealth I now attract
To me creatively to act
Money flowing right to me
My wallet overflowing I see

1. Consult with your subconscious using the pendulum.

2. Get into the Alpha state using your anchor.

3. Do opening a few Kundalini arousing breaths, to awaken some creative energy.

4. Begin to think about your desired manifestation, and really begin to visualize it somewhat, as in the Manifesting Synchronicity technique.

5. Now, get really creative, and come up with a simple rhyming spell, that encompasses all parts of your desired effect, writing it down in your journal. Don't be afraid to try a few drafts, until you think it's really perfect.

6. Check in with your subconscious, to make sure it likes the spell.

7. Return to normal awareness.

There is a power in the number three, so I recommended that you repeat your spell three times when you launch it in a ritual. The old saying, "Three times is a charm," summarizes this perfectly. There's something just right about

203

saying your spell three times. It just rhythmically flows right. It feels like the right number. Two is not enough, and four is too many. Three is also the natural number of cycles, beginning middle and end. However, you can accomplish this in two different ways. You can either run through the entire spell three separate times, or else say each line three times as you go along. Both seem to work well. Just do what feels right to you.

Exercise 78 – General Spell Work

This is a general outline to use when launching a simple spell. You can shorten it into a very minimal and simple operation, or elaborate it into a very complex rite. Remember, your subconscious enjoys effort and creativity, but too much effort can thwart your effectiveness by taking you out of the right state, and making you feel uncomfortable rather than enthusiastic and energetic. Simply follow these directions, and you should find yourself experiencing very good results.

1. Write your spell.

2. Consult with your subconscious using the pendulum.

3. Get into the Alpha state using your anchor.

4. Do opening preparations, including any combination of purification, consecration, chakra opening, Kundalini arousing breaths, circle casting and the pentagram ritual.

5. Make a statement of your intent, either out loud verbally, or thinking it through clearly in your mind.

6. Begin to invoke an appropriate magical atmosphere, using the Creating Magical Atmospheres technique, or using the pentagram or hexagram technique.

7. Recite your spell three times, directing the magical energy you've accumulated in a spiraling clockwise whirl, building and directing its force as you speak. Powerfully visualize this energy being charged by your spell. As you are doing this, visualize your desire, and place this visualization into the whirling energy.

8. As you finish the third time through your spell, send every bit of the energy you've accumulated up into the light above your head, knowing

that your superconscious will manifest your desires. You can travel up with the spell energy creatinging an ecstatic "gnosis" experience at this point if you wish.

9. Or you could also direct the spell energy toward your target, in which case, you must visualize the energy going up into the light of super-consciousness and then traveling to your target, or in the general area you wish to effect. Be careful about this, because you can easily descend into negative behavior in this way, trying to directly manipulate specific individuals.

10. Close your ritual space, preferably by performing appropriate banishing rituals for the energy of the spell, and the lesser pentagram ritual a second time, and withdrawing all of the energy of your protective circle back into yourself. All of your spell energy should already have been discharged toward you task, so this should place the balance of energy back to equilibrium.

11. Take some real outward actions toward getting what you have just projected, knowing that you are going to succeed. Don't omit this last step.

SIMPLE TALISMANIC MAGICK

Creating talismans is the art of binding a spirit or spiritual force into some object to vivify it with magical potential. This generally includes all things such as magical charms, amulets, rings, and many other similar magical objects. It is also simply the act of making any physical magical object. Most talismans take the form of a magical symbols or symbols carved or written upon, parchment, paper, papyrus, wood, stone or metal. The act of writing things down moves your ideas into the physical world. Your magical journal is a talisman. Your goals are talismans. Talismans very powerfully impact the subconscious. In this book we will cover making simple talismans out of paper, although you could easily adapt these same principles for making other sorts of charms, magical rings or any other thing you could imagine.

Exercise 79 - Sigils

Time Required: 15 to 40 minutes

The easiest and most direct way of making magical symbols, seals, magical monograms or sigils for use in talismanic magick is the one made popular by Austin Osman Spare and the good people who brought us Chaos magick. However, the technique is really much older than Spare, and a very similar technique can be found in Agrippa.[2]

I've already described this basic technique in my last book, but here is a quick recap. In this system there aren't any "correct" or "incorrect" sigils. Instead, you just use your creativity to create your own, based on a statement of your intent, or a sentence of desire.

1. So, first you must create a sentence that succinctly expresses what you want. The most important thing to remember with this statement is that it must be positive and clearly express what you really want. "It is my will to have a beautiful new girlfriend." You will then remove all of the repeating letters. In my little example this would look like this:

    IT IS MY WILL TO HAVE A BEAUTIFUL NEW GIRLFRIEND

    IT *S MY W*L* *O HAVE * B**U**F** N** G*R*****ND

    ITSMYWLOHAVEBUFNGRND

2. You will then stylize and combine these remaining letters into a single symbol that you like. It can be done in any number of ways, but should be as simple as possible. You can combine letters that are similar such as M and W or Y and V, to keep your symbol streamlined and tight. Just use your own aesthetic sense and creativity to create a sigil that seems pleasing and appropriate to your purpose. Here are a few ways you could sigilize the above.

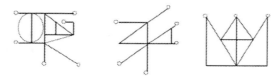

Diagram 19 - Various Sigilizations of ITSMYWLOHAVEBUFGRND

---

[2] *Three Books of Occult Philosophy* p. 562

206

3. All that's now left is to make your sigil into an aesthetically pleasing talisman and then to ritually charge it.

Words of Power

You can also use the above technique to create a "word of power." The garbled letters that you've created by removing repeating letters can be used as part of a spell, or repeated as a sort of mantra as you build up energy to manifest your desire. You can also rearrange the letters to make this word more sonorously pleasing. Your original intention will still be locked within.

A word like this could also be used to name a servitor or artificial elemental. That way, the name of the created being is directly connected to its purpose. We'll be creating artificial elementals next.

Exercise 80 - Talismanic Consecration

Time Required: 15 to 40 minutes

You can really use this easy technique to charge any object with magical energy, not just sigils created with the above method. You must simply have some object that you wish to charge with magical force for some specific purpose. You will also need a black cloth to wrap the talisman initially, and a cloth in the appropriate color for the energy you invoke to wrap it in later. You may also write a rhyming spell, if you wish, or you could simply charge your talisman with energy and intent.

1. Create or obtain an object you wish to charge for some magical purpose. Wrap it in a black cloth.

2. Consult with your subconscious using the pendulum.

3. Get into the Alpha state using your anchor.

4. Do opening preparations, including any combination of purification, consecration, chakra opening, Kundalini arousing breaths, circle casting and the pentagram ritual.

5. Unwrap your talisman from the black cloth and hold it in your hand.

6. Sprinkle a small bit of water on it to purify it, saying some words of purification appropriate to your purpose. As you are doing this, imagine that that it is cleared of all previous energy, a blank slate.

7. If you are burning incense, you can then pass your talisman through the incense smoke, using appropriate words of consecration. You may omit this if you are not burning incense.

8. Then rewrap your talisman in the black cloth.

9. Make a clear statement of your intent, either out loud verbally, or thinking it through clearly in your mind. This must include the specific purpose of the talisman, who it is for, and how long it will have to accomplish its job. You could also do this statement as a rhyming spell, but be sure to include all of that information.

10. Begin to invoke an appropriate magical atmosphere, using the Creating Magical Atmospheres technique, or using the pentagram or hexagram technique.

11. Once the desired force is all around you, unwrap your talisman and hold it up. Perceive the force that you desire beginning to accumulate in your talisman. Draw all of the energy in your circle into your talisman. If you have written a spell, you will recite it at this point while you are drawing the energy into your talisman. See the talisman glowing brightly with color of the energy, and feel it pulsing with power.

12. Once all of the energy in the whole circle is in your talisman, close your eyes and clearly visualize your talisman, and then begin to see an image of your accomplished desire behind the image of the talisman. See this image of the accomplished desire, move through your talisman until it is entirely in front of the talisman, filling your view.

13. Repeat this process of visualizing your talisman, then drawing an image of your completed desire through the image of the talisman until the imagined desire completely fills your view a number of times as quickly as possible until the image of the talisman automatically produces the image of your accomplished desire. You have now anchored this talisman to your desire.

14. Imagine your charged talismanic symbol and the image of your desire switching back and forth, finally rising up into the light of your su-

perconscious. You can travel up with the spell energy creating an ecstatic "gnosis" experience at this point if you wish.

15. Finally, wrap the talisman in an appropriately colored cloth for your purpose.

16. Close your ritual space, preferably by performing appropriate banishing ritual for the energy of the spell, and the lesser pentagram ritual a second time, and withdrawing all of the energy of your protective circle back into yourself. All of your spell energy should already have been discharged toward you task, so this should place the balance of energy back to equilibrium

17. Take some real outward actions toward getting what you have just projected, knowing that you are going to succeed. Don't omit this last step.

Once you have your charged talisman, you can hold onto it, give it to the person you created it for, or destroy it physically, setting it free to do its work on the astral plane. If you decide to destroy it, the easiest way to do this is simply by setting it on fire.[1] If you do this, just make sure that you are consciously setting it to work astrally rather than just destroying it. When you are destroying it, just hold onto the image of the talisman and its purpose, imagining that it is rising up into your superconscious.

Exercise 81 – Creating Artificial Elementals or Servitors

Time Required: 30 to 40 minutes

An artificial elemental or servitor is a talismanic creation that has a sort of consciousness of its own that it can use to creatively accomplish your desires. You can generate these artificial beings quite easily, sending them out into the world at your convenience to do whatever you wish. The nice thing about a servitor created in this way is that you can develop a relationship with it, directing it to accomplish your desires, and allowing it to do this in whatever way it can best accomplish your goals. These creatures are somewhat more flexible than talismans, and you can develop their use over time if you create one for long term use. When creating a servitor you must decide its purpose, name it, establish how long it has to accomplish what you want, and when it will disintegrate. You always want to create an end for your artificial creatures, even

---

[1] I offer several other Suggestions in *The New Hermetics.*

if that end is the day of your death. You shouldn't leave it floating around in your life if you don't need it. You can of course, dismantle your servitor early if you no longer want it. If your servitor is no longer serving you well, you should definitely dismantle it, disintegrating it in a ritual, and sending its energy back into the universe. You are in fact not creating anything. These servitors exist as parts of us, and you are really just activating some particular aspect of your being into temporary autonomy. You do not want to leave these energies activated, unless you are really aware of what you are doing and its consequences.

For your first few artificial elementals, you should probably create short term ones, ending them upon the completion of their tasks. Then, once you are getting good at creating them, you can create long-term elementals to serve all of your needs.

I keep a general servitor for each of the elements, who I can easily call upon to accomplish various tasks related to the elemental forces. If you create long term servitors such as these, you will want to occasionally "feed" them by recharging them in a ritual similar to the one in which you will charge them. For long-term elementals, you might want to have a physical home for it such as a statue, figurine or picture of your elemental. This will give you a reference point for working with it over time. You will simply place this object in your circle when creating the elemental, and identify it as the home of the elemental in your ritual.

The technique I am about to outline is somewhat different from the one in *The New Hermetics,* but you will probably find either effective. I consider this to be a somewhat superior revised method, but you will have to decide for yourself.

1. Decide the general and/or specific purpose that your elemental will serve.

2. Come up with a name for your elemental. It might be appropriate to choose a name that has something to do with its purpose, such as a "word of power" or anything else that has to do with its function.

3. Decide the amount of time it has to accomplish its mission and the date on which it will terminate.

4. If it is a long-term servitor, obtain an appropriate material base, an image, picture, sculpture etc. that can be the home of the servitor.

5. Consult with your subconscious using the pendulum.

6. Get into the Alpha state using your anchor.

7. Do opening preparations, including any combination of purification, consecration, chakra opening, Kundalini arousing breaths, circle casting and the pentagram ritual.

8. If you are using a material base, sprinkle a small bit of water on it to purify it, saying some words of purification appropriate to your purpose. As you are doing this, imagine that that it is cleared of all previous energy, a blank slate.

9. If you are burning incense, you can then pass your material base through the incense smoke, using appropriate words of consecration. You may omit this if you are not burning incense, placing the object on your altar.

10. Make a clear statement of your intent, either out loud verbally, or thinking it through clearly in your mind. This must include the servitor's purpose, its name, how long it has to accomplish what you want, and when it will disintegrate.

11. Begin to invoke an appropriate magical atmosphere, using the Creating Magical Atmospheres technique, or using the pentagram or hexagram technique, filling your circle with appropriate energy.

12. Once the desired force is all around you, close your eyes and begin drawing power from your superconscious and your subconscious by imagining energy coming up from your groin and belly and light coming down into your from above. Draw these two forces into the area of your solar plexus, feeling a strong dynamic power collecting there. This is the base for the consciousness of your elemental. Think again of the purpose and name of your elemental as you gather this force within, allowing yourself to move into a sort of one-pointed ecstatic consciousness, as you project your desires into this energy.

13. Hold out your hands in front of you, about 20 inches apart, and send this energy out of your solar plexus into the shape of a sphere between your palms.

14. Then begin to accumulate the planetary and/or elemental energies you've invoked that are swirling around in your circle into this sphere of energy between your palms. Gather all of the energy there, seeing and feeling your personal forces and the invoked forces swirling

211

together between your palms. Your hands can be around the material base if you have one.

15. Once you have fully gathered all of this energy, you will feel like you are holding a comet in your hands. Tell this baby elemental its name, its purpose, how long it has to do it, and when it will disintegrate.

16. At this point, you can shift the energy into some shape, such as an animal, human, some sort of geometric for or something that matches its material base. If you have a material base, you will now tell the elemental that this is its new home.

17. Once you have given the elemental its name and task, you must send it off to do its work. Imagine the elemental rising up into the light of your superconscious, up and out into the astral plane.

18. Close your ritual space, preferably by performing appropriate banishing ritual for the energy of the spell, and the lesser pentagram ritual a second time, and withdrawing all of the energy of your protective circle back into yourself. All of your spell energy should already have been discharged toward you task, so this should place the balance of energy back to equilibrium.

19. If you have consecrated a material base for your elemental, you can keep it wrapped in an appropriately colored cloth, or place it somewhere special in your home.

20. Take some real outward actions toward getting what you have just projected, knowing that you are going to succeed. Don't omit this last step.

Once you have created your elemental, you should try not to bother it as it is doing its work, unless you wish to give it further instructions. If you think about your elemental too much it will be continually hung up by your attention and not be able to do its job effectively. So, for the most part, you should just forget about your elemental until it finishes its job. If however, you need to communicate with your elemental, all that you need to do is go into the Alpha state and call it by name, imagining its color and form manifesting before you. You can then tell it whatever you want, then send it back off on its way. If it is a long term elemental and you have an image, you can just take out the image and communicate directly with the elemental that way.

CHAPTER NINE
Moving Objects
with Your Power

"Having learned to create astral forms, the
next step is to influence forms already existing, and this will be at first very difficult.
Phantasmal and fleeting as the astral is in
general, those forms which are definitely attached to the material possess enormous
powers of resistance, and it consequently requires very high potential to influence them."

-Aleister Crowley[1]

Telekinesis (also sometimes called psychokinesis) is the ability to move objects by means of psychic force. This is an area of magical and psychic development in which I have personally only had very modest success, but I wanted
to include a brief chapter on it for the sake of completeness. I have at least a little bit of repeatable positive experiences with all of the exercises in this chapter
except for the last two. I include these latter because I have it on fairly good
authority that they can work, if they are fully explored over a long period of
time.

Telekinesis seems to have an extremely seductive sway over many people,
almost to the point of unhealthy obsession. It is a very obvious sort of "miracle," and many people want to develop this ability at any cost. I have known of
several people, obsessed with the desire to develop telekinesis, supposedly for
some philanthropic reason such as "helping mankind."

However, telekinesis has few really practical applications, since it seems to
take a great deal of effort just to move a tiny object even a small amount. And
in the end, it seems like it would be far easier just to move the object with your

---

[1] *Magick: Book 4 Liber ABA*, p. 245

hand. There's a story about a young yoga student who spent many years trying to develop the ability to walk on water across a river. After decades of work, he eventually managed to do it. Just at that moment his master rode by him in a rowboat, saying "Wouldn't it have been easier to use a boat from the beginning? By now you could be enlightened!" In fact, from a spiritual perspective this story could really be applied to almost any of the techniques in this book.

But I am particularly reminded of this story whenever I play around with developing telekinesis. Over the next few pages I will outline a few experiments which should show you that it is possible to have a telekinetic effect on matter, and then give you a few practical applications for you to try. After that, we will discuss the abilities of levitation and teleportation, with a few practical suggestions that I've collected from others, even though I have never really experienced either myself.

I must warn you that telekinesis seems to be a rather fleeting and undependable phenomenon, at least for me. I have managed to succeed with these experiments on several separate occasions, but not necessarily every time I've tried. It may just be that I am particularly weak in this department and your success may be greater. However, I tend to think that this occasional lack of success may come from the impracticality of the experiments themselves. The subconscious is willing to go along with it a few times and produce the necessary phenomena, but once you have succeeded the subconscious balks at repeating it over and over again. You are also challenging the natural order of things with telekinesis, and the world seems to like remaining coherent as much as possible.

There are three basic techniques for telekinesis. That is to say, there are three ways to look at what you are doing, and these will give you the methods you can use to attempt moving matter. These three are attempting to establish identification with the object, attempting to manipulate the object through subtle astral energies, and simply using your imagination to will the object into movement. Of these three, the use of energy seems the easiest, and the others can somewhat be used in conjunction, so we will focus primarily on the generation and use of energy in this chapter. We will also add a bit of imagination and identification along the way, which you can use as much as you like at your own discretion. As Crowley says in the above quote, there is a tremendous amount of resistance to overcome, even in the simplest experiment, so do not feel disappointed if it takes you a few efforts to succeed, and results are inconsistent, even with these rudimentary experiments.

This being said, you also do not want to try overly hard, straining yourself psychically or physically. Instead, you must just remain relaxed and focused, holding on to the idea that you can do this, that it is possible, and that you will succeed. Too much stress will hinder rather than help your results.

Exercise 82 – Building Magnetism in the Hands

Time Required: 2 to 5 minutes

The simplest way to get into the right mental place to move objects is to imagine that your hands are becoming highly charged with astral, magnetic energy. This exercise will help you to develop this sensation.

1. Go into the Alpha state using your anchor.

2. Continue drawing the light down from your superconscious, and contain it in your belly, your Manipura chakra, collecting it like water in a pan.

3. At the same time, begin to breathe energy up from your Muladhara root chakra, containing this energy in your belly as well.

4. As you begin to feel this dynamic energy in your belly, bring your hands together as in prayer, and start to rub them vigorously for about 30 seconds, keeping your body relaxed, and continuing to collect energy.

5. Separate your hands slightly, feeling the tingle of energy between them. Move them closer and further apart without touching them, until you discover a sort of bouncy magnetic resistance between them.

6. As you do this, some of the energy in your belly will automatically start moving out into your arms and hands. This is natural, because you've moved your point of attention, the energy has simply followed. Now consciously start directing this energy up through your body and out to your hands, continuing to gently bounce them magnetically against each other, slowly separating them further and further apart.

7. All the while, continue collecting more and more energy in your belly, sending all of this energy out to your hands. After a couple of minutes, you will feel a strong magnetic force in your hands and fingers, even separated a foot or more from each other. You will then know that you are ready to begin.

You can also use this same exercise to concentrate elemental or planetary energies into your hands, simply by gathering this energy into you with your breath, rather than merely the vital force.

215

Exercise 83 – Telekinetic Pyramid

Time Required: 5 to 10 minutes

For this experiment, you will need a small perfectly square piece of paper (a post-it note works great!), a long needle and a small piece of clay.

You will first need to construct your Telekinetic Pyramid: (see Diagram 20)

1. Take your piece of square paper and fold it twice along the diagonal lines of the square, in the same direction each time. Fold it very tight so that the lines are crisp.

2. As you unfold it the second time it will naturally have a pyramid-like shape. You can tighten it a bit further at the center, to emphasize the central point further.

3. Take the needle, and poke the un-sharp side into the clay, so that the point of the needle is sticking out.

4. Press the clay onto a hard surface in front of you, so that the needle sticks straight up, and balance the center of the paper pyramid on the point of the needle. This is your telekinetic pyramid.

Now that you have constructed this simple telekinetic device, you will try to get the pyramid to spin on the needle using your power.

1. Place the device in front of you, in such a way that you can comfortably place your hands around it without any strain. It doesn't take much energy to make it move, but it should be still until you direct your attention to it. If it is dancing around on its own, this means that there is a draft in the room, or that your breath is disturbing it. You don't want either of these to mess up your experiment.

2. Once you've found a suitable place, you are ready to begin.

3. Consult your subconscious with the pendulum.

4. Get into the Alpha state using your anchor, and build up the magnetism in your hands, as above.

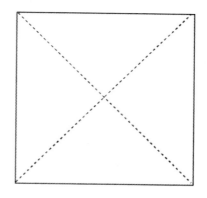

Diagram 20 - Telekinetic Pyramid

5. Cup your hands around the pyramid, and direct it to start spinning. Just will it to move, gently relaxing your attention on turning it with the magnetism of your hands. It may be helpful to imagine that the pyramid is just an extension of your own consciousness, identifying it as a part of yourself, and directing it that way. Do not strain. Once it starts turning one way, try to direct it in the other way.

6. Record your experience in your journal.

You can also try using just one cupped hand, or pointing at it with a finger, your outstretched hand, or directing your magnetic energy through your magick wand.

Exercise 84 – More Simple Telekinetic Testing

Time Required: varying

Use exactly the same technique as above on the following:

- Float a tiny piece of paper (the little circle left from a hole punch is perfect) in a small glass of water, and cup your hands around the glass. Try to move the paper in various directions.

- Cup your hands around a lighted candle and try to influence the movement of the flame. You can move it side to side, and make it bigger or smaller. For this experiment it might be useful to draw in red Fire energy to influence the flame directly, instead of mere magnetism. It is said that you can actually also cause an unlit candle to catch on fire in this way. I've never had any success, personally.

- Cup your hands around the smoke issuing from incense, and try to influence it as with the flame. You may wish to try some yellow Air energy for this as well.

- Cup your hands around a ping pong ball on a smooth flat surface, and try to get it to roll.

- Try moving the needle on a compass with the magnetism in your hands

- Hang your pendulum from a hook in front of you, setting it into motion with just your magnetism.

As with the last experiment you can also try using just one cupped hand, or pointing at it with a finger, your outstretched hand, or directing your magnetic energy through your magick wand.

Exercise 85 - Practical Applications

Time Required: varying

It actually seems far easier to affect things that are already in motion with a simple current of influence such as the kind you developed in a previous chapter. By collecting your magnetic energy as above, and sending it out on a wave of pure will, you can cause changes in the movements of physical objects. This

218

is also slightly more practical than the previous exercises. Try sending a current of your magnetic power out of you to affect the following while they are in progress. These are basically in descending order of difficulty:

- The flip of a coin

- The roll of a die

- A roulette wheel

- Speed up, slow down or stop an analog clock

- Change the direction of migrating birds (be sure to set them back on the right track!)

- Lottery numbers, as you are watching the drawing

- Traffic lights

- Try to affect the outcome of a Sports Event

Exercise 86 - Weather-Making

Time Required: 15 to 40 minutes

This is another more practical application of a specific kind of telekinetic effect. Magicians have used magical force for millennia to influence the patterns of weather to assist farmers and to cause troubles for their enemies. Weather magick can be somewhat tricky. In my experience, it is very easy to cause changes in the weather, but it is far less easy to change the weather in the way you would like it to be. Instead, you frequently cause greater problems than good. I used to have a knack for making things worse when I conducted weather magick workings. More recent experiments have been far more successful.

Many modern magicians consider this to be a disruptive and negative sort of magick that upsets the balance of nature and should be avoided. They feel that Mother Nature is perfectly capable of doing her work on her own, and often see it as a sort of transgression or betrayal of the Goddess. I don't entirely agree, but I am giving you this technique upon the promise that you will use it responsibly.

Also, don't overextend yourself. While it is possible and relatively easy to gather the necessary force to cause a rainstorm on muggy New England summer day, or in the Florida everglades, this is far less likely to work well in the Sahara. Likewise, if huge storm clouds loom upon the horizon, there is likely little you can do but perhaps make the shower somewhat briefer. On the other hand, you may be able to help the sun pop through on a cloudy day, or cause a few clouds to form on an extremely bright day. You may also find that you are a true weather magus, capable of far more than I am.

The basic technique for weather magick is quite simple. You merely need to accumulate the forces of the elements in whatever combination you would like to see manifest. In other words:

- Fire to warm

- Water to cool

- Fire and Air to get rid of rain

- Air and Water to create storms

- Fire and Water to create humidity

- Water and Earth to create hail

And so on and so on. These are just a few suggestions, and you can use your own creativity to come up with more. You can also use lunar forces to a certain extent in this work. This energy gathering can also be combined with a verbal (rhyming or not) spell if you wish. However, to gather enough energy to really have such a dramatic macrocosmic effect is no small feat. Do not attempt this lightly, as it may either not work at all, or drain you dramatically.

1. Consult with your subconscious using the pendulum.

2. Get into the Alpha state using your anchor.

3. Do opening preparations, including any combination of purification, consecration, chakra opening, Kundalini arousing breaths, circle casting and the pentagram ritual.

4. Make a statement of your intent, how specifically you intend to change the weather, either out loud verbally, or thinking it through clearly in your mind.

5. Potently draw the light of your superconscious into you, until you feel deeply connected with the true source of your power, a deep sense of cosmic strength.

6. Begin to invoke the appropriate magical energies, using the Creating Magical Atmospheres technique, or using the pentagram or hexagram technique. If you are using multiple forces, see and feel them combining dynamically as you invoke them. Invoke the dominant energy first.

7. Direct the magical energy you've accumulated in a spiraling clockwise whirl, building and directing its force tightly around you like a tornado. Powerfully visualize this energy being charged and directed by your will. As you are doing this, visualize your specific intention, and place this visualization into the whirling energy. If you have a spell, you will recite it three times while you are developing the energy. Visualize this energy as a column or cone of force that you are filling with more and more dynamic will. You should endeavor to feel the effect you are attempting to create (If you are creating sunshine, feel the heat, and the nice warm breeze, if a snowstorm, feel the bitter winds and cold wet snow).

8. Send every bit of the energy you've accumulated directly up into the sky above you, knowing that your force is transforming things immediately. You can travel up with the energy experiencing an ecstatic "gnosis" experience at this point if you wish. Imagine that this weather magick is like a powerful fire hose of energy bursting up continuously. Imagine that this energy is starting to whirl slowly in a clockwise spiral outward, continuously expanding and blasting up and out until it is whirling through the whole area you wish to affect.

9. Close your ritual space, preferably by performing appropriate banishing ritual for the energy of the spell, and the lesser pentagram ritual a second time, and withdrawing all of the energy of your protective circle back into yourself. All of your spell energy should already have been discharged toward you task, so this should place the balance of energy back to equilibrium.

10. Record your experience in your journal.

Exercise 87 - Levitation

Time Required: varying

I've never personally levitated, but many sources report that the following technique is the most reliable method. It is not actually a levitation technique per se, but rather a pranayama breathing technique that has levitation as one of its results. Aleister Crowley says of this technique, "As a development of this stage, the body rises into the air, and remains there for an appreciably long period, from a second to an hour or more."[1] Further, the Siva Samhita says, "...and when the practice becomes greater, the adept walks in the air."[2]

According to these and other sources, there are four distinct phases in the practice of this pranayamic breathing.

- First, you will become covered in sweat. This sweat is supposed to be healing, so you should rub it in, rather than wiping it off. You may also experience a sort of automatic rigidity at this phase.

- In the second stage, you will begin to shake and tremble violently, although you may not be aware of it, because you will be in an altered state.

- Then, you will find yourself briefly hopping up and down in place, or finding yourself hopping forward or backward, moving around in your room. Again you may or may not notice this until you are finished with your practice.

- Finally, you will find yourself floating in the air.

I have practiced this technique extensively, though I must admit perhaps not as extensively as I should have, and I have personally only experienced the first two stages. I have only been able to retain my breath for about 45 seconds, and this is apparently not long enough to experience the truly paranormal aspects of the technique. There will be more on this subject later.

This exercise is based upon the alternate nostril breathing that I briefly described much earlier in the Kundalini section. Again, it is similar to a technique from The New Hermetics, but you must take it quite a bit further if you wish to levitate with it.

---

[1] Ibid., p. 640
[2] *Siva Samhita*, p. 30

The best position for this exercise is "padmasana," better known as the lotus position, where we place our feet on both thighs, twisting into the famous yogic "human pretzel." This position naturally spreads our sit bones and supports our backs for this exercise. However, this position is quite uncomfortable for a lot of people, so a simple half lotus will do if you find the lotus position unbearable. Just sit cross-legged, and raise your top leg up onto your thigh. If even this is too uncomfortable, you can just sit cross-legged propped on the edge of a pillow, so that the pillow can give your back the necessary support.

You will not want to do this practice on a full stomach, as it will make you quite ill. You can eat a little bit, but not more than a few bites of food, and perhaps a little water or milk. Generally, you are supposed to eat a moderate vegetarian diet while conducting these practices.

It is traditional to perform this exercise 4 times a day. The first time you would perform this exercise is in the morning upon awakening, a second time at lunch time or noon, a third time before dinner or sunset, and a fourth time before going to bed at night. However, this is a lot, and you could start out a bit slower if you wish.

Take a seat in padmasana or some variation thereof. Sit up straight so that your spine is erect, your chest open, shoulders back, as if an invisible string attached to the crown of your head is pulling you toward the ceiling.

1. Go into the Alpha state using your anchor.

2. Close your right nostril with your right thumb, and exhale your breath completely through the left nostril. Then inhale through the same left nostril, filling your lungs very completely from the deepest recesses of your belly all the way to your collarbones. Do this calmly and consciously, do not force an uncomfortable amount of air into your lungs. All that you need do is fill your lungs to a comfortable fullness.

3. Now, hold your breath in your lungs, applying the three major "locks" of yoga, Mula Bandha, Uddiyana Bandha and Jalandhara Bandha. I've already described these. Contract your perineum, contract and lift your abdomen, and place your chin toward your chest. These three bonds will seal in the prana, but do not contract them aggressively, firm but easy. Hold your breath for as long as you possibly can, remembering that you are going to be exhaling slowly, so don't retain it so long that you have to gasp for air.

4. Seal the left nostril with your middle finger, and exhale very slowly through the right nostril. Exhale completely, using all the muscles of

223

your torso, including a secondary and more complete application of the Uddiyana Bandha, contracting and drawing in and up the abdomen, as if to touch the spine with the navel. This must be done with an easy strength, again firm but not aggressive. Do not hold the breath out.

5. Instead, keeping your left nostril sealed, inhale slowly through the right nostril.

6. Again, hold the breath in your lungs for as long as you possibly can.

7. Then seal the right nostril, and exhale your breath completely through the left nostril once again.

8. This is one cycle, and you should repeat it 9 more times for a total of ten cycles. This is to be repeated four times a day.

9. Record your experience in your journal.

The ideal ratio for this practice is 1:4:2. For every one second that you inhale, you should endeavor to retain the breath four seconds, and then exhale for two seconds. So, if it takes you four seconds to inhale, you will want to retain the breath for sixteen seconds, and exhale for eight. This must be extended longer and longer over time. 8:32:16, 16:64:32, 32:128:64. However, in practice it can be rather distracting to count your breath or look at a clock. Instead, you should eventually try to be concentrating on one or more of your chakras, or just being silently aware of your experience. So, you can just count your breath every once in a while to track your progress, instead, just attempting to get a sense of keeping the breath held in absolutely long as possible, then exhaling as absolutely slowly as you can possibly manage.

The key to this practice is the retention. You will want to retain your breath as long as you can, because it is in this stage that you will awaken your levitation abilities, or Vayu Siddhi. In order for this to happen, you will want to be holding your breath for over a minute, perhaps even longer. When you are holding your breath, your mind will slow down, and the subtle channels of energy known as Nadis will be cleansed and purified. Once you are able to easily hold your breath for over a minute, letting it out slowly over more than thirty seconds you will discover the paranormal effects of this practice.

Exercise 88 - Teleportation

Time Required: unknown

Teleportation or bi-location is simply astral projection which involves the crystallization of a new "physical" body from the energies that surround you in your astral body. I have heard many tales of this, but I have never seen it or experienced it in actuality. Once you have mastered astral projection, you can try to do this, though I have little acquaintance with it personally.

In your astral body, simply imagine the denser elements that surround you to be drawing to you, into your body of light, solidifying it. You can use the four elements for this, or simply use the dust or light particles in the air around you. Continue doing so until your body has a solid appearance. I wish I could give you more exact instructions for this, but I really don't know anything further about the subject.

CHAPTER TEN
Communicating With Non-Human Intelligence

"The Greeks call this 'the vision of Pan," the Chinese 'the great Tao,' Hindus 'Atman consciousness." The numinous, awe-ful, sublime 'God' 'Goddess' and 'Demon' figures who appear in the initial stages of this Awakening are Jung's 'archetypes of the collective unconscious' and are recognized as 'visitors from dream-time' by primitives, as 'them from Sidde' by witches, as Weird People in a thousand folk-traditions."

-Robert Anton Wilson[1]

In this chapter, you will learn a series of simple and effective techniques for communicating with spiritual entities, for bringing down some aspect of divinity or psychic authority into your body and life for the purposes of enlightenment and power. You will also learn some techniques for causing spirits to appear visibly to the psychic eye and in some cases even the naked eye. Instructions on some easy ways to test the accuracy of communications and the identity of the communicator are provided as well.

There is a popular subculture around today involving "angels," "extraterrestrial masters," and "space gurus" that communicate to mere mortals through special people called "channelers" or some such moniker. This movement has actually been around a lot longer than it might appear. In the past, the communications used be from "Apache Red Men," "Himalayan Mahatmas," or "Rosicrucian Adepts." The change in the region of the communicators over time merely reflects the fickleness of shifting cultural interests. The sort of commun-

---

[1] *Prometheus Rising*, p. 175

ication is very much the same. A hundred years ago this movement was called spiritualism or spiritism, and its practitioners were called mediums. A few years ago they were generally called channelers in common parlance, and the term medium is now making a big comeback.

As with the majority of professional psychics, a lot of these people were and are frauds. They charge exorbitant fees to give out questionable advice and to offer spurious communications with dead loved ones or invisible masters. But we need not dwell on this too heavily, because in the world of magick, truth and falsehood are extremely subjective terms. Some parts of a communication from any entity may be totally made up and used to serve the purposes of the seer, either consciously or subconsciously, while others may genuinely be from an inspired source. And it's not for me to decide which is which. I'd just advise caution when consulting any professional channeler or medium. The best thing to do is simply to learn these skills for yourself, so that you can be your own source of cosmic inspiration and information.

Often the beings that modern professional channelers seem to commune with are seemingly Hebraic Archangels or Prophets with a letter or two in their names adjusted, as if to make them seem a little more "jazzy." I am somehow reminded of the marketing for sports cars or sneakers by a lot of these "celestial beings." These entities usually seem to deliver the same general sort of message, a kind of pleasant and fluffy message of hope to the world. "We all must be good to each other, the world is evolving, becoming more enlightened and a golden age is soon to come, etc." There is nothing harmful in these messages, but also little that's particularly insightful.

I personally suggest that in your work you focus on contacting the spirits whose names I will provide in this chapter, rather than using the often sloppy techniques of channeling and mediumship in which you simply open yourself up to "whatever comes along." I also recommend that you call upon Angels, Spirits and other non-human intelligences with their names spelled in the usual way. Of course, you can always do what you want in the end, but there is often significance in the way that a spirit's name is spelled based on the numerology of the Qabala. I am not going to spend a great deal of time on this subject, but it is worthy of further study. There are several Qabalistic works in the bibliography and you could find a lot of useful information there. In this chapter we will discuss several methods of communicating with a number of different kinds of intelligence, who preside over the forces of the planets and the elements.

There are a number of good reasons for attempting to communicate with non-human intelligences. All gods, angels and spirits are essentially personifications of the natural forces that surround us. This was true in ancient times, and it is still true today. If you invoke Zeus or the airy archangel Raphael, you are invoking the majesty of the clouds and sky, which give forth rains to make the earth fruitful, and threaten us with lightning. By giving this force a name, you have a way of conceptualizing and connecting with it. By connecting with it, you can gain greater understanding of the force, and also gain some measure of that force in your own life. In *The New Hermetics*, I provided a simple method of connecting with the seven major Greco-Roman planetary deities for the purpose of personal empowerment, so I will not focus on that here. Rather, I will focus on communicating with the angels, spirits and elementals for the purpose of gathering information, and influencing events from their unique perspective. Communicating with non-human entities can be very valuable, educational and helpful in manifesting your desires. Probably the most powerful group of entities you can contact is the "Enochian" angels that were revealed to Dr. John Dee. However, this subject is complex enough to warrant a book of its own.

The following is a rather exhaustive list of entities, all of which can be contacted to understand the various aspects of the energies to which they are associated. Generally speaking, the Archangels represent the energy from a very exalted spiritual plane, the angels represent the energies on the Astral, while the Intelligences and Spirits represent the energies on the ethereal or sub-physical planes, and can most directly influence the physical world. The Spirits are generally considered to be somewhat nasty; they are often referred to as 'evil,' while the Archangels may be a bit too exalted for practical magick. By contacting the Archangels, you may gain some transcendental experience related to their particular domain. The Olympic Planetary Spirits and the Elemental Kings are leaders of large numbers of lesser spirits, and can be contacted for knowledge as well as to influence the world with their unique energy. These lists of entities represent a fairly complete set of beings to contact for a long time in your magick. Once you are quite experienced with these beings, you may decide to explore other beings such as the spirits of the Goetia or the Enochian Angels.

Archangels of Planetary Energies (Sephiroth)

Saturn –	Tzaphkiel	צפקיאל
Jupiter –	Tzadkiel	צדקיאל
Mars –	Kamael	כמאל
Sun –	Raphael	רפאל
Venus –	Haniel	האניאל
Mercury –	Michael	מיכאל
Moon –	Gabriel	גבריאל

Angels of Planets

Saturn –	Cassiel	כשיאל
Jupiter –	Sachiel	סחיאל
Mars –	Zamael	זמאל
Sun –	Michael	מיכאל
Venus –	Hanael	הנאל
Mercury –	Raphael	רפאל
Moon –	Gabriel	גבריאל

Intelligences of Planets

Saturn –	Agiel	אגיאל
Jupiter –	Iophiel	יהפיאל
Mars –	Graphiel	גראפיאל
Sun –	Nakhiel	נכיאל
Venus –	Hagiel	הגיאל
Mercury –	Tiriel	טיריאל
Moon –	Malkah be Tarshisim ve-ad Ruachoth Schechalim

מלכא בתרשישים ועד רוחות שחלים

Spirits of Planets

Saturn –	Zazel	זאזל
Jupiter –	Hismael	הסמאל
Mars –	Bartzabel	ברצבאל
Sun –	Sorath	סורת
Venus –	Kedemel	קדמאל
Mercury –	Taphtartharath	תפתרתרת
Moon –	Schad Barschemoth ha-Shartathan

שד ברשמעת השרתתן

Olympic Planetary Spirits

Saturn –   Arathor
Jupiter –   Bethor
Mars –   Phalegh
Sun –   Och
Venus –   Hagith
Mercury –   Ophiel
Moon –   Phul

See Appendix D for the sigils of the Olympic Planetary Spirits

Archangels of Elements

Fire –   Michael   מיכאל
Water –   Gabriel   גבריאל
Air –   Raphael   רפאל
Earth –   Auriel   אוריאל

Angels of Elements

Fire –   Aral   אראל
Water –   Taliahad   טליהד
Air –   Chassan   חשן
Earth –   Phorlakh   פורלאך

Rulers of Elements

Fire –   Seraph   שרף
Water –   Tharsis   תרשים
Air –   Ariel   אריאל
Earth –   Kerub   כרוב

231

Kings of Elementals

Fire –	Djin, king of the salamanders
Water –	Nichsa, queen of the undines
Air –	Paralda, king of the sylphs
Earth –	Ghob, king of the gnomes

Magical entities are perfectly real, with a strong emphasis on perfect. They are the undiluted essence of the idea they represent on different planes. Therefore, Bartzabel, the spirit of Mars, is a perfect personification of the martial concept on the lower astral plane. He is the fierceness of justice, strength, force, and violence. That he exists, "only in your mind" is perfectly obvious and does not in any way negate his existence. He is of the realm of ideas, and can only express himself on the purely material plane in a limited way.

It has been stated by many modern authorities on the subject of magick that "spirits," "angels," "elementals" and the like are simply aspects of the human unconscious mind that are transcendent or unbalanced in one way or another as the case may be. This seems like a fair assertion as long as we remember that the human mind encompasses everything in the sphere of sensation, so that rocks, friends, Thursday, green and so on are all equally no more than a part of the human mind. Drawing boundary lines in these matters is impossible and futile. As Aleister Crowley put it, "Thus, when we say that Nakhiel is the 'Intelligence' of the Sun, we do not mean that he lives on the Sun, but only that he has a certain rank and character; and although we can invoke him, we do not necessarily mean that he exists in the same sense of the word in which our butcher exists."[1] He then goes on to say, "When we 'conjure Nakhiel to visible appearance,' it may be that our process resembles creation- or, rather, imagination- more nearly than it does calling forth. The aura of man is called the 'magical mirror of the universe'; and so far as anyone can tell, nothing exists outside of this mirror."[2] But this should not lead you to think that these entities are just imaginary nothings. They are in fact, powerful aspects of the consciousness of the universe. They are illusions to be sure in a certain sense, but so is everything.

Quite simply, in terms of our four-part model of consciousness, The Archangels approximately represent the consciousness of their associated energies in the realm of the super-conscious mind (and above), the Angels in the conscious mind (and above), and the Intelligences and Spirits in the subconscious mind (and below). The Intelligences will represent the positive aspects of their energies, while the Spirits will represent more the negative side. The Olympic Plane-

---

[1] *Magick: Book 4 Liber ABA*, p. 142
[2] Idem.

tary Spirits fall somewhere in the middle of this scheme. The Elemental Kings and Rulers are perhaps somewhere near the Angels but really in the subconscious plane and with greater practical influence. The Old Gods such as Zeus, Odin or Astarte basically occupy the same space as the Archangels. This is of course just a metaphor.

Being perfect expressions of the "qualities," "feelings," or "ideas" that these entities embody on different planes, it is theoretically quite easy to establish contact with them. You must simply fill your senses with those things that put you in sympathy with the idea you wish to connect with. You can use number, symbol, incense, color and may other things to create the right "mood," but the easiest way to do this is simply to create a conducive magical atmosphere using the techniques you've already learned. In the traditional medieval scheme of magick it is necessary to conjure these entities in a hierarchical manner. If you wanted Kedemel, the spirit of Venus, to cause someone to fall in love with you, you would first need to invoke the proper name of God, in this case YHVH Tzabaoth, then invoke the Archangel Haniel, the Angel Hanael, the Intelligence Hagiel, and then finally Kedemel to do your bidding. While this might be effective, it is probably not entirely necessary for practical purposes. Simply creating the correct magical atmosphere, then using the telesmatic imaging technique that you will use in a few moments, you will find it quite easy to establish "contact," with these beings.

Nonetheless, for the sake of completeness, here are the appropriate divine names:

Names of God for the Planets (Sephiroth)

Saturn –	YHVH Elohim	יהוה אלהים
Jupiter –	El	אל
Mars –	Elohim Gibor	אלהים גבור
Sun –	YHVH Eloah Vedaath	יהוה אלוה ודעת
Venus –	YHVH Tzabaoth	יהוה צבאות
Mercury –	Elohim Tzabaoth	אלהים צבאות
Moon –	Shaddai El Chai	שדי אלחי

Names of God for the Elements

Fire –	YHVH Tzabaoth	יהוה צבאות
Water –	Elohim Tzabaoth	אלהים צבאות
Air –	Shaddai El Chai	שדי אלהי
Earth –	Adonai ha-Aretz	אדני הארץ

To create the magical atmospheres for contacting these beings, the colors previously presented will work quite well, but with the planetary energies you might wish to try the following colors for specific entities. These are from the color scales of the Hermetic Order of the Golden Dawn.

Planet	Divine Mind	The Archangels Superconscious	The Angels Conscious	The Spirits Subconscious
Saturn	Crimson	Black	Dark brown	Grey flecked Pink
Jupiter	Deep violet	Blue	Deep purple	Deep azure Flecked yellow
Mars	Orange	Scarlet red	Bright scarlet	Red flecked Black
Sun	Clear pink rose	Yellow (gold)	Rich salmon	Gold amber
Venus	Amber	Emerald	Yellow green	Olive flecked Gold
Mercury	Violet purple	Orange	Red-russet	Yellow-brown Flecked white
Moon	Indigo	Violet	Very dark Purple	Citrine flecked Azure

As you can probably see, the colors suggested before basically correspond to the Archangels. In a hierarchical sense this is appropriate, since by contacting the higher form of the energy, it is certainly possible to connect with its lower form. However, it might be useful to experiment. Honestly, I have not done this much in my own practice. For entities that occupy a more vague space in the planes, such as the Olympic Planetary Spirits, I would recommend using the usual colors. For the beings associated with the four elements, the usual colors should be fine.

When Encountering an Astral Being, be cautious and respectful. They are capable of a great deal, including changing your life or providing you with unique information and knowledge. If you consider them imaginary and useless, that will be true. If you consider them to be real and powerful, that will be so.

You are as powerful as any astral being, much more so in fact, but they are in their element on the astral, while it is just a visiting place for you. This makes it quite easy for them to manipulate and confuse you. Always remain in control of every encounter.

TELESMATIC IMAGING

In order to enter into useful communication with an astral being, it is easiest to build up a form in the "astral light" for the being to occupy, using the imagination, and then allowing the entity to occupy it and communicate or commune with you. This can be done simply by building up a form from the colorful energy you invoke in creating the magical atmosphere, or you could use the technique of telesmatic imaging. Although the former can be used quite effectively, in many ways the latter is superior since it gives you the opportunity to really think about the entity in terms of its name in the original Hebrew, and this will connect you with the entity in a very intimate and magical way from the beginning.

Telesmatic imaging is based on the esoteric associations of the Hebrew letters from the ancient magical text the Sepher Yetzirah. The letters are associated with the planets, the elements and the signs of the zodiac, and from these correspondences are also the esoteric keys to the twenty two major arcana of the Tarot. These correspondences then create pictorial suggestions for each letter. You will build up an image of the being you'll communicate with using these magical correspondences. By building up an image in this way, you are directly connecting with the subtle currents of magical energy that form this being, and your connection with the being is nearly automatic. Of this technique, the adepts of the Hermetic Order of the Golden Dawn have this to say, "And know thou that this is not to be done lightly for thine amusement or experiment, seeing that the Forces of Nature were not created to be thy plaything or toy. Unless thou doest thy practical magical works with solemnity, ceremony and reverence, thou shalt be like an infant playing with fire, and thou shalt bring destruction upon thyself."[1]

In terms of color, you could use the various color scales as above, with different colors depending upon the nature of the entity. I have not provided the complete color scale, but for simplicity's sake, I will only give the usual color attributions here, which are actually from the highest scale, associated with the divine mind. This should be more than sufficient for your regular use.

Most of these attributions are directly from the Hermetic Order of the Golden Dawn. Some are physical descriptions while others are more evocative of the "feeling" of the image you will create. It is helpful to be aware of the astro-

---

[1] Regardie, Israel, *The Complete Golden Dawn System of Magic*, Volume 5, p. 48

logical significance of these ideas, as well as a general familiarity with the Tarot. If you aren't familiar with these correspondences, hopefully the following descriptions will be helpful.

א A – Aleph – Bright-Pale Yellow – Air - Spiritual, Wings, Epicene, Slender

ב B – Beth – Yellow – Mercury – Active, Slight.

ג G – Gimel - Blue – Moon – Beautiful Yet Changeful, Full Face or Body

ד D – Daleth – Emerald Green – Venus - Very Beautiful, Full Face or Body

ה H – Heh – Scarlet – Aries - Fierce, Strong, Fiery

ו U, V, O – Vau – Red Orange – Taurus – Strong, Heavy and Clumsy

ז Z – Zayin – Orange – Gemini – Thin, Intelligent or Intellectual

ח Ch – Cheth – Amber – Cancer – Full face, not much expression

ט T – Teth – Greenish-Yellow – Leo - Strong and Fiery

י I, Y, J – Yod – Yellowish-Green – Virgo – Pale and Rather Delicate

כ K, C – Kaph – Violet – Jupiter - Big and Strong, Royal

ל L – Lamed – Emerald-Green – Libra – Well-Proportioned

מ M – Mem – Deep Blue – Water – Reflective, Dreamlike, Epicene

נ N – Nun – Green-Blue – Scorpio - Square and Determined, Dark

ס S – Samekh – Blue – Sagittarius - Thin, Expressive, Somewhat fierce

ע O, A – Ayin – Indigo – Capricorn - Rather Mechanical or Bestial

פ P – Peh – Scarlet – Mars – Fierce, Strong, Resolute

צ Tz – Tzaddi – Violet – Aquarius - Thoughtful, Intellectual

ק Q, K – Qoph – Ultra Violet Crimson – Pisces – Full, Dreamy

ר R – Resh – Orange – Sun – Proud, Dominant, Beautiful

ש Sh – Shin – Glowing Scarlet Orange – Fire – Fierce, Active, Epicene

ת Th – Tau – Indigo – Saturn or Earth – Dark, Epicene, Slow

So, to use these ideas to build up your image, you will need to look at the Hebrew spelling of the being you are invoking. You can find these Hebrew spellings in the lists of names above. You must remember that Hebrew is read from right to left, so the first letter will begin on the right side, and be read in reverse direction from English.

The first letter of the name will represent the head, descending downward so that the last letter represents the feet or lower portion of the figure. Let us say for example, that you are going to invoke אוריאל Auriel, the Archangel of Earth. The Hebrew Letters which form this name are א - A, ו - V, ר - R, י – I, א - A, ל - L. So, a telesmatic image of Auriel would look something like this:

א - A – Airy, winged, pale yellow with flowing golden hair

ו - V – Strong, broad face, ruddy cheeks, perhaps the horns of a bull

ר - R - Radiant shoulders, glowing like the sun, proud and beautiful

י – I – Body like a chaste young maiden in a green gown

א - A – With yellow golden wings

ל - L – Well proportioned legs and feet, with the sword and balance of justice at feet

Diagram 21 - The Archangel AURIEL

237

For longer names you will obviously need to use your creativity and common sense to divide up the portions of the image. You can imagine as an addition to this image that the angelic figure wearing a golden belt with the letters of their name engraved upon it. One of the best things you could do would be to enter the Alpha state, and use your creativity to make a rough sketch of such an image, as beautifully as you can. It is said that you should probably try not to sexualize the image, as this will attract lower forces than you want into your invocational magick, but this is subject to debate.

You can also use this telesmatic imaging for an advanced version of creating artificial elementals. Let your own creativity guide you in this matter.

You will notice that I have not given Hebrew letters for the Olympic Planetary Spirits or the Kings of the Elements. These beings are not of Hebrew origin, so this technique might not be the best for using them. You could transliterate the names fairly effectively, but it might just be best to use the simple technique of building up a regal, spiritual image directly out of the colors and energies you invoke initially.

For the Olympic Planetary Spirits, you will want to trace with your imagination the symbol that I've provided in Appendix 4 on their chest. This will place you in contact with their forces effectively. There are actually sigils or symbols for all of these entities that can be traced using the rose-cross lamen of the Golden Dawn, or using the Planetary Kameas. I will not go into these matters in this book, as the simple telesmatic imaging we've just discussed should place you strongly in sympathy with these forces.

Once you have developed a fairly strong image you are ready to begin your invocation.

Exercise 89 – Invocation of the Angelic Beings

Time Required: 30 to 60 minutes

With this exercise you can establish communication with any of the above mentioned Angels or Archangels. However, you should not use it with the Intelligences or Spirits of the Planets, or the Elemental Kings or Rulers. These beings should be communicated with through the techniques of evocation which we will cover in the next section.

This is a highly simplified invocational formula. You can of course expand upon it to include any ritual elements that you think important from your own experience. With the planetary energies, you may wish to invoke them on their appropriate days:

Monday: Moon
Tuesday: Mars

Wednesday: Mercury
Thursday: Jupiter
Friday: Venus
Saturday: Saturn
Sunday: Sun

There are also special appropriate hours for each of the planets throughout the day, but I have noticed little practical difference in any of these hours. I have generally found that night is the best time for this sort of work, but you may wish to work with Solar entities while the Sun is still visible. This is all really up to you, and will become clearer in your practical efforts.

Allow yourself to be open as you experience these entities, and do not try to force them to conform to your conscious expectations. They may quickly transform from your telesmatic image into something else entirely, and this may actually be a good sign. The telesmatic form is your projection, but once you have made contact this image may change to the way the being chooses to appear to you. However, the image should still be sympathetic with the energy you've invoked. If a Solar angel transforms into a black, watery dragon and you see images of storms, lightning and rotting corpses, something has gone wrong. In this case you should dismiss the Angel and banish the energies very completely, trying again another day.

If you are unsure of the being, you should test it by tracing an invoking polygon (pentagram or hexagram) appropriate to the energy of the being you invoked, drawing more energy into the being. This will make your vision more strong if you have the correct being, and it will cause the being to dissipate if you have a usurper or faker. This is the best way to test beings while in the middle of an operation. You may also judge by the nature of your communion with them, or the nature of their appearance, but even this at times can be deceptive.

Allow yourself to fully experience the personality of each of these beings as they come to you. These entities will have unique meaning for you in your magical universe, and if you give them the opportunity they can transform many aspects of your consciousness and life. These beings have real messages for you. Sometimes they may be irritable or weak and you should consider what this means about you and your relationships with these archetypal energies.

You should not necessarily expect the communication lines to be as clear as when you call to make an appointment with your dentist. These beings are archetypal symbol concepts, and may communicate to you through images, visions, shapes, colors, feelings or directly with words. At times the being may disappear and you'll just see a series of evocative images that the being is communicating to you. With some beings you may have a fairly direct conversation, in which the voice of the being (although technically inside you head) clearly seems to be coming from an outside source. At times, it may be difficult to distinguish the voice of the being from your own thoughts. All of these things indicate the nature of your natural connection to these forces. The more naturally you are in sympathy with the energy, the more easily you will be able to communicate with the being. You will also become more adept over progressive experiments.

It is often very difficult to discern real communication with these forces from mere fantasy. Don't spend a lot of energy on it while you are in the middle of your experiences as this will tend to cut you off, rather than enhance your experience. The best judgment of your success will be the quality of your experience. Did you learn things you previously did not know? Did you "feel" in communication with something other than yourself? You will receive symbols, words, feelings, in short: archetypal communication. Are you somehow altered by the experience? These are the best methods to determine your success, and should really only be considered after you are done with your work, and recording or reviewing your record. Ideally, you should have an assistant with you to record exactly what you are experiencing as you are going along.

1. Consult with your subconscious using the pendulum.

2. Get into the Alpha state using your anchor.

3. Do opening preparations, including any combination of purification, consecration, chakra opening, Kundalini arousing breaths, circle casting and the pentagram ritual.

4. Make a statement of your intent, naming the entity you intend to contact out loud, clearly and with conviction.

5. Potently draw the light of your superconscious into you, until you feel deeply connected with the true source of your power, a deep sense of cosmic strength.

6. Begin to invoke the appropriate magical energies, using the Creating Magical Atmospheres technique, or using the pentagram or hexagram technique.

7. Direct the magical energy you've accumulated in a spiraling clockwise whirl. Powerfully visualize this energy being charged and directed by your will to experience communion with the entity you've chosen. Begin to accumulate the energy into an amorphous shape in front of you, in an appropriate direction in your temple (either in an elemental

direction, in the east, or in a section that corresponds to where the planet is currently in the sky).

8. You can now begin invoking the being. (You may call the beings using their hierarchies at this point if you wish.) You should have a pillow or small chair in your workspace that you can sit in to allow as full relaxation and visualization as possible. You may close your eyes at this point, or just begin to focus on your third eye to develop your visualization. You can use your Alpha state anchor again at this point, taking a moment to deepen and focus your state.

9. You may use a spell (or hierarchy) to initially invoke the being if you wish, or you can simply "vibrate" the name of the being. In either case, you will need to "vibrate" the name of the entity three times, either at the end of the spell, or in lieu of the spell. To do this you will imagine the name of the entity in shimmering white letters in your heart from the white light above you as you inhale, and as you exhale, you say the name slowly and melodiously causing a vibration as you imagine the white light letters going out with your breath. Send this breath energy into the amorphous shape, and see your telesmatic image developing in the amorphous energy before you. Three times is of course the ideal, but you can do it more times if you need to in developing your vision.

10. Once you have visualized the being before you, you may feel it entering and mingling with you. This is fine, as long as you make sure that you clearly separate yourself when you dismiss the being. If it seems uncomfortable, end the experience by dismissing and doing appropriate banishings and closing your circle. If everything seems okay, you may proceed.

11. The being will be there, even if your visualization seems shaky or unclear, and it may quickly start looking quite different from your telesmatic image. Ask this being if it will communicate with you. When it agrees, ask the being to tell you how you can get along with it most beneficially, if it has any advice for you, if it will help you to accomplish your goals, work with you in the transformation of your life, or whatever you would like to know. The answers may come in any number of ways, as described above.

12. If the being seems hostile, aggressive, or unwilling to communicate, ask how you can relate more positively with it. Please be sure to consider

any advice you receive, however strange it might appear, and thank the figure.

13. When you feel that the conversation is over, dismiss the being, thanking it for its participation, and asking that it will return to communicate more in the future if need be. See the figure dissolving away.

14. Close your ritual space, performing appropriate banishing rituals for the energy of the being, and the lesser pentagram ritual a second time, and withdrawing all of the energy of your protective circle back into yourself. Do not under any circumstances omit the banishing for any reason. Make sure that all of the energy you've invoked has dissipated.

15. Record your experience in your journal.

Exercise 90 — Evocation with the Magick Mirror

Time Required: 40 to 60 minutes

When you wish to communicate with beings of a "lower" nature, such as the Planetary Spirits or Intelligences, Elementals or Demons, you will want to evoke rather than invoke them. You don't want to have them in your magical circle, invading and perhaps causing obsession. Instead, you will draw them into an area outside you circle. The tradition method of doing this is by evoking them into a triangle. The shape of the triangle is the most stable geometric form, implying a strong limiting force, so the ancient magicians used it as a symbol for containing "evil" spirits. This technique is designed for lower beings, but you could use it for Angels or even Gods as well if you wish.

Please keep in mind that our primitive metaphysical concepts of "good" and "evil" are for the most part priestly creations for the purpose of governing and controlling the masses. They have no useful place in any kind of transcendental philosophy. The difference between a demon and an angel is simply a matter of their sphere of influence. Demons and Lesser Spirits are those aspects of consciousness whose natures are of a preconscious and unreasoning character. "Greed," "lust," "hunger" and any kind of wild primal desires are incarnated in these creatures. They are desires as yet unfulfilled, in relation to the particular sphere in which they work. In other words, a Venusian Demon will represent lust and debauchery, while a Jupiterean Demon is unchecked ambition and over-indulgence. But this is the secret of their great power. They are the mighty constituents of the deep places of the subconscious mind, the primal sources of our drives to be and do more. They are seen as evil only by those who are frightened to look at the truth of the darker places in their own unconscious needs.

The great danger in congress with demons and elementals is of course the possibility of obsession. The fear is that their low ways will somehow rub off on you, causing you to behave in horrible, bestial ways. However, most likely you are already obsessed by legions of "demons" and "elementals," swarming through your every waking moment. Much of your magical work must be spent in ridding yourself of these unwanted hangers-on in your sphere of awareness.

The power of evocation is that it allows you to begin a useful relationship with these "beings." Rather than whispering their demands into your ears with you remaining unaware of their influence, you can draw them out, and command them to obey your Will. In this way, you can actually increase your personal evolution, rather than descending down to the level of a Demon.

For this technique you will need a magick mirror and a "triangle of evocation." As I mentioned before, the magick mirror can be made from any number of things.

Diagram 22 - Traditional Triangle of Evocation

This is an image of the traditional form for the triangle. The words along the edges are medieval magical formulae that mean little today, and can be replaced with words that you find more appropriate, or perhaps even omitted altogether. This does not have to be large, somewhere between two and three feet on each side. The mirror can either be placed within the triangle or else can be made a part of the triangle by making the circle in the middle a black mirrored surface.

You will place this triangle outside your circle, in the appropriate direction from which your being will be evoked. The triangle should have a candle on either side, appropriate incense burning in front of it, and the mirror should be placed in such a way that it does not reflect anything, merely offering a field of blank darkness.

This technique is very similar to the last, except that you will be visualizing the entity in the mirror, outside of your circle, rather than in direct contact with you.

1. Consult with your subconscious using the pendulum.

2. Get into the Alpha state using your anchor.

3. Do opening preparations, including any combination of purification, consecration, chakra opening, Kundalini arousing breaths, circle casting and the pentagram ritual.

4. Make a statement of your intent, naming the entity you intend to contact out loud, clearly and with conviction.

5. Potently draw the light of your superconscious into you, until you feel deeply connected with the true source of your power, a deep sense of cosmic strength.

6. Begin to invoke the appropriate magical energies, using the Creating Magical Atmospheres technique, or using the pentagram or hexagram technique, but do not bring this energy into the circle. Instead, visualize it circling as a column within the confines of your magick triangle.

7. Direct this energy into the magick mirror. Begin to accumulate the energy into an amorphous shape in the mirror.

8. You can now begin evoking the being. You should have a pillow or small chair in your workspace that you can sit in to allow as full relaxation and visualization as possible. Begin to focus on your third eye to develop your visualization. You can use your Alpha state anchor again at this point, taking a moment to deepen and focus your state.

9. You may use a spell to initially evoke the being if you wish, or you can simply "vibrate" the name of the being. In either case, you will need to

244

vibrate the name of the entity three times, either at the end of the spell, or in lieu of the spell. To do this you will imagine the name of the entity in shimmering white letters in your heart from the white light above you as you inhale, and as you exhale, you say the name slowly and melodiously causing a vibration as you imagine the white light letters going out with your breath. Send this breath energy into the amorphous shape in the mirror, and see your telesmatic image developing in the amorphous energy before you. Three times is of course the ideal, but you can do it more times if you need to in developing your vision.

10. Once you have visualized the being in the mirror, you can begin your communication. If the being begins to invade your circle in any way, end the experience by dismissing and doing appropriate banishings and closing your circle. If everything seems okay, you may proceed.

11. The being will be there, even if your visualization seems shaky or unclear, and it may quickly start looking quite different from your telesmatic image. Ask this being if it will communicate with you. When it agrees, ask the being to tell you how you can get along with it most beneficially, if it has any advice for you, if it will help you to accomplish your goals, work with you in the transformation of your life, or whatever you would like to know. The answers may come in any number of ways, as described above.

12. If the being seems hostile, aggressive, or unwilling to communicate, ask how you can relate more positively with it. Please be sure to consider any advice you receive, however strange it might appear, and thank the figure.

13. When you feel that the conversation is over, dismiss the being, thanking it for its participation, and asking that it will return to communicate more in the future if need be. See the figure dissolving away.

14. Close your ritual space, performing appropriate banishing rituals for the energy of the being, and the lesser pentagram ritual a second time, and withdrawing all of the energy of your protective circle back into yourself. Do not under any circumstances omit the banishing for any reason. Make sure that all of the energy you've invoked has dissipated.

15. Record your experience in your journal.

Exercise 91 – Distorted Image Magick Mirror Technique

Time Required: 40 to 60 minutes

This technique is essentially the same as the last, except that you will position the magick mirror in such a way that it reflects your face when you sit to begin your visualization. The image of the being will form from the visual distortions created by staring continuously at your reflection in the mirror. This is a simplified form of the technique made popular by Poke Runyon and his Ordo Templi Astarte. This technique will be greatly assisted if the light is very dim in the room where you are working, perhaps just illuminated by the two candles on either side of the triangle. You should also endeavor to stare at your own reflected image fixedly relaxing your eyes and allowing your third eye to develop the telesmatic image. You can focus your attention on one of your eyes, or at your nose or the center of your forehead. Just keep your eyes on the same point, and let yourself go with the flow.

1. Consult with your subconscious using the pendulum.

2. Get into the Alpha state using your anchor.

3. Do opening preparations, including any combination of purification, consecration, chakra opening, Kundalini arousing breaths, circle casting and the pentagram ritual.

4. Make a statement of your intent, naming the entity you intend to contact out loud, clearly and with conviction.

5. Potently draw the light of your superconscious into you, until you feel deeply connected with the true source of your power, a deep sense of cosmic strength.

6. Begin to invoke the appropriate magical energies, using the Creating Magical Atmospheres technique, or using the pentagram or hexagram technique, but do not bring this energy into the circle. Instead, visualize it circling as a column within the confines of your magick triangle.

7. Direct this energy into the magick mirror. Begin to accumulate the energy into an amorphous shape in the mirror.

8. You can now begin evoking the being. You should have a pillow or small chair in your workspace that you can sit in to allow as full relax-

ation and visualization as possible. Stare at your reflected image in the mirror. Begin to focus on your third eye to develop your visualization. You can use your Alpha state anchor again at this point, taking a moment to deepen and focus your state.

9. You may use a spell to initially evoke the being if you wish, or you can simply "vibrate" the name of the being. In either case, you will need to vibrate the name of the entity three times, either at the end of the spell, or in lieu of the spell. To do this you will imagine the name of the entity in shimmering white letters in your heart from the white light above you as you inhale, and as you exhale, you say the name slowly and melodiously causing a vibration as you imagine the white light letters going out with your breath. Send this breath energy into the amorphous energy in the mirror and your reflected image. Three times is of course the ideal, but you can do it more times if you need to in developing your vision.

10. Eventually, your image will begin to blur and transform into the image of the being, and you can begin your communication. The being will be there, even if your visualization seems shaky or unclear. If the being begins to invade your circle in any way, end the experience by dismissing and doing appropriate banishings and closing your circle. If everything seems okay, you may proceed.

11. Ask this being if it will communicate with you. When it agrees, ask the being to tell you how you can get along with it most beneficially, if it has any advice for you, if it will help you to accomplish your goals, work with you in the transformation of your life, or whatever you would like to know. The answers may come in any number of ways, as described above.

12. If the being seems hostile, aggressive, or unwilling to communicate, ask how you can relate more positively with it. Please be sure to consider any advice you receive, however strange it might appear, and thank the figure.

13. When you feel that the conversation is over, dismiss the being, thanking it for its participation, and asking that it will return to communicate more in the future if need be. See the figure dissolving away.

14. Close your ritual space, performing appropriate banishing rituals for the energy of the being, and the lesser pentagram ritual a second time, and withdrawing all of the energy of your protective circle back into yourself. Do not under any circumstances omit the banishing for any reason. Make sure that all of the energy you've invoked has dissipated.

15. Record your experience in your journal.

Exercise 92 – Evocation to Physical Manifestation

Time Required: 40 to 60 minutes

This technique is a variation on the above, except that you will not use a mirror at all, instead visualizing the entity evoked appearing visibly in the triangle outside your circle. This image will most likely be with your third eye, but if you have a knack for it, the being may take on a somewhat visible appearance within the triangle. An outside observer might see this as a sort of visible mist or blur of shadow, or the shape of the being within the triangle. Some people seem to be better at this than others. Some people also seem to be naturally better at "seeing" these things than others. As a teenager, when I was just beginning to experiment with magick and had yet to develop much skill or technique, I performed an evocation like this, with little result at all to me. But I had a friend in the circle with me who saw the being so clearly that it scared the pants off of him and we had to quickly end the experiment.

You will burn copious amounts of appropriate incense for this technique. The being will be able to use the fine matter of the incense to help in its manifestation. As I mentioned before, here are some incenses that might be appropriate:

Saturn: Myrrh
Jupiter: Cedar
Mars: Tobacco (or Dragon's Blood, Red Pepper or other hot scents)
Sun: Frankincense
Venus: Benzoin
Mercury: Sandalwood
Moon: Camphor

Fire: Cinnamon
Water: Cedar
Air: Sandalwood
Earth: Myrrh

These are just suggestions. You can also obtain pre-mixed blends either in stick, cone or raw form from many occult and new age shops.

1. Consult with your subconscious using the pendulum.

2. Get into the Alpha state using your anchor.

3. Be sure to light your incense.

4. Do opening preparations, including any combination of purification, consecration, chakra opening, Kundalini arousing breaths, circle casting and the pentagram ritual.

5. Make a statement of your intent, naming the entity you intend to contact out loud, clearly and with conviction.

6. Potently draw the light of your superconscious into you, until you feel deeply connected with the true source of your power, a deep sense of cosmic strength.

7. Begin to invoke the appropriate magical energies, using the Creating Magical Atmospheres technique, or using the pentagram or hexagram technique, but do not bring this energy into the circle. Instead, visualize it circling as a column within the confines of your magick triangle.

8. Accumulate the energy into an amorphous shape in the triangle and begin evoking the being. You should have a pillow or small chair in your workspace that you can sit in to allow as full relaxation and visualization as possible. Begin to focus on your third eye to develop your visualization. You can use your Alpha state anchor again at this point, taking a moment to deepen and focus your state.

9. You may use a spell to initially evoke the being if you wish, or you can simply "vibrate" the name of the being. In either case, you will need to "vibrate the name of the entity three times, either at the end of the spell, or in lieu of the spell. To do this you will imagine the name of the entity in shimmering white letters in your heart from the white light above you as you inhale, and as you exhale, you say the name slowly and melodiously causing a vibration as you imagine the white light letters going out with your breath. Send this breath energy into the triangle, and see your telesmatic image developing in the amorphous energy before you. Three times is of course the ideal, but you can do it

more times if you need to in developing your vision. See the being coming together visibly in the incense smoke.

10. Begin your communication. If the being begins to invade your circle in any way, end the experience by dismissing and doing appropriate banishings and closing your circle. If everything seems okay, you may proceed.

11. The being will be there, even if it seems shaky or unclear, and it may quickly start looking quite different from your telesmatic image. Ask this being if it will communicate with you. When it agrees, ask the being to tell you how you can get along with it most beneficially, if it has any advice for you, if it will help you to accomplish your goals, work with you in the transformation of your life, or whatever you would like to know. The answers may come in any number of ways, as described above.

12. If the being seems hostile, aggressive, or unwilling to communicate, ask how you can relate more positively with it. Please be sure to consider any advice you receive, however strange it might appear, and thank the figure.

13. When you feel that the conversation is over, dismiss the being, thanking it for its participation, and asking that it will return to communicate more in the future if need be. See the figure dissolving away.

14. Close your ritual space, performing appropriate banishing rituals for the energy of the being, and the lesser pentagram ritual a second time, and withdrawing all of the energy of your protective circle back into yourself. Do not under any circumstances omit the banishing for any reason. Make sure that all of the energy you've evoked has dissipated.

15. Record your experience in your journal.

Exercise 93 – Pendulum Communion

Time Required: 20 to 40 minutes

In this exercise, you will connect with higher intelligences using the pendulum, to allow them to communicate directly with you, without the usual filters of your own desires and expectations getting in the way. This is a very useful technique, particularly if you have the tendency to influence your visions toward your own desires, and want to get some accurate information. Of course this technique is far from infallible, and you can still end up influencing things toward your preconceived notions, but it at least adds another layer of filtering.

For this technique, you do not need to use telesmatic imaging, so if your visualization skills are somewhat weak, this technique might be ideal for you. You can use this technique to communicate with specific entities, or merely connect with the "Solar Angels," or the "Venusian Spirits" in a more freeform way, although the instructions will call for you to commune with a particular being.

This is the technique I used for my mother when I produced the numbers that won her several thousand dollars in the lottery. I succeeded a second time with her, and she won a smaller amount of money, but in trying to use this technique for my own selfish ends, it did not work at all. I don't know if it's even such a good idea to abuse the Angels to obtain lottery numbers and such, but you will have to judge that for yourself. If you do decide to use this for such a purpose, don't necessarily expect to win the very first day that you play the number. Continue playing it for a few weeks before you give up on it. It took my mother a week or two each time before she won.

Only use this technique with Angels or other higher beings. It is inadvisable for inexperienced magicians to bring demons or elementals directly into the body consciousness like this.

1. Consult with your subconscious using the pendulum.

2. Get into the Alpha state using your anchor.

3. Do opening preparations, including any combination of purification, consecration, chakra opening, Kundalini arousing breaths, circle casting and the pentagram ritual.

4. Make a statement of your intent, naming the entity you intend to contact out loud, clearly and with conviction.

5. Potently draw the light of your superconscious into you, until you feel deeply connected with the true source of your power, a deep sense of cosmic strength.

6. Begin to invoke the appropriate magical energies, using the Creating Magical Atmospheres technique, or using the pentagram or hexagram technique, filling your circle with the energy.

7. You should have a pillow or small chair in your workspace that you can sit in to allow as full relaxation and visualization as possible. Begin to focus on your third eye to develop your visualization. You can use your Alpha state anchor again at this point, taking a moment to deepen and focus your state.

8. Take the pendulum in your hand.

9. Imagine that you are giving up control of your arm, moving your astral sense of your arm out of the physical arm, and rest it at your side. This is simple to do, just imagine it. Don't make it harder by thinking overmuch and testing. Of course you can still move your arm, even after you've moved your "astral" arm. That's not the point. The point is to release some of your conscious and subconscious control of your arm, to make room for an outside intelligence to use it.

10. You can now begin invoking the being. You may use a spell to initially evoke the being if you wish, or you can simply "vibrate" the name of the being. In either case, you will need to "vibrate the name of the entity three times, either at the end of the spell, or in lieu of the spell. To do this you will imagine the name of the entity in shimmering white letters in your heart from the white light above you as you inhale, and as you exhale, you say the name slowly and melodiously causing a vibration as you imagine the white light letters going out with your breath.

11. Imagine that the energy of the being is filling your arm, by seeing the appropriate color moving in and feeling the possession.

12. Communicate with the being via the pendulum. You may wish to test it in some way, but for the most part this is relatively unnecessary.

13. When you feel that the conversation is over, dismiss the being, thanking it for its participation, and asking that it will return to communicate more in the future if need be. Feel the being leaving your body completely, and dissipating away.

14. Close your ritual space, performing appropriate banishing rituals for the energy of the being, and the lesser pentagram ritual a second time, and withdrawing all of the energy of your protective circle back into yourself. Do not under any circumstances omit the banishing for any reason. Make sure that all of the energy you've invoked has dissipated.

15. Record your experience in your journal.

Exercise 94 - Automatic Writing

Time Required: 20 to 40 minutes

This is a variation of the above, where you will use a pen to allow the being to write with your possessed hand rather than manipulate the pendulum. This is a slightly more advanced technique and you may wish to experiment with pendulum technique before attempting this one.

As you begin to communicate with the entity, the pen may not move of its own accord right away. Instead, you may just sense words coming into your mind. If you experience this, let your hand record what you are experiencing. Soon the being will begin to take up the task itself. Just keep recording what you are experiencing, and it will flow more and more naturally. You should use a smooth flowing pen in this practice, so that it can glide easily over the surface of the paper where you are recording your communication. You will also want to bring several sheets of paper into your circle as the communication may be copious or in large characters and pictures. You could also simply use your journal, if this is convenient. You can experiment with using your non-dominant hand for this, but it's not strictly necessary.

1. Consult with your subconscious using the pendulum.

2. You can write the details of your operation at the top of the first sheet of paper if you wish.

3. Get into the Alpha state using your anchor.

4. Do opening preparations, including any combination of purification, consecration, chakra opening, Kundalini arousing breaths, circle casting and the pentagram ritual.

5. Make a statement of your intent, naming the entity you intend to contact out loud, clearly and with conviction.

6. Potently draw the light of your superconscious into you, until you feel deeply connected with the true source of your power, a deep sense of cosmic strength.

7. Begin to invoke the appropriate magical energies, using the Creating Magical Atmospheres technique, or using the pentagram or hexagram technique, filling your circle with the energy.

8. You should have a pillow or small chair in your workspace that you can sit in to allow as full relaxation and visualization as possible. Begin to focus on your third eye to develop your visualization. You can use your Alpha state anchor again at this point, taking a moment to deepen and focus your state.

9. Take a pen in your hand, and place the point at the top of your paper

10. Imagine that you are giving up control of your arm that holds the pen, moving your astral sense of your arm out of the physical arm, and rest it at your side. Again, this is simple to do, just imagine it. Don't make it harder by thinking overmuch and testing. Of course you can still move your arm, even after you've moved your "astral" arm. That's not the point. The point is to release some of your conscious and subconscious control of your arm, to make room for an outside intelligence to use it.

11. You can now begin invoking the being. You may use a spell to initially evoke the being if you wish, or you can simply "vibrate" the name of the being. In either case, you will need to "vibrate the name of the entity three times, either at the end of the spell, or in lieu of the spell. To do this you will imagine the name of the entity in shimmering white letters in your heart from the white light above you as you inhale, and as you exhale, you say the name slowly and melodiously causing a vibration as you imagine the white light letters going out with your breath.

12. Imagine that the energy of the being is filling your arm, by seeing the appropriate color moving in and feeling the possession.

13. Communicate with the being, asking it what you will. The pen may move of its own accord, or you may feel like you are hearing sounds or seeing pictures. Allow the pen to record these. As you progress, the movement of the pen will become more and more automatic.

14. When you feel that the conversation is over, dismiss the being, thanking it for its participation, and asking that it will return to communicate more in the future if need be. Feel the being leaving your body completely, and dissipating away.

15. Close your ritual space, performing appropriate banishing rituals for the energy of the being, and the lesser pentagram ritual a second time, and withdrawing all of the energy of your protective circle back into yourself. Do not under any circumstances omit the banishing for any reason. Make sure that all of the energy you've invoked has dissipated.

16. Record your experience in your journal.

A note of caution: once you begin working in this way, you may find yourself caught up in constant urges to write from the spiritual source. If you are not clear about dismissing the communicating being you could find yourself being kept up at night, constantly filled with the need to write words from the spirit. Do a banishing and a grounding and centering.

Exercise 95 - Channeling

Time Required: 40 to 60 minutes

Channeling is allowing direct communication to your mind from an outside spiritual intelligence. It can actually be one of the most dangerous things you can do. This danger actually only presents itself when you do channeling in a sloppy way.

Channeling is really just a particular form of invocation. Most instructions for channeling are very vague, and invite you to accept communication from whatever comes along. I recommend that you avoid this messy kind of work because you will attract very low sorts of psychic intelligences. These astral phantoms will be more than happy to tell you that they are the prophet Ezekiel, or some other such noble personage, and give you all sorts of happy news from the great beyond, but it will mostly just be a lot of nonsense. Meanwhile they will be siphoning off your energy, and constantly demanding more and more of your time. This may seem innocuous, particularly at first, but this can easily lead to a dangerous obsession. Many professional channelers suffer from this very problem, and most of their information is this same sort of nonsense. If you are really interested in channeling, I suggest that you basically follow the instructions for invocation preceding, perhaps with the following modifications to allow the being to communicate with you very directly.

1. Consult with your subconscious using the pendulum.

2. Get into the Alpha state using your anchor.

3. Do opening preparations, including any combination of purification, consecration, chakra opening, Kundalini arousing breaths, circle casting and the pentagram ritual.

4. Make a statement of your intent, naming the entity you intend to contact out loud, clearly and with conviction.

5. Potently draw the light of your superconscious into you, until you feel deeply connected with the true source of your power, a deep sense of cosmic strength.

6. Begin to invoke the appropriate magical energies, using the Creating Magical Atmospheres technique, or using the pentagram or hexagram technique.

7. Direct the magical energy you've accumulated in a spiraling clockwise whirl. Powerfully visualize this energy being charged and directed by your will to experience communion with the entity you've chosen. Begin to accumulate the energy into an amorphous shape in front of you, in an appropriate direction in your temple (either in an elemental direction, in the east, or in a section that corresponds to where the planet is currently in the sky).

8. You can now begin invoking the being. You should have a pillow or small chair in your workspace that you can sit in to allow as full relaxation and visualization as possible. You may close your eyes at this point, or just begin to focus on your third eye to develop your visualization. You can use your Alpha state anchor again at this point, taking a moment to deepen and focus your state.

9. You may use a spell to initially invoke the being if you wish, or you can simply "vibrate" the name of the being. In either case, you will need to "vibrate the name of the entity three times, either at the end of the spell, or in lieu of the spell. To do this you will imagine the name of the entity in shimmering white letters in your heart from the white light above you as you inhale, and as you exhale, you say the name slowly and melodiously causing a vibration as you imagine the white light letters going out with your breath. Send this breath energy into the amorphous shape, and see your telesmatic image developing in the amorphous energy before you. Three times is of course the ideal, but you can do it more times if you need to in developing your vision.

10. Once you have visualized the being before you, feel it entering and mingling with you. Allow yourself to become one with the being. Commune with the being for as long as you want, receiving knowledge and understanding of the being from within. You may ask questions of the being, or just feel at one with it, receiving knowledge in a transcendental way.

11. When you feel that the communion is over, dismiss the being, thanking it for its participation, and asking that it will return to communicate more in the future if need be. See the figure dissolving away. Make sure that you clearly separate yourself when you dismiss the being.

12. Close your ritual space, performing appropriate banishing ritual for the energy of the being, and the lesser pentagram ritual a second time, and withdrawing all of the energy of your protective circle back into yourself. Do not under any circumstances omit the banishing for any reason. Make sure that all of the energy you've invoked has dissipated.

13. Record your experience in your journal.

This technique is ideal for use in groups, in which you let the others ask questions of the being, while you allow yourself to be completely possessed, letting the being answer questions with your mouth. Again, this should probably not be done with negative or lower beings unless you are prepared for the impact.

CHAPTER ELEVEN
Seeing the Future

"The vast majority of people who go to 'for-
tune-tellers' have nothing else in mind but the
wish to obtain supernatural sanction for their
follies. Apart from Occultism altogether, everyone knows that when people ask for advice, they only want to be told how wise they
are. Hardly anyone acts on the most common-
sense counsel if it happens to clash with his
previous intentions."

-Aleister Crowley[1]

The only real time is now, this very moment that you are in. The past is
gone. It cannot be retrieved. It is just a memory. Equally, the future does not
exist, and will only exist when it becomes now. For this reason, seeing the future is a shaky proposition at best. Nothing is written in stone, and we can always alter the path we are currently walking. Certain things seem inevitable, but
even these can be changed if we really want to and drastically change our behavior. Billions of factors change the path of manifestation every second. The most
we can really hope for in seeing the future is to get a sense of where things are
headed right now, with the actions we are currently taking in our lives. We can
also get a sense of what sort of unexpected curve balls life is about to throw us.

Do not expect to see your entire destiny with any of these techniques,
because you are creating this destiny constantly, and it changes with every new
decision that you make. Instead, try to use future thinking to see where your
current actions are leading you. I have placed this brief chapter toward the end
of the book, in the hopes that you will have developed a certain natural ability
to distinguish between the subtle energies of consciousness at this point, and
that you will be able to take your future visions with a grain of salt.

---

[1] *Magick: Book 4 Liber ABA*, pp. 245-246

Precognition and prognostication are the arts of the seer. Throughout history, great leaders, warriors, kings, businessmen and even hopeful lovers have sought out the advice of wise people whose vision allowed them to see a little more of what was to come than the rest of humanity. It still happens to this day. Many world leaders still consult astrologers, psychics, and their modern, statistical heirs, the futurists. In this chapter we will explore a few simple ways for you to develop metaphysical future vision consciousness within yourself.

Exercise 96 - Developing your Intuition- the Gift of Prophecy

Time Required: 10 to 20 minutes

This is a simple technique for receiving flashes of insight, directly from your superconscious. This will happen fast, in flashes of images and ideas. You must be fairly sensitive to receive these effectively.

Basically, you just have to think of what you'd like to know about, focus upward through the crown of your head to the light of your superconscious mind, and allow whatever images that come to pop into your mind. Just allow impressions to drop in. You will likely receive a multitude of sensations flooding in, a fast series of impressions that you will need to notice quickly.

1. If possible, use your pendulum to make sure your subconscious and superconscious are willing to work right now. There will of course be times when this is not convenient or necessary.

2. Use your anchor to go into the Alpha state.

3. If possible, do a few Kundalini arousing breaths.

4. Tell your superconscious that you want to obtain insight about whatever subject you need to know about. This can really be anything, not just foretelling the future. You can use this technique to solve problems, obtain creative ideas and a plethora of other things directly from the supreme creativity of your superconscious mind.

5. Shift your gaze inward to the top of head, focusing into the light above to receive direct information from your superconscious mind. Relax your attention there, letting your mind flow, allowing whatever comes into your mind to appear. Images may be brief, momentary.

6. You may again ask for the specific information if you are not receiving anything, or clarification of anything you receive. But you should not

refuse or ignore any images that you see no matter how vague or momentary. If you do not understand something, or feel that you have missed something, simply ask for more. These images and thoughts may be highly symbolic, and you can sort it all out later.

7. Do not analyze, simply observe what comes, keeping it in your mind, not forgetting anything.

8. Return to normal consciousness slowly and deliberately, intentionally remembering all that you have experienced.

9. Immediately write down whatever you have observed. It is important to write it all immediately, because you will tend to forget it quickly, much like dreaming.

To really get the hang of this technique, try these practical applications:

• Ask your superconscious what the next week, month or year will be like

• What are the life lessons you are now working on?

• Look at the upcoming world situation

• Intuit the right place to go or be to experience something profound

• See how to get ahead in your career

• Invent something

• Receive new ideas

• Learn how to do something you can't figure out

• What are the motives behind someone who's bugging you?

Exercise 97 – Future Timeline

Time Required: 15 to 40 minutes

This is a simple exercise to help you get in touch with where you are heading in your life right now. It may be a bit unpleasant if you are honest with it, and are not heading down the right path. But this is a good thing, because you may be able to steer yourself away from problems, or motivate yourself to take new actions in your life.

1. Use your pendulum to make sure your subconscious and superconscious are willing to work right now.

2. Use your anchor to go into the Alpha state.

3. If possible, do a few Kundalini arousing breaths.

4. Imagine that you are standing in front of a mirror, looking at yourself, as you did in the exercise at the beginning of this book. Visualize yourself exactly how you are right now. Begin to think about your life, what you are doing day to day, how you are habitually feeling and what you are habitually doing. Are there ways in which you are not getting the most out of your life right now? Are there things which you are doing and feeling that are not positive? Are there things that you should be doing that you are putting off or avoiding? Are there habitual emotions that are limiting you from getting the most out of your life?

5. Shift your gaze inward to the top of head, focusing into the light above. Imagine yourself floating up into this light so that you are moving outside of space and time for the moment. See your future and your past lying beneath you, along some sort of a timeline. This could be a tunnel or passage way, or a series of images, whatever seems appropriate to you.

6. Imagine that you are now floating down into the future on your timeline, so that you are moving ahead five years. Again see yourself standing in front of a mirror, five years older than you are now. Imagine yourself having carried all your emotions, beliefs, thoughts and limitations that you discovered in the last section with you for the last five years. How is your life? Are you heading in the direction that you would like? Do you have all that you want? How have your emotions and thoughts affected events? See, hear and feel how your life will be if you hold onto your limitations for the next five years. Feel the pain that these limitations will cause you, holding onto them for five more years. What will you miss out on? Relationships? Experiences? Opportunities?

7. Do not analyze, simply observe what comes, keeping it in your mind, not forgetting anything.

8. You may extend this further, traveling fifteen or twenty years ahead, dragging with you all of your limitations and negative beliefs. Is this the way you want your life to be?

9. Return to normal consciousness slowly and deliberately, intentionally remembering all that you have experienced.

10. Immediately write down whatever you have observed. It is important to write it all immediately, because you will tend to forget it quickly, much like dreaming.

For most people, this exercise will be a wake up call. We all allow our limitations to severely hamper our actions, and looking at these limitations over the course of our lives can inspire us to real change. If you are honest and really see what the future may hold if you don't change some of your behaviors and thoughts, you may discover a whole new series of magical operations that you need to begin.

This technique can also be used in another way. You can think about new and empowering beliefs and powers that you are invoking into your life, and see how these positive new things can affect your future for the brighter.

Exercise 98 - How to Induce Prophetic Dreams

Time Required: must be performed at bedtime

This is just a simple variation on dream programming that will allow you to receive dream images that relate to your future. You may want to know something specific, or just wish to see where things are heading in general.

1. When you are interested in receiving a prophetic dream, think about the subject of your interest constantly throughout the day, turning it over and over in your mind. Obsessively puzzle with it as much as possible all day long, all the way up to when you go to bed.

2. When you are getting ready for bed, write at the top of a blank page of your journal, "tonight I will dream about my future...(your subject)."

3. Consult with your subconscious using the pendulum about whether it understands your intention, and is willing to play along.

263

4. Shift your gaze inward to the top of head, focusing into the light above to receive direct information from your superconscious mind. Relax your attention there, letting your mind flow, allowing whatever comes into your mind to appear. As you are drifting off to sleep, continue thinking about this subject, letting images relating to this subject play through your mind until you fall asleep.

5. When you awaken, write down any dreams whether they relate to your future or not.

Wait a day or two to analyze whether your dreams have any relationship with your question. If you do not get satisfactory results the first time, you can try three or four more times, but if nothing comes, it means that your superconscious is keeping this information from you. Don't push too hard.

THE TRUE VALUE OF DIVINATION

I was originally contemplating giving instructions on a number of different oracles or systems of divination in this space, but this could easily fill a book of its own. So, I've decided to merely give a quick explanatory note on the general principles of divination, so that you can explore whatever systems you prefer.

Divination can generally be defined as the use of any outside tool to encourage a connection with the world of spirit that will in turn control operations of your hand or brain to obtain some information about the past, present or future. This then includes using the Tarot, Astrology, Bibliomancy, Geomancy, I Ching, reading tea leaves or even a coin toss. You ask a question of the universe, and use the oracular device to interpret the universe's answer.

The wonderful thing about divination is that it places so much of the task of receiving psychic information directly into the hands of the universe. You shuffle cards, or toss coins, or throw runes or bones or whatever, and the forces of the universe give you an answer of their own accord. The skeptic will call this "random chance," but it is a meaningful chance, because you have imbued it with a question, and some answer invariably comes, even if it seems ridiculous or unrelated. I'm sure we have all asked the "Magic Eight Ball" numerous questions throughout our lives. Even this is a genuine oracle, if approached as such. You will frequently be amazed at the direct connection between the question and answer you receive from any oracle.

But, as one of my teachers recently reminded me, if you consult any oracular device you are making a compact with the universe. The universe is going to provide some sort of answer to whatever you ask, whether you like the answer or not. For instance, if you make a coin toss, you are karmically bound to obey that toss. If you ignore this, you are insulting the spirit of the oracle. I once ignored an oracle for years, and my life really started to stagnate. Once I obeyed the oracle, my life improved dramatically. It is necessary for you to understand that an oracle is a genuine source of information from the consciousness of the universe. It is neither a game nor an illusion.

Oracles are real. Divination has real power to provide you with important insights. But most methods of divination take a good deal of time to learn. Reading ready-made answers to oracles out of a book is next to useless. It is only once you have internalized the meanings of the components of an oracle that their spiritual power really comes to life. You must learn the stories of each element of the divinatory process. If you are using the Tarot, you must become individually intimate with each one of the cards. If you are interested in I Ching or Geomancy, each of the symbols must be memorized and understood. All of these symbols will come to have unique meanings for you, and these meanings will also change over time. One of the best ways that I know of to get in touch with these elements ids through the process of visiting them astrally. I provided complete and simple directions for exploring the Tarot like this in the Practitioner level of *The New Hermetics*. These same directions could easily be adapted for any divinatory process.

Once you have made the components of these systems a part of yourself and your inner world, reading their messages becomes real magick. The individual symbols will just be gates, and you will receive unique messages from each one, every time you use them. When using any divination device, always trust your very first impressions, both at the start, before you've even begun, and through every turn of the process. These quick flashes of insight are where the message resides.

Truthfully, if you opened yourself up, getting into the alpha state, you could use any form of divination to a certain degree with no training, simply casting cards or coins or whatever, then allowing whatever impressions come. This requires a good deal of confidence to accomplish, and that confidence comes most easily when you are intimately familiar with your system of divination.

CHAPTER TWELVE
The Other Side

> "Necromancy has its name because it works on the bodies of the dead, and gives answers by the ghosts and apparitions of the dead, and subterraneous spirits, alluring them into the carcasses of the dead by certain hellish charms, and infernal invocations, and by deadly sacrifices and wicked oblations."
>
> -Francis Barrett[1]

In this final chapter, we will explore the ultimate mystery, that of the world beyond life, the other side, the realm of the dead. This is one of the most controversial aspects of magick, for a number of reasons. First, we will explore both past lives and communicating with the dead, which would seem to contain a paradox or inconsistency. How can you communicate with someone who is dead if they are reincarnated? This in fact is not an inconsistency, because in communicating with the dead, we are not contacting their essential essence, their higher nature, that part of them that might reincarnate, but rather just their astral shade or phantom, which can remain in the astral light after death, even if the person's true spirit might be reincarnated, or elevated to some higher plane.

Further, many people do not believe in reincarnation at all, whether for religious reasons or because they just think it seems unlikely or preposterous. You certainly do not have to explore past lives if you feel fundamentally opposed to the concept. However, the real value in past life exploration is not discovering that we were Marie Antoinette in a previous life. The real value lies in discovering archetypal themes that relate to our current life. Whether the past incarnations are real or elaborate creations from our unconscious, within the stories we that discover there are useful lessons to apply in our current lives.

---

[1] *The Magus,* Vol. 2, p. 69

You can get just as much out of the techniques by just considering these past lives to be metaphorical fairy-tales from your unconscious which may help you to see your life in a new light. Over progressive past life explorations, you will discover that these archetypal stories present us with new ways of looking at challenges that we face in our current lives, and may uncover challenges that we've never consciously acknowledged. In my personal past life work, I have consistently noticed a tendency for violence in my past lives. I have been a brutal soldier or warrior a number of times, as well as a quack physician who performed strange operations. In my current life I have had a lot of trouble expressing my anger and violent urges, but I never consciously realized this problem until I explored past lives using the techniques that you will find in this chapter. Now I am able to work on this hidden, violent tendency in myself consciously in a way I might never have discovered if it weren't for these past life regressions. I have never bothered to verify my past lives, because I think it is rather unimportant, personally. You may take this as far as you want. I have heard of a number of people who have discovered very accurate relations between their visions and some actual person from the past.

Also, a lot of magicians and lay people alike believe that talking to the dead is somehow wrong, that it disturbs the natural order and should be avoided like the plague. Necromancy is often thought to attract very low, vampiric, astral larvae of a most unwholesome character into the life of the regular practitioner. Of spiritism, a watered down form of necromancy, Aleister Crowley writes, "They make themselves perfectly passive, and, so far from employing any methods of protection, deliberately invite all and sundry spirits, demons, shells of the dead, all the excrement and filth of earth and hell, to squirt their slime all over them."[1] Certainly this subject is not something to be trifled with lightly. However, if there is something you need to know, or someone you need to connect with, there is little danger if it is used with magical caution.

PAST LIVES

As I've just mentioned, the purpose of these techniques is to discover the universal themes and large-scale patterns that you have been playing out in your life, by looking back at "previous incarnations," throughout history. As Aleister Crowley writes, "There is no more important task than the exploration of one's previous incarnations."[2] These may or may not be real lives, but they will give you an opportunity to explore consciousness in a new and novel way. Hopefully, over the course of a few experiments you will discover some consistent

---

[1] *Magick: Book 4 Liber ABA*, p. 281
[2] ibid. p. 173

themes that will give you insight about the patterns that have brought you to where you are currently in your life.

Exercise 99 - Past Life Regression

Time Required: 40 to 60 minutes

In approaching this, you can have some specific issue, phobia, or consistent pattern of problems in your life in mind, and attempt to discover how these things may relate to an experience or series experiences in a past life. Or, you can just travel backwards, obtaining whatever vision comes to you. Either way, it may take a few experiments to really discover some important themes or patterns.

1. Consult with your subconscious using the pendulum.

2. Get into the Alpha state using your anchor.

3. Do opening preparations, including any combination of purification, consecration, chakra opening, Kundalini arousing breaths, circle casting and the pentagram ritual. Not all of this is really necessary for this experience. Do only as much as you will to do.

4. Make a statement of your intent to experience a past life.

5. Sit or lie down comfortably, bringing yourself into the Theta state as deeply as possible, while remaining in control of the experience.

6. Recall something that happened yesterday, something simple and pleasant, and move back into this experience as fully as possible. See, hear and feel your past surroundings from yesterday vividly.

7. Now, move back to a week or so ago, recalling some pleasant event.

8. Now, move back to a month or so ago, recalling vividly some pleasant event.

9. Go back a year, perhaps to your birthday or some other pleasant day.

10. Now go back to your early teens, then back to the age of 9 or 10.

11. Go to age 5 or 6, and 4 then 3 then 2 then 1. And now visualize yourself in the warm, dark experience of the womb.

12. And go back even further seeing a light, and as you pass through this light look down at your feet.

13. Simply notice what comes. Look at your body. See where you are. Allow yourself to explore your surroundings, trying to get a sense of experience. Things may just come in flashes, or a whole story may unfold.

14. Allow yourself to go to an "important event" that took place in this life, something that you need to learn about. Experience whatever images come and feel free to explore for as long as you want. You may ask yourself what the message from this life was all about. Explore whatever you want.

15. Return to normal consciousness slowly and deliberately, intentionally remembering all that you have experienced.

16. Immediately write down whatever you have observed. It is important to write it all immediately, because you will tend to forget it quickly, much like dreaming.

Exercise 100 – Past Life Timeline Alternative Method

Time Required: 40 to 60 minutes

This is a variation on the previous exercise, using a method similar to the future timeline that you explored in the last chapter. You will simply visualize a line of time, go back up it and visit childhood then keep going back. The advantage of this technique is that you do not have to be in such a deep altered state as you were in the previous exercise, so you can more easily remain in control and remember what has occurred. The disadvantage of this technique is that it may remain much more of a fantasy, and could prevent you from obtaining as deep insights as the previous exercise. However you may find it even more useful.

1. Use your pendulum to make sure your subconscious and superconscious are willing to work right now.

2. Use your anchor to go into the Alpha state.

3. Do opening preparations, including any combination of purification, consecration, chakra opening, Kundalini arousing breaths, circle casting and the pentagram ritual. Not all of this is really necessary for this experience. Do only as much as you will to do.

4. Imagine that you are standing in front of a mirror, looking at yourself. Visualize yourself exactly how you are right now. Begin to think about your life, what you are doing day to day, how you are habitually feeling and what you are habitually doing.

5. Shift your gaze inward to the top of head, focusing into the light above. Imagine yourself floating up into this light so that you are moving outside of space and time for the moment. See your future and your past lying beneath you, along some sort of a timeline. This could be a tunnel or passage way, or a series of images, whatever seems appropriate to you.

6. Imagine that you are now floating down into the past on your timeline, so that you are moving back five years. Again see yourself standing in front of a mirror, five years younger than you are now. Begin to think about your life then, what you were doing day to day, how you were habitually feeling and what you were habitually doing. How were you different then? How the same?

7. Again, shift your gaze inward to the top of head, focusing into the light above. Imagine yourself floating up into this light outside of space and time, looking down at your future and past timeline.

8. Float down further into the past on your timeline, moving back to your early teens. Again see yourself standing in front of a mirror, as a young teen. Begin to think about your life then, what you were doing day to day, how you were habitually feeling and what you were habitually doing. How were you different then? How the same?

9. Again, shift your gaze inward to the top of head, focusing into the light above. Imagine yourself floating up into this light outside of space and time, looking down at your future and past timeline.

10. Float down further into the past on your timeline, moving back to your early childhood. Again see yourself standing in front of a mirror, as a small child. Begin to think about your life then, what you were doing

day to day, how you were habitually feeling and what you were habitually doing. How were you different then? How the same?

11. Again, shift your gaze inward to the top of head, focusing into the light above. Imagine yourself floating up into this light outside of space and time, looking down at your future and past timeline.

12. Float down further into the past on your timeline, moving back beyond the beginning of this life. Again see yourself standing in front of a mirror, but it will not be you. Who is this person at whom you are now looking? Begin to think about this life, what you were doing day to day in this past life, how you were habitually feeling and what you were habitually doing. How were you different then? How the same?

13. Do not analyze, simply observe what comes, keeping it in your mind, not forgetting anything.

14. You may extend this further, traveling further back, experiencing other periods in this life, or other lifetimes altogether.

15. Return to normal consciousness slowly and deliberately, intentionally remembering all that you have experienced.

16. Immediately write down whatever you have observed. It is important to write it all immediately, because you will tend to forget it quickly, much like dreaming.

Exercise 101 – Seeing Past Lives in the Magick Mirror

Time Required: 40 to 60 minutes

This is such an extremely simple and strangely effective technique that I almost don't even need to bother writing it out step by step. It is based on the same principle as the distorted image technique for contacting spirits.

1. Use your pendulum to make sure your subconscious and superconscious are willing to work right now.

2. Sit in front of your magick mirror (a dark mirror) at night, with only the light of a candle or two, looking at your reflection in the mirror.

3. Use your anchor to go into the Alpha state.

4. Do opening preparations, including any combination of purification, consecration, chakra opening, Kundalini arousing breaths, circle casting and the pentagram ritual. Not all of this is really necessary for this experience. Do only as much as you will to do.

5. Simply stare at your image in the mirror unblinkingly, allowing your eyes to tear if they must, but continuing to stare at the image without shifting your gaze. Eventually, perhaps after fifteen minutes or a half hour, your face will start to change shape, and you will see a new face in the mirror.

6. This is the face of one of your past lives. You may now ask about this life, and the details w ill begin to come to your mind. You may continue this practice as long as it is comfortable. Don't strain yourself.

7. Return to normal consciousness slowly and deliberately, intentionally remembering all that you have experienced.

8. Immediately write down whatever you have observed and discovered.

NECROMANCY

According to many of the great magical scholars, both ancient and modern, the practice of necromancy can be dangerous and caution should be taken. In my experiments in this direction I have noticed no real problem, but I suppose that there are some potential dangers. First and foremost, you must keep in mind that you are not really going to be communicating with the real essence of the individual you are going to talk to. Instead, you will be communicating with their astral shell, shade or shadow, that part of themselves that is left behind in the astral plane, made up of the memories of the past of the individual. This could also simply just end up being your own memories or fantasies of the person, projected through the lens of your imagination. But this practice could easily become addictive, particularly if it is a person who is sorely missed.

The other small danger is that some other unbalanced spiritual intelligence could easily masquerade as the deceased person, and ingratiate itself into your life for the purposes of sucking your energies away from you. Such a spirit might start giving you advice and demanding things from you and could become very destructive to you. So, for both of these reasons it is highly recommended that you not get into the habit of contacting the same deceased person over and over again. If you have something you need to know, or something you need to get off your chest, communicating with a deceased spirit is relatively harmless. But if you just wish to maintain and continue your relationship through this process, you will probably end up getting into trouble.

Autumn is traditionally the best time for necromancy, and Halloween the absolute ideal time. However, the night of the new moon is also suitable, when the darkness is greatest, and the shades of the dead are a bit more active. Many writers recommend a long period of preparation for necromancy, where you set up a shrine and go through various preparatory rituals. I think this is rather unnecessary, but it might be a good idea to set up your workspace for necromancy a week in advance, spending a little time each day thinking about the person you are going to contact. This will effectively build up the energy and anticipation for the ritual. But, you could honestly do it rather informally and still most likely get some results.

Exercise 102 - Necromancy of Love

Time Required: 40 to 60 minutes

For this practice you should burn some pleasant, sweet smelling incense, evocative of pleasant memories of the past. If you know of a scent that the person enjoyed in life, this would of course be ideal. Set up a little shrine in your temple or workroom for the person you will communicate with, including as large a photograph as you can find. Cover this photo with a white cloth, preferably of silk. Surround the photo with flowers, and any precious things that belonged to the person you will contact. You may wish to leave this shrine for a week or so, spending a little time with it each day, to really build up the atmosphere.

On the day that you will conduct your working, bring an offering of food and drink to the shrine, and serve yourself some too. This is sometimes called a "dumb supper."

You will need to write a spell to evoke this person, using your memories and reflections on the person's life. Set up your triangle of evocation in the west, the direction of the dead. Place two white candles at the triangle, one on either side.

You can use any of the visualization methods of evocation, a crystal ball, a mirror, clairvoyance, or attempt physical manifestation.

1. Consult with your subconscious using the pendulum.

2. Uncover the image of the person, and bring it into your working area.

3. Get into the Alpha state using your anchor.

274

4. Do opening preparations, including any combination of purification, consecration, chakra opening, Kundalini arousing breaths, circle casting and the pentagram ritual.

5. Make a statement of your intent, naming the person you intend to contact out loud, clearly and with conviction, looking at the image.

6. Potently draw the light of your superconscious into you, until you feel deeply connected with the true source of your power, a deep sense of cosmic strength.

7. Direct this energy into the triangle of evocation. Begin to accumulate the energy into an amorphous shape.

8. Recite your spell three times, looking at the image before you, conjuring up all the force you can, and directing it into the energy in the triangle.

9. Go to each of the four cardinal points clockwise, starting in the north and ending in the west, calling the person's name, inviting them to join you.

10. You should have a pillow or small chair in your workspace that you can sit in to allow as full relaxation and visualization as possible. Begin to focus on your third eye to develop your visualization. You can use your Alpha state anchor again at this point, taking a moment to deepen and focus your state.

11. Say the person's name slowly, three times, feeling their presence in the triangle.

12. Look to the triangle. The shade of the person will manifest in some way, although it may not be that clear.

13. You can now begin to communicate. The answers may come in any number of ways, images, words, or feelings. Just remain open and receive what comes.

14. When you feel that the conversation is over, dismiss the shade, thanking it for its participation, and setting it free from you. See the shade dissolving away.

15. Go again to the four quarters, saying "good bye (person's name), return now to the shadows."

16. Close your ritual space, performing the lesser pentagram ritual a second time, and withdrawing all of the energy of your protective circle back into yourself. Do not under any circumstances omit the banishing for any reason. Make sure that all of the energy you've evoked has dissipated.

17. Record your experience in your journal.

Exercise 103 - Necromancy of Knowledge

Time Required: 40 to 60 minutes

The purpose here is to obtain information from someone that you do not necessarily know, but that you cannot obtain in any other way. This could be in the case of some spiritual master or great thinker of the past, whose ideas you wish to understand better, or who died with some secret that you need to know. This technique is exactly the same as the last, but you omit the "dumb supper," and use black candles instead of white. All the other steps are identical. You shouldn't just use this lightly, and you must certainly take any information you receive with a grain of salt.

1. Consult with your subconscious using the pendulum.

2. Uncover the image of the person, and bring it into your working area.

3. Get into the Alpha state using your anchor.

4. Do opening preparations, including any combination of purification, consecration, chakra opening, Kundalini arousing breaths, circle casting and the pentagram ritual.

5. Make a statement of your intent, naming the person you intend to contact out loud, clearly and with conviction, looking at the image.

6. Potently draw the light of your superconscious into you, until you feel deeply connected with the true source of your power, a deep sense of cosmic strength.

7. Direct this energy into the triangle of evocation. Begin to accumulate the energy into an amorphous shape.

8. Recite your spell three times, looking at the image before you, conjuring up all the force you can, and directing it into the energy in the triangle.

9. Go to each of the four corners clockwise, starting in the north and ending in the west, calling the person's name, inviting them to join you.

10. You should have a pillow or small chair in your workspace that you can sit in to allow as full relaxation and visualization as possible. Begin to focus on your third eye to develop your visualization. You can use your Alpha state anchor again at this point, taking a moment to deepen and focus your state.

11. Say the person's name slowly, three times, feeling their presence in the triangle.

12. Look to the triangle. The shade of the person will manifest in some way, although it may not be that clear.

13. You can now begin to communicate. The answers may come in any number of ways, images, words, or feelings. Just remain open and receive what comes.

14. When you feel that the conversation is over, dismiss the shade, thanking it for its participation. See the shade dissolving away.

15. Go again to the four quarters, saying "good bye (person's name), return now to the shadows."

16. Close your ritual space, performing the lesser pentagram ritual a second time, and withdrawing all of the energy of your protective circle back into yourself. Do not under any circumstances omit the banishing for any reason. Make sure that all of the energy you've evoked has dissipated.

17. Record your experience in your journal.

IN CLOSING

You now have enough magical practices to occupy you for a very long time. Hopefully you are working through these techniques slowly and methodically, developing your powers gradually and thoughtfully. All of the powers of heaven and earth are now at your fingertips. There is no law beyond Do what thou wilt.

I wish to finally share an extended quote from the secret instructions of the Hermetic Order of the Golden Dawn that will hopefully be of some assistance to you on your continuing journey.

"Thou therefore who desirest magical gifts, be sure that thy soul is firm and steadfast, for it is by flattering thy weakness that the Evil One will gain power over thee. Humble thyself before thy God, yet fear neither man nor spirit. Fear is failure and the forerunner of failure; and courage the beginning of virtue. Therefore fear not the spirits, but be firm and courteous with them, for this too may lead you into sin. Command and banish the Evil ones. Curse them by the Great Names of God, if need be; but neither mock nor revile them, for so assuredly thou wilt be led into error... To obtain magical Power, learn to control thought. Admit only true ideas which are in harmony with the end desired, and not every stray and contradictory idea that presents itself. Fixed thought is a means to an end; therefore pay attention to the power of silent thought and meditation. The material act is but the outward expression of the thought, and therefore it hath been said that 'the thought of foolishness is sin.' Thought therefore is the commencement of action, and if a chance thought can produce much effect, what cannot fixed thought do?... Establish thyself firmly in the Equilibrium of Forces, in the center of the cross of the elements, that Cross from whose centre the creative word issued in the birth of the dawning universe... Be thou therefore prompt and active as the Sylphs, but avoid frivolity and caprice. Be energetic and strong like the Salamanders, but avoid irritability and ferocity. Be flexible and attentive to images like the Undines, but avoid idleness and changeability. Be laborious and patient like the Gnomes, but avoid grossness and avarice. So shalt thou gradually develop the powers of thy Soul and fit thyself to command the spirits of the elements. For wert thou to summon the Gnomes to pander to thy avarice, thou wouldst no longer command them, but they would command thee. Wouldst thou abuse the pure creatures of God's creation to fill thy coffers and to satisfy thy lust for Gold? Wouldst thou defile the Spirits of driving Fire to serve thy wrath and hatred? Wouldst thou violate the purity of the Souls of the Water to pander to thy lust and debauchery? Wouldst thou force the Spirits of the evening breeze to minister to thy folly and caprice? Know that with such desires thou canst but attract the evil and not the good, and in that case the evil will have power over thee."

Love is the law, love under will.

APPENDIX A
Three Types of
Magick Wands

There are infinite ways to construct a magick wand, and many authorities believe that their way is the "one correct way." You will have to use your own judgment and experience to determine your own preference. Below you will find three examples of simple wands that I have found useful.

Simple Branch of Tree

The easiest way to make a magick wand is simply to cut a small branch from a tree. Traditionally there are a few kinds of tree that are considered "most magical." These are: almond, hazel, oak, willow, yew and a few others. Different trees suit different temperaments. Find a suitable tree, and cut off a young branch. Use your growing intuition to determine whether it is an appropriate tree, and try to get the tree's permission to do this, using your subconscious and perhaps even consulting the pendulum. It is traditional to cut the branch with a single stroke, but this may be easier said than done. Then you will strip the bark, smooth down the wood, rub it down with an appropriate oil, and consecrate it in some way.

Diagram 23 - Simple Branch Wand

Magnetized Rod through Dowel

Another fairly simply procedure that is purported to empower your wand with greater force is to insert a magnetized steel or iron rod down the length of your wand's shaft. You can use a branch cut from a tree as above, or use a wooden dowel for this. The traditional manner for getting the metal rod through the wood is to super heat it so that it burns a passage as you work it down through the wand. This is impractical and hard to do in practice. A much easier approach is simply to cut the wand into sections, and drill a hole down the center than will neatly accommodate the diameter of your magnetized rod. The "south pole" of your magnetized rod faces the front of the wand.

Diagram 24 - Magnetized Rod through Dowel

Crystal Wand

This is the type of wand that I generally use, not because it is necessarily any more effective than anything else, but simply that I first constructed it many years ago when I was a young teenager, and it has great sentimental value, and years of use to back up its strength. I first learned of this wand from a book of rather questionable value called *Crystal Power*[1], which stated that this type of

---

[1] Smith, Michael G., *Crystal Power*, (St. Paul, MN; Llewellyn Books, 1985)

wand was used in ancient Atlantis, and the technology behind it was responsible for all of the great and unimaginable achievements of that civilization. While this has always seemed rather mythological to me, I built a wand like this as a teenager, and it has remained with me since. This is a fairly easy wand to construct, but you will need a few materials: a small clear quartz crystal with a point, a copper tube 8 to 15 inches in length whose diameter will neatly fit the crystal, an end cap for the copper tube, several feet of leather strap, and glue.

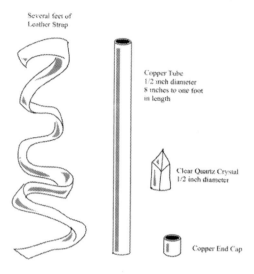

Several feet of
Leather Strap

Copper Tube
1/2 inch diameter
8 inches to one foot
in length

Clear Quartz Crystal
1/2 inch diameter

Copper End Cap

Diagram 25 - Crystal Wand Materials

With these materials in hand, you will glue the crystal so that it points out of the copper tube, and glue the end cap to the other end. Then you glue the leather strap around and around the tube, to insulate it.

The idea behind this wand is that the hollow tube is used to collect your energy; the leather strap will help to insulate and keep it in the rod, while the crystal will focus and amplify it as you project the energy outwards. In some ways, this wand reminds me a little of one of Wilhelm Reich's orgone contraptions. You will have to judge for yourself how effective this wand will be for you.

Diagram 26 - Crystal Wand

APPENDIX B
A Simple Consecration Ritual

It may be a good idea to ritually consecrate your magick and psychic tools, such as the wand that we just discussed, so that they have been cleared of outside energies, and specifically charged for your specialized ritual use. The following simple procedure will be sufficient. You will need a small basin of water in your ritual space, as well as appropriate incense or oil.

1. Use your anchor to go into the Alpha state.

2. Perform a circle casting, and whatever other opening preparations you think appropriate.

3. Take the object you are consecrating in your hand.

4. Either immerse it into the basin of water, or if that is inappropriate (if the object is delicate or made of paper) simply sprinkle a bit of water on the object.

5. Say to yourself "I cleanse this (object), so that I may purify this (object), so that I may use it to accomplish my work," or something similar. You could also specifically mention the work you are going to use it for.

6. Visualize and feel the water sucking away all negativity. Imagine vividly that all previous uses, images, thoughts and worries that don't relate to your special work with this object are now disappearing, magnetically drawn into the water.

7. Take up some burning incense in your hand (In a censer or incense holder. Don't burn yourself!). You could also use holy oil.

8. Place your object into the smoke of your incense, smelling it and feeling the warm tickle of it filling the object, (or anoint the object with oil) saying, "I consecrate this (object) to my work, and this work alone that it may be accomplished with the power of the great animating consciousness of the universe," or some such other words that you

devise. Feel and visualize the light from your superconscious filling your whole body as you say this, and feel this energy filling your object with the inspired power of your superconscious mind.

9. Close your circle.

10. Record your experience in your journal.

You may find it useful to invoke appropriate energies into your tools. For example, the energy of Fire might be suitable for your Wand (as Fire rules thw Will), or Lunar energy might be useful for your pendulum (as the Moon rules the subconscious). But these further matters will be up to your own creativity and specific needs.

APPENDIX C
Unicursal Planetary Hexagrams

Here are two different versions of the planetary hexagrams, using a unicursal rather than a double-triangle hexagram. It should also be noted that the signs of the Zodiac may be invoked by the hexagrams of their ruling planet. This is, of course, also true of the traditional hexagrams. You can also invoke the signs of the Zodiac with their appropriate elemental pentagrams. The difference in this will depend on whether you wish to stress their terrestrial or celestial nature.

The first versions of the unicursal hexagrams use the same type of lineal pattern as the pentagrams, and are from Israel Regardie[1], while the second use a similar pattern to the traditional hexagrams with some necessary modification of course:

---

[1] *The Complete Golden Dawn System of Magic*, Volume 4, pp. 29-32

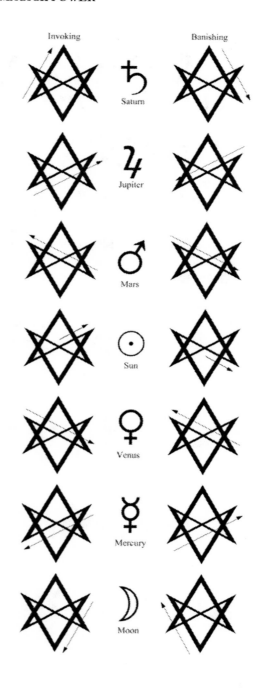

Diagram 27 - Unicursal Hexagrams of the Planets - First Version

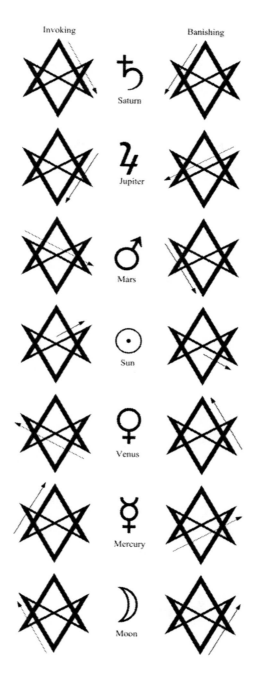

Diagram 28 - Unicursal Hexagrams of the Planets - Second Version

APPENDIX D
The Sigils of the
Olympic Planetary Spirits

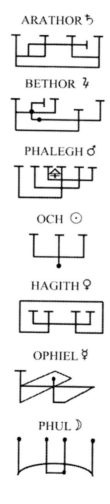

ARATHOR ♄

BETHOR ♃

PHALEGH ♂

OCH ☉

HAGITH ♀

OPHIEL ☿

PHUL ☽

Diagram 29 - The Olympic Planetary Spirits and their Sigils

291

BIBLIOGRAPHY
And Suggested Readings

Agrippa, Henry Cornelius. *Three Books of Occult Philosophy* (St. Paul, MN; Llewellyn Books, 1993)

Bandler, Richard and Grinder, John. *Frogs into Princes,* (Moab, UT: Real People Press, 1981)

————. *The Structure of Magic,* (Palo Alto, CA: Science and Behavior Books, 1975)

————. *The Structure of Magic 2,* (Palo Alto, CA: Science and Behavior Books, 1976)

Bardon, Franz. *Initiation into Hermetics,* (Wuppertal, Germany: Ruggeberg-Verlag, 1993)

————. *The Practice of Magical Evocation,* (Wuppertal, Germany: Ruggeberg-Verlag, 1991)

Barrett, Francis. *The Magus* (Secaucus, NJ: Citadel Press, 1967)

Carroll, Peter. *Liber Kaos,* (York Beach, ME: Samuel Weiser Books, 1992)

————. *Liber Null and Psychonaut,* (York Beach, ME: Samuel Weiser Books, 1987)

Chaney, Earline. *Kundalini and the Third Eye* (Upland, CA: Astara, 1980)

Crowley, Aleister. *777 and other Qabalistic Writings,* (York Beach, ME: Samuel Weiser Books, 1973)

————. *The Equinox Vols. 1-10,,* (York Beach, ME: Samuel Weiser Books, 1999)

————. *Liber Aleph vel CXI* (York Beach, ME: Samuel Weiser Books, 1991)

————. *Magick: Book 4 Liber ABA* (York Beach, ME: Samuel Weiser Books, 1998)

————. *Magick Without Tears* (Phoenix, AZ: New Falcon Publications, 1991)

Duquette, Lon Milo. *Enochian Sex Magick* (Phoenix, AZ: New Falcon Publications, 1991)

Garfield, Patricia. *Creative Dreaming* (New York: Ballantine Books, 1974)

Gawain, Shakti. *Creative Visualization* (New York: Bantam Books, 1978)

Harary, Keith and Weintraub. Pamela. *Have an Out of Body Experience in Thirty Days* (New York: St. Martin's Press, 1989)

————. *Lucid Dreams in Thirty Days* (New York: St. Martin's Press, 1989)

Hill, Napoleon. *Think and Grow Rich* (New York: Fawcett Columbine, 1988)

Huson, Paul. *Mastering Witchcraft* (New York: Perigree, 1970)

Jung, Carl G. *Alchemical Studies* (Princeton, NJ: Princeton University Press, 1967)

————. *The Archetypes and the Collective Unconscious* (Princeton, NJ: Princeton University Press, 1969)

————. *The Portable Jung* (New York: The Viking Press, 1971)

King, Francis (editor). *Ritual Magic of the Golden Dawn* (Rochester, VT: Destiny Books, 1997)

Kraig, Donald Michael. *Modern Magick* (St. Paul, MN: Llewellyn Books, 1992)

La Berge, Stephen. *Lucid Dreaming* (New York: Ballantine Books, 1985)

Leary, Timothy. *Game of Life* (Tempe, AZ: New Falcon Publications, 1995)

Levi Zahed, Eliphas. *Transcendental Magic* (London, Bracken Books, 1995)

Lidell, Lucy. *The Sivananda Companion to Yoga* (New York: Fireside, 1983)

Long, Max Freedom. *The Secret Science at Work* (Marina del Ray, CA: DeVorss, 1953)

Mead, G.R.S. *Thrice Great Hermes: Studies in Hellenistic Theosophy and Gnosis* (York Beach, ME: Samuel Weiser Books, 1992)

Monroe, Robert A. *Journeys Out of the Body* (New York: Doubleday, 1977)

Murphy, Joseph. *The Power of Your Subconscious Mind* (Paramis, NJ: Prentice Hall, 1963)

————. *Psychic Perception: The Magic of Extrasensory Power* (New York: Parker Publishing Company, 1971)

Newcomb, Jason Augustus. *21st Century Mage* (Boston, MA: Weiser Books, 2002)

————. *The New Hermetics* (Boston, MA: Weiser Books, 2004)

————. *Sexual Sorcery* (Boston, MA: Weiser Books, 2005)

Ophiel. *The Art and Practice of Astral Projection* (York Beach, ME: Samuel Weiser Books, 1974)

Regardie, Israel. *The Complete Golden Dawn System of Magic* (Phoenix, AZ: New Falcon Publications, 199o)

————. *The Middle Pillar* (St. Paul, MN: Llewellyn Books, 1987)

————. *The Tree of Life* (York Beach, ME: Samuel Weiser Books, 1972)

Reich, Wilhelm. *Character Analysis* (New York, Pocket Books, 1976)

————. *The Function of the Orgasm* (New York, Farrar, Strauss and Giroux, 1973)

Richards, Steve. *Levitation* (Wellingborough, Northamptonshire UK, The Aquarian Press, 1980)

Robbins, Anthony. *Unlimited Power* (New York: Ballantine Books, 1986)

Sanders Jr., Pete A. *You Are Psychic!* (New York: Fireside, 1999)

Schneider, Michael S. *A Beginner's Guide to Constructing the Universe* (New York: HarperPerrenial, 1995)

Selby, John. *Kundalini Awakening* (New York: Bantam Books, 1992)

Smith, Michael G. *Crystal Power* (St. Paul, MN; Llewellyn Books, 1985)

Starhawk. *The Spiral Dance* (New York: Harper and Row, 1989)

Sui, Choa Kok. *Pranic Healing* (York Beach, ME: Samuel Weiser Books, 1990)

Vasu, Rai Babadur Srisa Chandra (translator). *The Siva Samhita* (New Delhi: Munshiram Manoharlal, 1999)

Vivekananda, Swami. *Raja Yoga* (New York: Ramakrishna-Vivekananda Center, 1982)

Wilson, Robert Anton. *Prometheus Rising* (Phoenix, AZ: Falcon Press, 1983)

ABOUT THE AUTHOR

Jason Augustus Newcomb has devoted his life to gaining and sharing an increased understanding of the Western Mystery Tradition, both how it relates to modern consciousness studies, and its relations with other forms of esoteric spirituality. Jason is a long-time initiate of Western Mystery Schools, both visible and invisible, and has explored magic and mysticism in its varied forms for the past twenty-two years... in this incarnation. Jason's goal is to participate in the evolution of humanity in whatever small way Divine Providence has ordained for him. He is devoted to helping people expand both personally and spiritually, seeing these as essentially in the same continuum. He is the author of the books: 21st Century Mage, The New Hermetics, and Sexual Sorcery; and has produced an extensive series of audio CDs offering instruction in magical practice and hypnosis. Jason has created numerous CDs that go along with many of the practices in this book. He is also a licensed Neuro-Linguistic Programming Practitioner a certified Clinical Hypnotherapist. In his most creative moments he is also a painter, sculptor, novelist, screenwriter and filmmaker. Jason now lives with his wife Jennifer and their one-year-old daughter Aurora in Sarasota, FL.

You can visit Jason's website at www.newhermetics.com for more information.

Printed in the United States
116887LV00011B/134/A